teach® yourself

twentieth century usa

D1100023

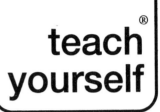

twentieth century usa
carole bryan jones

For over 60 years, more than
40 million people have learnt over
750 subjects the **teach yourself**
way, with impressive results.

be where you want to be
with **teach yourself**

For UK order enquiries: please contact Bookpoint Ltd, 130 Milton Park, Abingdon, Oxon OX14 4SB. Telephone: +44 (0) 1235 827720. Fax: +44 (0) 1235 400454. Lines are open 09.00–18.00, Monday to Saturday, with a 24-hour message answering service. Details about our titles and how to order are available at www.teachyourself.co.uk

For USA order enquiries: please contact McGraw-Hill Customer Services, PO Box 545, Blacklick, OH 43004-0545, USA. Telephone: 1-800-722-4726. Fax: 1-614-755-5645.

For Canada order enquiries: please contact McGraw-Hill Ryerson Ltd, 300 Water St, Whitby, Ontario L1N 9B6, Canada. Telephone: 905 430 5000. Fax: 905 430 5020.

Long renowned as the authoritative source for self-guided learning – with more than 40 million copies sold worldwide – the **teach yourself** series includes over 300 titles in the fields of languages, crafts, hobbies, business, computing and education.

British Library Cataloguing in Publication Data: a catalogue record for this title is available from the British Library.

Library of Congress Catalog Card Number: on file.

First published in UK 2005 by Hodder Education, 338 Euston Road, London, NW1 3BH.

First published in US 2005 by Contemporary Books, a Division of the McGraw-Hill Companies, 1 Prudential Plaza, 130 East Randolph Street, Chicago, IL 60601 USA.

This edition published 2005.

The **teach yourself** name is a registered trade mark of Hodder Headline.

Typeset by Transet Limited, Coventry, England.
Printed in Great Britain for Hodder Education, a division of Hodder Headline, 338 Euston Road, London NW1 3BH, by Cox & Wyman Ltd, Reading, Berkshire.

Hodder Headline's policy is to use papers that are natural, renewable and recyclable products and made from wood grown in sustainable forests. The logging and manufacturing processes are expected to conform to the environmental regulations of the country of origin.

Impression number   10 9 8 7 6 5 4 3 2 1
Year   2010 2009 2008 2007 2006 2005

contents

01

the USA at the beginning of the twentieth century

This chapter will cover:
- the American Constitution and its influence on the country's history
- the federal nature of the US government
- US political institutions and their role in government.

The first thing the foreigner has to take in about America is simply the size of the place, and the variety of life that goes on inside it.

Alistair Cooke, a British-born reporter who became famous for his *Letter from America* radio broadcasts to the BBC during the twentieth century, hit the nail on the head. The United States of America is one of the biggest countries in the world, indeed the whole of England can be fitted into just one of the 50 states – the state of Texas – three times! Cooke noted that the East coast of the USA passed through a variety of geographical features – skiing country in the north, through fertile farmland, to semi-tropical swamps and warm winter resorts in the south; on the West coast there are vast virgin forests in the north, while in the south there are deserts; in between the two coasts there are mountains, prairies and great plains.

Yet in 1903, the potential of the USA's huge economic power was only just becoming apparent; in military terms the USA was amateurish, with its fleet being described as a collection of 'old washtubs' by one politician of the time; power still lay in the hands of the 'old world' – European states such as Britain, Germany and France were considered the major players on the world stage, the USA was merely one of the supporting actors.

Gradually, the USA's military power grew to match that of its economic might, and the country's role was decisive in both the world wars of the twentieth century (1914–18 and 1939–45). Following the Second World War there developed a potentially deadly rivalry between the USA and the Soviet Union; the Cold War, which existed between these two super powers for over 45 years, at times threatened the entire planet because of their reliance on nuclear weapons as a deterrent and as a defence. However, by 1991 the Soviet Union as a single entity had ceased to exist and at the end of the millennium it seemed as though the USA was the world's only unchallenged super power.

Henry Luce the founder of *Time* magazine, called the twentieth century the 'American Century'. Yet although the USA was transformed into the most powerful and influential country in the world internally, for much of the century it retained divisions between rich and poor, black and white, divisions which many would argue persist to the present day. In order to understand why this situation should exist in the 'land of the free' and the 'land of opportunity' it is important to understand something of the early history and politics of the country.

The American Constitution and federalism

American society holds certain ideas which are rooted in the early history of the country. In 1776, 13 British colonies in North America declared their independence from the mother country and fought a successful revolution against their former rulers. Following the revolution in order to govern the country they drew up a Constitution which is generally regarded as the model of democracy. This Constitution, ratified in 1787 although subsequently amended to suit changing circumstances, still defines the framework of government in the USA today. One of the key features of the Constitution is the federal system of government which means that each state retains its own government but that there is also a central (or federal) government for the whole country.

In 1787, each state was self-governing and independent but to 'form a more perfect union, establish justice, insure domestic tranquillity, provide for the common defence (and) promote the general welfare', they joined together in the United States of America and gave up certain limited powers to the federal government. These powers were in the spheres of foreign affairs, defence, taxation, the currency and the postal service and the regulation of inter-state and international trade; all other powers of government were retained by the states as 'states rights'. The states wanted to ensure that the government of the USA could never become too powerful or tyrannical and so the Constitution limits the powers of government and clearly defines the rights of citizens. These rights are outlined in the first ten amendments to the Constitution and are known as the 'Bill of Rights'. Within the Bill of Rights, freedom of religion, of speech, of the press, and of assembly is guaranteed, as is the right to petition the government. Citizens can also carry weapons for self-defence and have the right to a fair trial.

The federal nature of the government means that power is shared between the federal (or central) government and the state governments. The federal government is divided into three parts – the legislature or law-making body (Congress), the executive or governing body (President) and the judiciary which is in charge of justice and the court system. An inbuilt series of 'checks and balances' ensures that no branch of government becomes too powerful. Each body acts as a check on the other two, for example, the President can negotiate a foreign treaty,

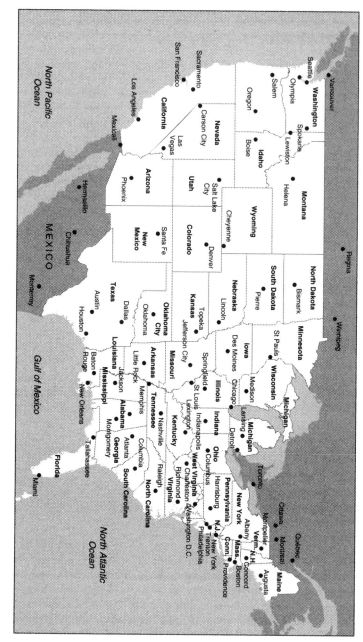

figure 1 a map of the USA

but Congress must approve it in order to bring it into operation; the President can veto a law passed by Congress, but Congress can overrule this veto by a two-thirds majority.

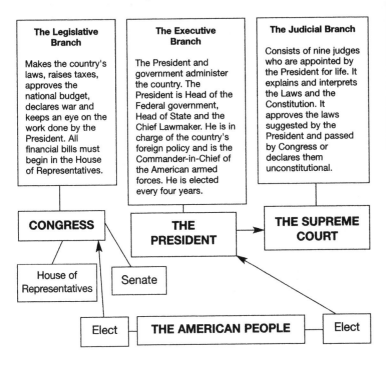

figure 2 judiciary/executive/legislature

Changing the constitution

It seems strange that a Constitution written in the eighteenth century and designed for a small agricultural nation could still be relevant to a major industrial nation over 200 years later. The secret lies in the ability of the states to amend the constitution if three-quarters of the states agree and the power of the Supreme Court to interpret the Constitution according to the mores of the contemporary society. The Supreme Court has the power to veto acts of federal and state government if it believes that the Constitution is being infringed. Occasionally this power has been used to hinder rather than facilitate reforms.

Political parties

There are two main political parties in the USA: the Republicans and the Democrats. However, unlike European political parties they do not stand for opposing political principles. Often their policies seem identical but the main difference lies in the way the parties respond to the conflicting demands of the various sections of public opinion, for example, business, trade unions, agricultural or state interests. The American voter often supports one party on one issue and the other party on a different issue; similarly they might vote for a congressman from one party and the other party's presidential candidate. At the beginning of the twentieth century, the Republicans were regarded as the more conservative party with a tendency to support business interests, while the Democrats were seen as the more progressive party which tended to support labour interests and to be more amenable to making changes in the traditional structure of US society.

The voters

The American people vote for the President, congressmen, senators, state governors, members of the state governments and, in some states, some public officials such as judges. The fifteenth amendment (change) of the Constitution in 1870 gave voting rights in theory to all male citizens regardless of their race, colour or religion. However, in practice many states avoided this by ruling that voters had to be literate or resident in the state for a certain length of time before they could register to vote. It was not until 1920 that American women won the right to vote; it was 1924 before Native American Indians were declared full citizens of the USA and thus eligible to vote; in 1965 the Voting Rights Act gave the federal government power to send federal representatives into an area to place the names of African-American citizens on the electoral rolls thus ensuring that African-American voters in many southern states finally gained the vote.

It would be complacent to view the system of voting in the USA at the end of the twentieth century as reformed beyond all recognition compared to the situation that existed at the beginning of the twentieth century as there are clearly several areas which need to be reformed further. In his book *Stupid White Men* (2001), the author and film director Michael Moore has publicized the view that during the Presidential election of 2000 many American voters were deliberately disenfranchised. In Florida, the Secretary of State in charge of the elections instructed Database Technologies to examine the state's electoral rolls and remove anyone suspected of being a felon. Thousands of felons, the majority of whom were African Americans, were removed from the electoral roll together with thousands of citizens who had never committed a crime and thousands who had only committed misdemeanours. In total, 173,000 registered voters in Florida were disenfranchised including the elections supervisor of Madison County, Florida! Michael Moore is convinced that this campaign of disenfranchisement was a deliberate ploy on the part of the Bush camp. The topic of voter registration remains one of considerable concern to many within US society, and both sides in the 2004 presidential election employed thousands of lawyers to scrutinize electoral procedures, but further controversy was avoided.

02

the USA in 1900

This chapter will cover:
- the end of the Gilded Age and the advent of progressivism
- progressive Republican Presidents – Roosevelt and Taft
- the work of Woodrow Wilson.

The period immediately prior to the twentieth century is sometimes known as the 'Gilded Age'. The analogy is subtle. Gilt often loses its lustre by becoming tarnished or it rubs off to reveal the base material beneath; in the same way, in spite of the prosperity brought by industrialization and economic progress in the USA at the end of the nineteenth century, there was also an atmosphere of political corruption and industrial exploitation and there were wide gaps between the rich and poor. It was a period of rapid industrialization and urbanization which saw an influx of immigrants from Europe bringing with them challenges as well as much needed cheap labour. Change was so rapid that US society and politics could barely keep up. Government economic policy prior to 1900 had been characterized by the principle of laissez-faire – the idea that government had no business interfering in people's lives by passing legislation unless the nation's interests were directly threatened; business should be left alone to run its own affairs and, similarly, workers were free to bargain with their employers regarding wages and working conditions. Due to the lack of government regulation of the economy, some large businesses, or trusts, had increased their power to such an extent that they had become monopolies which could fix prices and get rid of any competition. Their power threatened free enterprise and the public interest, especially as some dominated the political process using bribery and corruption common even in 'high places'.

Progressivism

Slowly, reform became a priority and some historians refer to the first two decades of the twentieth century as the 'progressive era'. Unfortunately these historians do not agree on any definition of progressivism, its causes, its supporters, the extent of its success nor even its timescale. Generally, the Progressive movement was made up of different groups of people including middle-class professionals, the media (or 'muckrakers' as Theodore Roosevelt called them), members of the Protestant clergy and some politicians including Presidents Theodore Roosevelt (1901–9), William Taft (1909–13) and Woodrow Wilson (1913–21).

The Progressive movement had no specific programme and many 'progressive' measures varied according to local circumstances. In Wisconsin, the Republican Governor Robert

La Follette clashed with powerful vested interests in the railroads and local politics, while in Cleveland, Ohio, the Democrat Tom Johnson worked hard to reform both city politics and social deprivation – to national acclaim. Generally speaking, progressives were anxious to reform political corruption, the monopolies of big business and the urban deprivation of the big cities; they seem to have held the belief that the political and social environment could be influenced and improved by sensible direct action on the part of the government at all levels. However, they should not be confused with socialists; the progressives were fervently pro-democracy and accepted capitalism, but at the same time they were keen to see moderate change in the areas mentioned above – business, politics and society.

Nearly all progressives wished to regulate big business or 'bust' the power of the trusts (a combination of firms or corporations reducing competition and controlling prices throughout a business or an industry), but they could not agree how to do this. They were opposed to corrupt party machines and the influence of big business on politics but they could not agree on the extent of the political reforms needed – some even opposed giving women the vote. Progressives wanted the government to help the less fortunate in society, especially as some religious progressives believed that poor social conditions could lead to evil, the rise of socialism or class struggle. There were many attempts to clear slums, develop better health and safety at work, improve educational and leisure facilities, improve the hours and wages of women and children who worked, and to ensure a basic welfare provision for widows and orphans. Yet they could not agree on the value or otherwise of Prohibition (the ban of alcohol).

On a federal level the work of the progressives tends to be seen in the work of Presidents Roosevelt, Taft and Wilson. These Presidents used their executive position to further the cause of progressivism and bring about a number of progressive reforms in the federal government.

President Theodore (Teddy) Roosevelt 1901–9

In complete contrast to the cuddly, comforting safe toy named after him, the teddy bear, President Roosevelt, or T. R., as he was known, was quite an adventurer. His chequered career encompassed such jobs as rancher, author, assistant secretary of the navy, the leader of the Rough Riders in the Spanish–American war, a war hero, Police Commissioner and Governor of New York – and all this before he became the twenty-sixth President of the United States at the age of 42 when President William McKinley was assassinated in September 1901. McKinley had been standing in a receiving line greeting the public in Buffalo when an anarchist named Leon Czolgosz shot him twice at point-blank range. Despite early hopes that he might survive the attack, a week later the President died, whispering the words of his favourite hymn, 'Nearer my God to Thee, Nearer to Thee.'

With Theodore Roosevelt in the White House, the nineteenth century was over and the modern era had begun. Conservative Republican, Mark Hanna, complained to a colleague, 'Now look! That damned cowboy is president of the United States!'

At first, Roosevelt seemed to reassure the rather conservative Republican Party elders by keeping the cabinet he had inherited from McKinley but his State of the Union address when he came to office in 1901 made it quite clear that here was a man who had a 'progressive' vision for the role of the federal government. He called for greater federal control of business and inter-state transport, a civil service in which promotion was based on merit rather than seniority or political sponsorship, and a greater effort to conserve the natural resources of the nation.

Roosevelt's 'square deal'

Roosevelt was one of the first Presidents to use the term 'deal' when setting out his policies; he talked of a 'square deal' to help all Americans – workers and businesspeople, consumers and producers. His Square Deal policy tried to be even-handed to both capital and labour – 'We stand for the rights of the man of wealth and for the rights of the wage-worker'; in fact Roosevelt probably satisfied neither and much reform was left to the presidency of Woodrow Wilson.

In 1902, Roosevelt supported striking miners in eastern Pennsylvania in their efforts to gain a pay increase, an eight-hour day and union recognition by threatening to use federal troops to run the mines should the mine owners not agree to submit themselves to a board of mediation. The mine owners partically agreed to the miners' demands allowing a 10 per cent pay increase and a nine-hour day rather than an eight-hour day, but union recognition was withheld.

His genuine support for the conservation of the country's natural resources, and his desire to limit the transferral of public land to private ownership became apparent when Roosevelt backed the 1902 Newlands Act (which raised money to finance irrigation projects by the sale of land) and added 60 million hectares (148 million acres) to federal forest reserves and established several national parks. Between 1905 and 1909 approximately 48.5 million hectares (120 million acres) of land were taken into public ownership. These policies gave the impression that Roosevelt was backing 'the people' rather than big business interests in mining, timber and oil, and the fact that he was such a youthful, dynamic individual with a young family contributed to his 'progressive' image.

In the sphere of big business, Roosevelt was not against very large corporations but he was keen to ensure fair play and that consumer interests were placed at the forefront of business practice. The Pure Food and Drug Act of 1906 and the Meat Inspection Act of 1908 both sought to ensure that consumers' health was protected from the dangers of false labelling and unsanitary meat-processing conditions. Roosevelt also took action against some big business practices by enforcing the terms of the 1890 anti-trust legislation and by setting up a Bureau of Corporations to investigate allegations against trusts. Twenty-four official charges were brought against the trusts during Roosevelt's presidency – twice as many as any previous administration. The Elkins Act of 1903 and the Hepburn Act of 1906 helped strengthen previous legislation concerned with inter-state commerce; the former emphasized the illegality of secret rebates on the railroads by making both the recipient and the giver open to prosecution; it also made the railroad agent responsible for any changes in the published rates. The Hepburn Act strengthened and extended the power of the Interstate Commerce Commission by enabling it to inspect the books of railway companies and establish the maximum rates they could charge.

Some historians have questioned Roosevelt's commitment to reform, seeing him as a reactionary who championed the cause of reform in order to stave off revolution. He wrote that, 'We seek to control law-defying wealth, in the first place to prevent it doing evil, and in the next place to avoid the vindictive and dreadful radicalism which if left uncontrolled it is certain in the end to arouse.' However, conservatives viewed him with great suspicion which must strengthen his progressive credentials, and his commitment to conservation cannot be doubted. Roosevelt was certainly a self-publicist but his encouragement of reform and his attempts to persuade big business to reform itself certainly contributed to the cause of progressivism. He can be credited with inventing one of the most crucial elements of the modern presidency: the use of the media to appeal directly to the people. He was an extremely popular President who seemed to have a genuine concern for the underdog in US society, but he refused to stand for a third term as President, and gave his support to William Howard Taft as the Republican candidate.

President William Howard Taft 1909–13

The contrast between Roosevelt and Taft could not have been more striking. While the former was young, energetic and adventurous, the latter weighed over 127 kg (20 stones) and gave the impression of being slow and rather ponderous. When he moved into the White House in 1909, Taft found many of the building's fixtures (including hundreds of doors) 'inadequate' for his needs and he ordered renovations. In particular, the President ordered the installation of a special bathtub large enough to accommodate four average-sized men when, after using the original bathtub for the first time, he got stuck and required considerable assistance to get out!

Taft seemed to lack Roosevelt's political skills, which had successfully managed the split within the Republican Party between the progressives and the conservatives. To many of the progressives Taft appeared to support the conservatives, however, he continued Roosevelt's conservation policies and the extension of merit as a basis for career advancement in the civil service. With regard to the prosecution of big business misdemeanours, Taft's administration saw more 'trust-busting' than that of the Roosevelt years. Using the anti-trust legislation, the Standard Oil Company of New Jersey was deemed to have an illegal monopoly over oil refining and was consequently dissolved; similarly the American Tobacco Company was forced to reorganize.

The Mann-Elkins Act of 1910 further strengthened the powers of the Interstate Commerce Commission and extended its authority to telephone, telegraph and wireless companies. The efforts to improve employment conditions continued with the formation of the Departments of Labor and Commerce, and the federal government led the way when an eight-hour day was introduced for all employees on government contracts. In 1913 a graduated income tax was introduced by the sixteenth amendment to the Constitution.

All of the above would seem to strengthen Taft's progressive credentials, yet some progressive leaders felt that he was less committed to the progressive cause than he might have been, especially in the areas of tariff reform and conservation. Taft had reduced the tariff from 57 per cent to an average of 40 per cent in 1909, which pleased some farmers and workers in the West who had seen prices rise faster than wages, but many progressives were disappointed having argued for a much greater reduction. The decision to return various parcels of land in Wyoming and Montana to private ownership and allow parts of Alaska to be claimed by private individuals for the purpose of mining convinced progressives that Taft had abandoned Roosevelt's principles of conservation. Two federal conservationists, Louis Glavis and Gifford Pinchot, protested and were dismissed. As Taft sided more frequently with the conservative Republicans in Congress, progressive leaders plotted revenge.

The 1912 presidential election

In 1911, Theodore Roosevelt made a surprise decision to run as a candidate for the nomination as the Republican candidate in the forthcoming presidential election. In spite of great support for Roosevelt in the primaries, Taft dominated the party convention and was duly chosen as the Republican candidate. Undeterred, Roosevelt turned to the newly-formed Progressive Republican League and was nominated by them as their presidential candidate. This party was known as the Bull-Moose Party since the term was frequently used by Roosevelt in his speeches to denote someone who was energetic and forthright. However, apart from their stance on tariffs, trusts and conservation, there was little difference between the policies or 'platforms' presented by the Republicans and the Progressive Republicans. A voter presented with the choice between the 'New Nationalism' of the Republicans and the 'New Freedom' of the Progressive Republicans would have been hard pressed to differentiate between the two, with the result that the election was fought on personalities rather than specific differences in the platforms. Not everyone approved of Roosevelt's decision to stand for a third term. While campaigning in Milwaukee in

October 1912, Roosevelt was shot in the chest by an insane saloon-keeper who opposed his third-term candidacy. Though 'bleeding like a wounded bull moose', the former President remained bent on completing the speech he had planned to give. 'I will deliver this speech or die,' he declared. 'One or the other.'

The Republican vote was split and Woodrow Wilson (the Democrat candidate) was able to take advantage of this and won the election for the Democrats for the first time in 20 years. In the comic monologue, *My Policies* (1915), Aaron Hoffman poked fun at the political and personal style of Theodore Roosevelt:

> But you must admit that the Bull Moose Party during its short but eventful life served this country well. If it wasn't for us and mostly me – you wouldn't have Woodrow Wilson as your president to-day…I had no feeling against Mr Taft. He's a brilliant man – honourable – the highest type of intellectual American but he had one unpardonable fault – he wouldn't do a damn thing I said.

The 1912 election is important because it marked the end of the Gilded Age. All of the candidates supported political reform, lower tariffs and regulation of big business – it was a clear victory for progressive policies.

President Woodrow Wilson 1913–20

Elected to the post of President of the USA in 1913 at the age of 54, this university professor had little experience of politics prior to his adoption as the Democratic candidate. However, Woodrow Wilson succeeded in gaining 435 electoral college votes against 88 for Teddy Roosevelt and only 8 for William Taft. Although this seems like a huge victory, if we look at the actual number of votes cast by the people, Wilson's total of 6,283,019 was less than the combined votes for Taft and Roosevelt which stood at 7,604,463. Wilson had served just two years as Governor of New Jersey before winning the White House and he became the first southern-born President since the Civil War.

He became President of the richest country in the world – a country that was blessed with an abundance of natural resources such as coal, oil and metals; one that had a plethora of talent in the scientists, engineers and inventors, such as Ford and the Wright brothers, who could make use of these natural resources; one that had an extravagance of financiers and industrialists such as Rockefeller and Carnegie who controlled vast industrial empires and had personal fortunes greater than the national income of many countries in the 'old world'. This combination of 'blessings' ensured that the USA was a prosperous nation which was booming in the early part of the twentieth century.

Yet, not all the citizens of the USA shared in the industrial wealth of the nation; there was also a dark side to this prosperity and stability. In spite of the efforts of Roosevelt and Taft, beneath the veneer lay a grinding poverty. Slums and inner city tenements were to be found next to the new streets of the cities; children and immigrants slaved for long hours and low pay in dangerous conditions with little hope of recompense should they be injured at their work; certain businesses had such power that they gained a monopoly over what they were selling thus stifling individual enterprise.

In the political sphere all was not as it seemed – there were many corrupt politicians who were open to bribery, sold public land for private gain and awarded valuable contracts to their friends, or to the highest bidder. Mining and lumber companies seized public land without paying or being taxed. Even farming had become the preserve of big business with the machinery and equipment needed to farm on a profitable, competitive scale being beyond the reach of the ordinary homesteader and leaving him or her unable to compete. East coast bankers were unwilling to lend money to small enterprises and the customs duties which protected US goods from competition from abroad also made it difficult for the farmer to sell produce to a foreign market as other countries raised tariffs on US goods in return.

The New Freedom

Woodrow Wilson was aware of these problems, declaring that 'evil has come with the good. With riches has come inexcusable waste'. He believed that any American should have the freedom to manage their affairs as they wished, so long as this freedom was extended to all, and not limited to a privileged few. He was aware that in the space of half a century life in the USA had changed so rapidly that real freedom was in danger of disappearing. His 'New Freedom' attacked the huge corporations and favoured trust-busting rather than business regulation and he was in favour of tariff reduction. Although Wilson claimed the federal government should be free to become involved in the affairs of the states, the corporations and individuals, he tended to oppose its involvement in social or welfare matters; these, he believed should be the preserve of the state governments.

There seems to be two phases to Wilson's policy making during his first term in office. From 1913–14 he persuaded his recalcitrant colleagues to support the passage of measures such as the 1913 Underwood-Simmons Tariff (which reduced tariffs); the Federal Reserve Act (which created a central banking system); the 1914 Clayton Anti-trust Act (which extended the number of business practices which were illegal and made it clear that strikes, picketing and boycotting were not illegal); he introduced the first permanent income tax law and he gave the Federal Trade Commission (1914) more power over trusts.

Yet these measures were not seen as enough by many who felt that further reform was needed to improve the welfare of many Americans; it would take action by the federal government to make concrete improvements in this sphere rather than waiting for the individual states to do it. With the 1916 election looming and the prospect of perhaps running against Theodore Roosevelt (who had re-joined the Republicans) or at the very least a united Republican Party, Wilson introduced a series of measures designed to steal a march on Roosevelt's 'New Nationalism' which had already advocated several welfare improvements. Wilson declared his support for votes for women; railroad workers gained an eight-hour maximum day through the Adamson Act (1916); the Federal Farm Loan Act (1916) helped farmers to get long-term mortgage loans at a lower rate than those offered by commercial banks; financial assistance was provided to federal employees who were absent from work because of illness or injury thanks to the Workman's Compensation Act (1916), and finally a Child Labour Act (the Keating-Owen Act 1916) barred goods made using child labour from inter-state commerce.

By the end of his first term in office Wilson had completed much of his Republican predecessors' progressive agenda and secured re-election in 1916. Wilson campaigned on 'Peace, Prosperity and Progress' and gained 9.2 million votes; his opponent, Charles Hughes won 8.5 million votes – the result was so close that the *New York Times* mistakenly declared Hughes the winner the day after the election! Although his success in keeping the USA out of the World War raging since 1914 did much to enhance his popularity with the electorate, it was ironic that Wilson took the country into that war in April 1917.

The USA at war 1917–18

During the war the federal government became involved in many national activities such as the running of the railways and telephone lines, the production of food, the conservation of fuel and the increase of income, inheritance and corporate taxes. Civil liberties were curtailed as the Espionage Act of 1917 and the Sedition Act of 1918 made criticism of the war effort illegal. Left-wing trade unions were targeted and over 1,500 people, including Eugene Debs the Socialist leader, were imprisoned.

Propaganda against Germany was spearheaded by the Committee on Public Information and indirectly the campaign for Prohibition was given a boost since much of the US brewing industry was dominated by Germans!

President Wilson's wife Edith set an example to the rest of the country and proved her resourcefulness when, during the war, she bought a flock of sheep to crop the White House lawn, and auctioned their wool for the benefit of the Red Cross. The auction netted $100,000.

By 1918 and the end of the war, the role of the federal government in the lives of the American people had significantly increased; the eighteenth amendment (1917) which introduced Prohibition finally became law and the nineteenth amendment was introduced which resulted in votes for women in 1920.

Wilson post war

With the advent of peace, Wilson began to lose the support of the American people. They had entered the war in order to safeguard their country and they had little sympathy with Wilson's dream of a new world made safe from war. The time spent in Versailles re-drawing European frontiers and creating the League of Nations was regarded with suspicion by the American public and many felt that the League might drag the USA into yet another war not of their concern, rather than actually preventing war. The Republicans now controlled the Senate and refused to ratify the Treaty of Versailles, the opposition to it being led by Senator Henry Cabot Lodge who believed many of Wilson's ideas were woolly minded and ill-thought out. Cabot Lodge's 14 'reservations' on Wilson's ideas for the creation of a League of Nations claimed that the League compromised the USA's sovereignty and freedom of action. Wilson refused to be intimidated and set off on a gruelling whistle-stop tour of the USA to gather support from the people for his plans. This tour was ill-advised as Wilson had already suffered a stroke while in Versailles; on 26 September 1919 he suffered a second stroke in Pueblo Colorado, and a third even more debilitating stroke followed in October. Wilson spent the last 17 months of his second term lying or dozing in the White House, unable to carry out his duties. His wife Edith unobtrusively performed many of his presidential functions. By the presidential election of 1920, Wilson's style of government was out of fashion, the public seemed to have lost its appetite for domestic reform and were more concerned with restoring stability and order in a country raked with 'Red Scares', strikes, rioting and racial strife. The Democrat candidate, James Cox, found that the disillusioned electorate blamed the Democrats for rising prices, industrial conflict and economic problems and these were the issues which concerned them, not the League of Nations which was the Democrats' main campaign issue. The Republican candidate, Warren Harding, had run an uninspiring campaign promising a return to 'normalcy' – whatever that was supposed to mean! The party was acutely aware of Harding's shortcomings and one Republican grandee, Senator Penrose, suggested Harding be kept at home and not be allowed to make any speeches: 'If he goes on tour, somebody's sure to ask him questions and Warren's just the sort of damned fool that will try to answer them.' Yet Harding won the 1920 election with a greater margin than any previous presidential candidate.

Woodrow Wilson, an idealist and a consummate politician, remained an invalid for the rest of his life and died three years later on 3 February 1924.

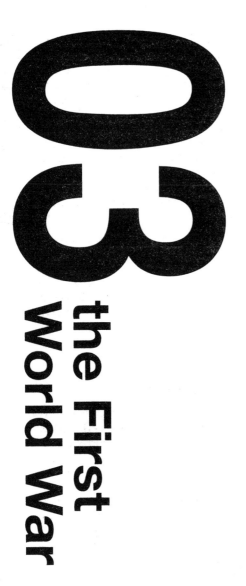

03

the First World War

This chapter will cover:
- the reasons the USA entered the war
- US involvement in Europe
- the effect of the war on the USA.

When, in 1914, war broke out in Europe between the Central Powers (Germany, Austria-Hungary and later Turkey) and the Allies of the Entente (Britain, France, Russia and later Italy), most Americans believed that the USA's distance from Europe would be sufficient to keep it out of the war. Since the country was made up of millions of immigrants originally from Europe, the US President Woodrow Wilson had no wish to become involved in a war which could alienate a large sector of the American populace, whichever side the USA chose to support. Publicly, Wilson insisted that the war in Europe was nothing to do with the USA but privately his sympathy lay with Britain, France and Belgium rather than the Central Powers. The allies were 'fighting our fight' as he put it.

The USA was not entirely neutral during the years 1914–17. The country continued to trade with Britain, lending the country money at a high rate of interest to purchase US goods and, by 1915 nearly one in three British shells fired on the Western Front in France had been made in the USA. However, the USA's wish to keep out of the European conflict was severely compromised by a number of incidents in the opening years of the war.

The sinking of the *Lusitania*

In 1915, Germany became increasingly convinced that the USA, in spite of her declarations of neutrality, was supplying the Allies with arms and ammunition. On 7 May 1915, the Cunard passenger liner *Lusitania* was torpedoed by a German U-boat. The British Admiralty had secretly subsidized the liner's construction in 1903 and she had been built to Admiralty specifications on the understanding that should war break out, the ship would enter government service. As war clouds gathered in 1913, the *Lusitania* had gone into dry dock in Liverpool to be fitted for war service which included the installation of ammunition magazines and gun mounts on her decks. The mounts, concealed under the teak deck, were ready for the addition of the guns when needed.

On May 1 1915, the ship had left New York City en route for Liverpool. Unbeknown to her passengers, almost all of her hidden cargo consisted of munitions and contraband destined for the British war effort. On May 7, as the ship neared the coast of Ireland, a torpedo fired by the German submarine U-20 hit her side; the torpedo exploded on impact but was followed by a mysterious second explosion which tore the liner apart. At the time it was believed to be a second torpedo, but it has since been confirmed as an internal explosion. The cause of this second explosion has never been completely explained.

Within 18 minutes, the giant ship slipped beneath the waves. Of the 1,924 aboard, 1,198 died including some 128 Americans. There was a public outcry and Wilson sent a strongly worded protest to Berlin. Germany insisted that the *Lusitania* had been secretly carrying ammunition bound for the British war effort, but did promise not to attack passenger ships without warning, and the USA remained out of the war.

In the same year, several US merchant ships were torpedoed by German U-boats by mistake but Wilson still endeavoured to keep the USA out of the war. In the presidential elections in November 1916, he campaigned on the slogan: 'He kept us out of the war'. Within six months of being re-elected, Wilson had changed his stance and had become convinced that the USA should enter the war on the side of the Allies. What had caused this change in direction?

The Zimmerman telegram

In January 1917, British intelligence intercepted a telegram from the German foreign minister, Alfred Zimmerman, to the German Ambassador in Mexico. It seemed to suggest that Germany was prepared to back Mexico's plans to invade and seize Arizona, New Mexico and Texas if, in return, Mexico would enter the war on Germany's side. Germany had been using unrestricted submarine warfare (the sinking of any shipping coming near the Allies in an attempt to starve them of food and materials), but only infrequently because of fierce US opposition. In theory, the USA's official neutrality meant that trading continued with all belligerents; in practice their trading partners tended to be the Allies rather than Germany and, consequently, US shipping was a frequent victim of the German U-boats.

The German High Command was under no illusion that renewed unrestricted submarine warfare would in all likelihood cause the USA to declare war on them, but gambled on undermining the British war effort before a US army could arrive in Europe in force. The alliance with Mexico and Japan, as proposed in the Zimmerman telegram, intended to create a new front in the area of the Pacific and Central America. This would distract the US and help the German war effort by dealing a psychological blow to the Allies who were by now in desperate need of US military assistance on the Western Front. The 'secure' channel by which the telegram was sent was not as secure as the Germans believed; when British intelligence intercepted the telegram, they recognized the effect it would have on US public opinion and presented it to the USA on 24 February 1917; it was released to the world's press on 1 March. Mexico and Japan immediately denied having anything to do with the proposal but Zimmerman admitted the telegram's authenticity on 3 March. This was accompanied by press reports that German immigrants had been sabotaging US factories, and this stirred up more anti-German feelings and led to renewed calls for Prohibition since there were so many German breweries in America.

Unrestricted submarine warfare

On 31 January 1917, Germany had imposed a zone around the British Isles which was patrolled by submarines prepared to sink any enemy ship together with any suspected of supplying Britain with war material. President Wilson had promptly cut diplomatic links with Germany, the first step to war. This declaration of unrestricted submarine warfare, together with the sinking of four unarmed US ships on 12 and 19 March and the publication of the Zimmerman telegram, increased the American public's hostility towards Germany and facilitated Wilson's attempts to persuade Congress to declare war on Germany. In his speech to the combined assembly of the Senate and the House of Representatives on 2 April 1917, Wilson reminded the assembly that US ships had been sunk with the loss of American lives and declared that neutrality was at an end: 'We must fight for the peace of the world…The world must be made safe for Democracy.'

The Allies looked to the USA for salvation with the expectation that the industrial strength of the USA would replenish the supply of war material necessary for victory and that fresh US troops could revitalize the exhausted Allied forces. The French writer, Jean de Pierrefeu, wrote of the entry of the USA into the war: 'Life arrived in torrents to revive the mangled body of France bled white by the countless wounds of four years'.

In most areas these expectations were unrealistic. The USA was unprepared for its entrance into the armed conflict especially since many inside the USA believed that their country's contribution to the war would be largely economic. In April 1917, the US army numbered less than 300,000 which included all the National Guard units that could be pressed into national service. The army's arsenal of war supplies was non-existent. Prior to 1917, the USA had built no more than 800 planes and yet Clemenceau, the French leader, called upon the country to produce 2,000 planes per month immediately. The Allies, in addition, expected the US to provide an unlimited supply of manpower that they could absorb into their divisions which were nearing collapse under the strain of war. George C. Marshall, the future army chief of staff, recalled that of the 200 men in each company that landed in France, 180 were raw recruits, and that not only did some companies have no weapons some had not even heard of the weapons they did have!

Wilson selected General John J. Pershing (called 'Black Jack' after he commanded the famous 10th Cavalry which recruited African-American troopers nicknamed 'buffalo soldiers' in the 1890s) to head the American Expeditionary Force (AEF). Pershing left for Europe with a mandate from Wilson to co-operate with Allied forces under the following proviso: 'that the forces of the United States are a separate and distinct component of the combined forces the identity of which must be preserved.' In other words, there would be no wholesale integration of US soldiers into the British and French armies as the Allied commanders had hoped. The USA would fight under its own flag and its own leadership. This proved to be a bone of contention among the Allies for the rest of the war. The French had sent experienced English-speaking officers to give the new arrivals some advice and tips about the art of modern fighting using such things as machine guns, barbed wire and creeping artillery barrages, information obtained after three years of bloody experience. The British General Ivor Maxse offered to teach the US troops about tactics learned through bitter experience which could be employed by small units using grenades and light machine guns rather than rifles. Pershing received this advice politely enough but was determined to fight battles 'the American way'. After all, what useful advice could an army that had consistently failed to break the enemy's defences offer him?

The USA's build-up was slow – Pershing had called for a million men, Congress replied it could muster 420,000 by spring 1918. The Selective Services Act introduced conscription in May 1917 and initially men aged 21–30 were called up. Some 3.5 million were called up during 1917 and 1918 and over 1.5 million volunteered. Over half of these served on the Western Front. The anticipated cornucopia of military supplies from the USA never materialized and in the main the 'doughboys', as the US soldiers were called, fought with equipment supplied by the Allies. A War Industries Board was set up under the authority of the financier Bernard Baruch, and this organized supplies and raw materials for the war effort. And yet all the artillery the Americans used at the battles of Saint-Mihiel and the Argonne was French or British, the troops crossed the Atlantic in British ships, the transport trucks were British and French and not a single US war-plane fought on the Western Front. This was because space on the transatlantic ships was needed for food for a starving Britain, which meant that the Americans could supply men or equipment but not both, and as the German spring offensive in 1918 threatened the Allies with defeat, troops were the priority. US troops saw their first action in May 1918 in fighting along the River Marne.

The Battle of the Marne

Over 85,000 US soldiers took part in the Battle of the Marne during the summer of 1918. The German attack on the Marne had been launched by General Erich von Ludendorff on 15 July but the Germans failed to break through and the Allied General Ferdinand Foch was able to organize a counter-attack using 24 divisions of the French army, and soldiers from the USA, Britain and Italy. The Americans commanded by Pershing halted the German advance at Bellau Wood and Chateau-Thierry. On 20 July the Germans had begun to withdraw and by 3 August they were back to where they were when the combined Spring Offensive began in March. The arrival of the US troops had a profound psychological effect on both the Allies and the German troops revitalizing the former and dispiriting the latter. Allied casualties during the Battle of the Marne were heavy: French 95,000; British 13,000; and US 12,000. It is estimated that the German army suffered an estimated 168,000 casualties.

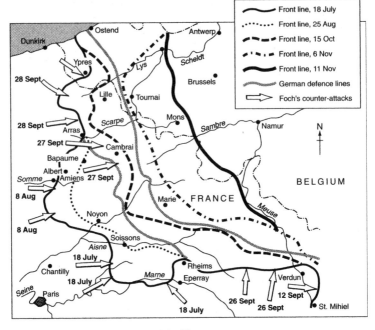

figure 3 the battle in the area of the Marne

St Mihiel

The German-held area around St Mihiel in eastern France was the location of the US army's first offensive. Here Pershing and 300,000 troops assembled in early September. When the German High Command became aware that the attack was imminent, they ordered a partial withdrawal of troops which was still in progress when the US army attacked on 12 September. The advancing US and French troops were supported by over 1,400 aircraft and on the first day the main attack advanced 9 km (5.5 miles) to reach Thiancourt. By 16 September, the entire St Mihiel salient was under Allied control.

The Battle of the Argonne

During the summer of 1918, the Allies had been successful in offensives on Amiens and Albert and, in an attempt to cut off the entire German 2nd Army, Marshal Foch ordered an attack at Meuse-Argonne. Pershing was given overall command of the operation and the AEF was given the main attacking role. 400,000 US troops from the successful St Mihiel campaign were brought down to take part in the Meuse-Argonne offensive on 26 September 1918. More than 300 tanks were used by the US 1st Army in the offensive and the advance was supported by 500 aircraft from the US Air Service. Two-thirds of the soldiers involved in the advance were battle weary having only recently arrived from St Mihiel. Small wonder the troops only advanced 3 km (2 miles) along a 64 km (40 miles) front on the first day. The offensive failed to 'take off' and eventually came to a halt on 30 September. The offensive was resumed on 4 October with the Americans pushing through the Argonne Forest. This time the US troops, supported by 3,000 guns and 189 tanks launched an attack on the 64 km (40 miles) front, succeeding in advancing 9.5 km (6 miles) on the first day – an amazing feat. The success of the fresh US troops contrasted starkly with the exhausted Allies who had been fighting for four years but this success was short-lived. The logistics of supplying the army with 3,000 tonnes of shells per day on inadequate roads destroyed by shells proved to be too much; there were reports of US soldiers starving on the battlefield and of US wounded dying of thirst since it was impossible to remove them to dressing stations and field hospitals because of the traffic jams on the roads approaching the front. The geography of the area also hindered the offensive – so dense was the woodland in the area that it was almost like a natural fortress. The US army was unable to continue its success of the first day and took 21 days to cover the next 5 km (3 miles) before grinding to a halt. The reasons for this were numerous but poor supply routes were a major factor as was the inexperience of the US troops. Pershing was puzzled by the failure of the Argonne offensive; his diary recorded his conviction that if the army kept on pounding, the Germans would be forced to yield, a sentiment which Allied generals had ceased to share. The Germans held their ground until 4 November when they began to retreat. Fresh US troops were moved to the front and had advanced 32 km (20 miles) when the Armistice was announced on 11 November 1918.

The US Home Front

In 1917 the nation had to be mobilized for war and from April 1917 the government closely controlled US industries, thus abandoning laissez-faire temporarily. The government increased taxes on the rich; it intervened to settle disputes between workers and employers; it introduced propaganda exercises such as 'Meatless Tuesdays' and 'Wheatless Mondays' to encourage the public to save food, with the slogan 'Food will win the war'. The Committee on Public Information (CPI) was established to direct propaganda and to promote the idea that the USA was defending democracy and decency against the despicable 'Hun', as the Germans were called. To pay for the war, the government issued 'liberty bonds' promising that after the war those who had loaned money would be repaid with interest. The CPI whipped up hatred of Germany to such an extent that school authorities banned the teaching of German in schools and, in Boston, music by Beethoven and other German composers was banned because of the composers' nationality. The Espionage Act (June 1917) made it illegal to obstruct recruitment into the armed forces and set a fine of $10,000 and 20 years' imprisonment for interfering with the recruiting of troops or for the disclosure of information dealing with national defence. Additional penalties were included for the refusal to perform military duty. Over the next few months around 90 went to prison under the terms of this act, many of them members of the anti-war movement and left-wing political figures such as Eugene V. Debs and Emma Goldman. Debs was sentenced to ten years for a speech made in Canton, Ohio, on 16 June 1918 attacking the Espionage Act by claiming it was unconstitutional. The Sedition Act (May 1918) introduced heavy penalties for anyone who used 'disloyal language' about the government or armed forces. Over 1,500 people were imprisoned under the terms of the act including over 450 conscientious objectors. Rose Pastor Stokes (a radical and wife of a millionaire) was sentenced to ten years in prison for writing a letter to the *Kansas City Star* deploring the profiteering which went on and hinting at government connivance. Soon afterwards Kate Richards O'Hare (a socialist and reformer) was sentenced to five years for making an anti-war speech in North Dakota.

US losses

By the end of the war 36,931 US soldiers had been killed in action; 2,900 were missing; and 59,000 had died from disease. Naturally these figures, together with the return of troops following the armistice in November 1918, had a great impact on American public opinion which demanded that the USA turn its back on Europe and any other conflicts outside the USA, and adopt a policy of isolationism. More than 2 million troops eventually reached Europe but a large number arrived too late to see any action. The US forces suffered 264,000 casualties during the war. It has been calculated that 112,432 Americans died. Of these, around 50 per cent died from disease, mainly in the influenza epidemic that swept Europe at this time.

As the US 'doughboys', many of them wounded, sailed back to the USA, President Wilson sailed in the opposite direction to be present at the peace conference which was held in Versailles. Not only was he anxious to ensure that his 'Fourteen Points' – or proposals for a fair and just peace – formed the basis of the peace treaty, but he was also keen to present the conference with detailed plans for a new peace-keeping organization, the League of Nations. He believed that this organization could prevent a world war breaking out in future and was anxious that the USA formed the cornerstone of such an organization.

The Treaty of Versailles

When the Germans petitioned for peace, they did so to the Americans rather than to the British or French, in the hope that the Americans would be more lenient. After all, the Americans had not been fighting so long, they had not been fighting on home territory and President Wilson had issued his views on the principles needed for a just peace, namely his 'Fourteen Points' – or proposals for a fair and just peace, Wilson had declared that the USA's purpose in entering the war was to make the world safe for democracy; this reflected the high ideals of many Americans and the belief that their democratic system of government was worthy of being copied by all other countries. Wilson saw the USA's entry into the war as a chance to create a new world order with US democratic ideals as its foundation. His 'Fourteen Points' called for a new set of international rules based on principles such as the right of self-determination (the right to self-government), freedom of the seas, free trade, a negotiated disarmament and an end to secret diplomacy.

Wilson's 'Fourteen Points', although much heralded by the Allies, did not form the basis of the Treaty of Versailles. Greeted in Europe as a saviour, Wilson's idealistic principles failed to impress Britain and France. Britain had lost 900,000 men and had been nearly bankrupted by the cost of the war, and France had not only fought Germany twice in the space of less than half a century but had also lost 1.4 million lives during the most recent conflagration in addition to the material damage caused by the fighting. Rather than conducting the negotiations in an atmosphere of reconciliation, a spirit of revenge prevailed; the victorious Allies were anxious to 'make Germany pay' for all the damage done during the war especially as they had to pay back the money loaned to them by the USA during the war! The 'Big Four' – Wilson, Lloyd George (Britain), Clemenceau (France) and Orlando (Italy) – quarrelled bitterly about the terms of the peace settlement, with the Europeans determined to ensure that their territorial and reparation (compensation for damage) demands were met. Having fought the war for four years, they were not content to permit the USA, who had only joined in the fighting in 1918, to dictate the peace. Because of this, many of Wilson's high ideals were ignored or only half-heartedly put into action where they suited the Allies best. Eventually Wilson was pushed into a much less liberal peace than he had originally hoped for, particularly with regard to reparations. The Reparations Commission established Germany's debt at $33 billion in 1921, but it should be remembered that this money was not only going to rebuild the devastated towns and villages of France and Belgium but also to pay off the US loans the Allies had received during the first three years of the war and which the Americans were demanding be paid back with all speed. Had Wilson been a little more accommodating with regard to war loans perhaps the final reparations figure would have been less severe.

The League of Nations

Wilson proposed the establishment of a world organization to settle international disputes – an association of self-governing states 'to promote international cooperation and to achieve international peace and security' – that is, to settle international disputes peaceably and without recourse to war. Collective security was the principle at the heart of this organization – should one state attack another, other states would intervene to aid the victim. Wilson himself drafted the Covenant of the League of Nations and he made sure that it was written into the

Treaty of Versailles and the four other treaties which made up the Paris Peace Settlement. It was his sincere hope that the League could balance out any unfairness in the peace treaties.

Wilson returns to the USA

On his return from Europe in July 1919, Wilson presented the Treaty of Versailles and the Covenant of the League of Nations to the Senate for ratification. Only approval from the Senate would allow the USA to join the League, but within the Senate many were opposed to an organization which they believed would drag the USA into European conflicts – conflicts which did not concern or benefit the USA. One group of opponents known as the 'Irreconcilables', led by Senator Borah, held strongly isolationist views and were totally opposed to the League. A second group of opponents led by Senator Henry Cabot Lodge was not so extreme in its suspicion of the League, but they wanted major changes, known as the 'Lodge Reservations', to be made to the Covenant before they would give their support.

Wilson refused to consider making any changes; in his opinion the 'Lodge Reservations' undermined the League and he totally rejected them. Instead he decided to take his arguments directly to the people of the USA, embarking on a punishing schedule of public speaking where he proposed to make 37 one-hour speeches in 22 days. The combined strain of the war and the peace had taken its toll on Wilson and in September he suffered a series of strokes. This once erudite, charismatic public speaker was reduced to stumbling over his words and crying with frustration. During vital debates in the Senate Wilson issued instructions from his sickbed in the White House refusing to compromise in spite of the efforts of moderates to introduce small amendments which would satisfy the majority of senators and thus ensure acceptance of the Treaty. Wilson's reply to these compromises was stubborn: 'Better a thousand times to go down fighting than to dip your colours to dishonourable compromise.' He ordered the Democrats to vote against the proposed modifications and enough of them obeyed him to result in the required two-thirds majority needed to accept the Treaty being short of only seven votes. In November 1919 and March 1920, the Senate voted against US membership of the League and refused to accept the terms of the Covenant.

The USA's isolationism 1919–33

By the 1920s Americans were far more wary of foreigners, and several policies of the early 1920s can be seen to reflect this wariness; immigration restrictions and the Fordney-McCumber tariffs (see Chapter 5) reflected the mood of the nation and the view of President Calvin Coolidge that 'America must be kept American'. Yet in spite of being suspicious of becoming involved in European entanglements, US foreign policy in the 1920s cannot be said to be completely isolationist. Although the USA was not officially a member of the League of Nations, US observers attended more than 40 meetings of the League's Assembly and supported much of the League's work, particularly in the humanitarian spheres of health and labour.

Even before the end of the war, the appearance of the new Communist state in Russia following the 1917 Revolution worried Americans. They felt that their Democratic ideals and economic prosperity might be threatened by the contrasting political and economic ideals of the Communist state, and Wilson sent 7,000 US troops to Russia to fight on the side of the White anti-Communist army against the Bolshevik (Communist) Red army. These troops remained in Russia until 1920, and although they had little effect on the Russian civil war, they succeeded in creating a suspicion of Americans on the part of the Russians which lasted until the late twentieth century. The USA was the last great power to recognize the Union of Soviet Socialist Republics (USSR) in 1933 and even then it was more because of a fear of Japanese designs on China and the Far East than because of an acceptance of the Communist state.

American fear of Japanese ambitions was one of the reasons behind the Washington Naval Conference in 1922 which aimed to maintain the status quo in the Far East. In all, three treaties were signed at this conference: the USA, Britain, France and Japan agreed to consult on matters regarding the Pacific; the USA, Britain, Italy, France and Japan agreed to limit their naval capacity regarding battleships to a ratio of $5:5:1\,{}^3/4:1\,{}^3/4:3$; a further treaty between nine powers that had interests in the Pacific agreed to respect Chinese territorial integrity. These agreements not only calmed fears of Japanese ambitions but also strengthened the principle of disarmament, permitting the Republicans to reduce military spending and cut taxes, and seemed to ensure that the kind of naval race which had led to the First World War would not occur again.

The USA had emerged from the First World War with the strongest economy in the world and with a vastly expanded share of worldwide trade, but economic considerations also meant that the USA could not completely cut herself off from the rest of the world. In 1922, the Germans announced that they could not meet the reparation payments and this lead to the occupation of the Ruhr by French troops attempting to force payment of the reparations, or to take them in kind from the industries that lay in the Ruhr. The Germans responded with passive resistance which in turn led to hyperinflation as industrial production shut down. The crisis threatened to destroy the German economy and result in the outbreak of violence until a conference was organized to sort out the chaos. Charles Dawes, a banker from Chicago, presided over the conference which rescheduled Germany's reparations payments and saw US loans of $200 million being given to Germany to rebuild her industry and economy, and thus keep up with her reparation repayments. In 1928, a further conference resulted in the Young Plan which cut the reparations payments to $9 billion to be paid off over 59 years. The USA was forced to take these steps because without German reparation payments to Britain and France, the USA would not be repaid the loans she had made to the Allies during the war.

The USA emphasized her commitment to world peace when, in 1928, the Kellogg-Briand Pact was signed renouncing war. For all its high sounding proclamations, the Pact had little worth, lacking as it did the mechanism for the enforcement of peace. The USA, while approving the Pact by a Senate majority of 85–1, made it quite clear that the Pact would have no effect on the Monroe Doctrine nor on America's self-defence and this 'get out clause' ensured that the Pact, though commendable in intention was, in reality, worthless.

The USA had emerged from the First World War as the leading economy of the world, yet there were problems to be faced at home. Four million soldiers were demobbed in 1919 just as industries started to lay off workers, since the demand for war materials had dried up. Prices had doubled during the war, but wages had not kept pace, with the result that workers demanded higher pay and went on strike to make their point. At the same time, there was a wave of race riots – also a reaction to the economic circumstances in which African Americans found themselves after the war. To add to this volatile mix came the influx of left-wing immigrants and the establishment of two communist parties in 1919. When anarchists began a wave of bomb attacks many were terrified that revolution was spreading to the USA. It was not surprising that Americans wanted to turn their back on Europe and concentrate on domestic matters and the 'return to normalcy'.

04

problems and challenges in the 1920s

This chapter will cover:
- immigration – the 'open door' closes
- prohibition and gangsters
- the revival of the Ku Klux Klan
- cultural change.

In 1913, 17-year-old Joseph Henry Bryan left his home in rural Denbigh, North Wales, to travel 80.5 km (50 miles) to the port of Liverpool. There he boarded *The Adriatic*, a ship bound for New York. The ship's manifest shows that he travelled alone and that his fellow travellers came from all over Europe. The records of arrival on Ellis Island show that Joseph Henry Bryan was met by his father who had crossed the Atlantic two years earlier and was now living in Waterbury, Connecticut. Evidently William Bryan had gone on ahead to earn enough money to send for the rest of the family. As Joseph Henry was the eldest son, he was the first to join his father and together the two men earned enough money to send for Elizabeth Bryan (wife and mother) and the two younger children.

This story is not a unique one – the 25 million records on Ellis Island tell many stories of families who parted in the 'old world' to be reunited in the USA. But what had attracted this Welsh family to the USA? The Bryans had their roots in farming which, at the beginning of the twentieth century, was in a parlous state and, like many other economic refugees, they left Wales to seek a higher standard of living in the USA.

The booming US economy at the beginning of the twentieth century attracted a flood of immigrants but by then it had become clear that the USA was no longer the 'melting pot' envisaged by French-born US author, agriculturalist Jean de Crevecoeur in 1782; increasingly the immigrants clung to their old languages and traditions rather than discarding them and becoming English-speaking 'Americans'. Assimilation was hampered by the clearly identifiable ethnic districts, or ghettos, which formed in the big cities and by the fact that attitudes towards immigrants had changed. Some Americans felt that the huge pool of cheap labour created by the immigrants would affect the labour market and lead to a decrease in wages. Anti-immigrant feeling had increased during the war, especially against Germans, and the Russian Revolution in 1917 made Americans increasingly suspicious of immigrants from eastern Europe for fear they would bring communism to threaten the democracy of the USA. This fear of communists, or 'Reds', grew after the war as a series of strikes swept the country and convinced many Americans that a communist revolution was imminent. When the home of the Attorney General Mitchell Palmer was bombed by a group of anarchists, the media became hysterical and whipped up fears of a potential conspiracy to undermine US democracy. Palmer organized a series of raids, rounding up anyone he believed was a 'Red'. As many as 1,000 people were rounded up and arrested, many under arrest warrants which were signed after the arrests. Of these, 556 were deported in spite of evidence that the majority of them were not communist supporters. The arrests were not only targeting individuals but also looking for information from membership lists, and files and Palmer urged Congress to pass a severe sedition bill – it refused. The Palmer raids proved hugely controversial, with the *New York Times*, 1920, complaining

> Without warrants of arrest men were carried off to the police stations and other temporary prisons, subjected there to secret police-office inquisitions commonly known as the 'third-degree', their statements written categorically into mimeographed blanks, and they were required to swear to them regardless of their accuracy.

In spite of the fiasco of the Palmer raids, the 'Red Scares' continued during the 1920s. There was a problem with anarchists. Thirty-eight people were killed by a bomb on Wall Street on 16 September 1920, and earlier that year the cause célèbre involving two Italian immigrants, Nicola Sacco and Bartolomeo Vanzetti, began its seven-year run.

On 15 April 1920, two men, one a paymaster for a shoe factory, the other his armed guard, were attacked, shot and robbed of the $15,000 payroll they were carrying; both men later died. On 5 May 1920, two Italian-born labourers, Sacco and Vanzetti, were arrested for the crime; they were known to be anarchists who had opposed the USA's entry into the war, avoided military service, had supported strikes and, in the case of Vanzetti, had previous criminal convictions. The judge who presided over the trial, Judge Webster Thayer, a conservative Republican, was clearly biased against the two men because of their Italian extraction and their political beliefs, and his adverse comments about the men during the trial made it obvious that he was determined to find them guilty. On very weak, circumstantial evidence, such as their guilty demeanour, the fact that they were carrying guns and that 61 eye witnesses said two Italian-looking men did it, Sacco and Vanzetti were convicted and sentenced to death. The trial attracted a lot of worldwide attention and there followed a seven-year struggle to prove that the men were innocent and that they had been discriminated against because of their ethnic origin and their political views, which they were perfectly entitled to hold in a democracy. In spite of these efforts, Sacco and Vanzetti were executed in the electric chair on

24 August 1927. In the 1970s the two men were granted a formal pardon by the Governor of Massachusetts who accepted that a mistrial had taken place.

The case added to the already hysterical attitude in US society at the time, and it finally convinced politicians that the 'open-door' immigration policy needed to be limited. This received great support from rural and small town communities whose inhabitants were predominantly white Anglo-Saxon Protestants (WASPs) who agreed wholeheartedly with President Coolidge's assertion that 'America must be kept American'. In 1921, the Emergency Quota Act was passed which reduced immigration from eastern and southern Europe by establishing a quota: new immigrants were permitted entry in proportion to the number of people of the same nationality who had been in the USA in 1910. Exceptions were made for artists, actors, academics, nurses and other professionals. This act was extended in 1924 by the National Origins Act which reduced the quota to 2 per cent of the 1890 census and was biased in favour of immigrants from northern Europe who tended to be WASPs. By 1929, only 150,000 immigrants per year were allowed admission, 85 per cent from northern and western Europe and none from Asia.

Prohibition

In a country where big business was so powerful and rights and freedom of the individual so highly prized, it seems amazing that an act which attacked the seventh largest industry in that country and enforced a certain way of living upon all of its inhabitants could have been passed into law by politicians who tended to favour laissez-faire policies and who had sworn to uphold the American Constitution and Bill of Rights. Yet the eighteenth amendment to the Constitution, which banned the production, transportation or sale of alcoholic beverages, was passed in 1917, followed by the 1919 Volstead Act, which defined liquor as drinks containing 0.5 per cent alcohol. By January 1920, the Prohibition of alcohol applied to the whole of the USA. The 'Noble Experiment' had been passed after only three days' debate by a Congress that had been lobbied unmercifully by a number of pressure groups. The Temperance Movement had been foremost in the pressure applied to government, and the Women's Christian Temperance Union and Anti-Saloon League campaigned with great success in the mainly rural areas of the South and West, threatening not to vote for political candidates who did not support the 'Dries' (as the supporters of Prohibition were called). They believed that the only way to end drunkenness, alcoholism, crime, acts of violence and poverty was to ban the sale of alcohol, a belief shared by many deeply religious Americans. The First World War spurred on the campaign with accusations that brewing used the equivalent of 11 million loaves of barley per day, grain which could have been used to feed the USA's Allies during the war. Since many of the brewing firms such as Schlitz, Pabst and Busch were German, the USA's enemy during the war, some claimed that it was unpatriotic to drink alcohol.

Once the National Prohibition Act came into nationwide effect at midnight 16 January 1920, John Kramer became the first Prohibition Commissioner with the job of enforcing the Act. Congress gave him $2.2 million which paid for a mere 1,500 agents; by 1926 this amount had risen to $10 million and by 1929 there were 3,000 agents and $12 million being spent on enforcing Prohibition. The task was impossible; the agents were poorly paid and open to bribery; one in 12 agents was sacked for taking bribes – it was discovered that they had been taking bribes because they were being taken to work in chauffeur-driven cars! Criminal elements took over the production, distribution and sale of alcohol and the small number of agents were soon overwhelmed by these criminal forces. Gangsters made over $2 billion a year from the illegal liquor trade and they were quite prepared to bribe politicians, judges and the police, and to settle any disputes with other gangs through the use of violence. Between 1926 and 1927, there were 130 gangland murders. Corruption in US society was at an all time high during this period, and once bribes were taken by officials, this put them in the pockets of the gangsters permanently and enabled other rackets such as gambling and prostitution to flourish. Corruption even reached into the federal government and some of President Harding's advisers were involved.

With land borders and coastlines of 30,000 km (18,640 miles), it was difficult to stop the smuggling of alcohol by bootleggers. The name 'bootlegger' originated in the seventeenth century when smugglers used to hide drink in their high leather boots to avoid paying taxes. The twentieth century bootleggers were as inventive as their earlier counterparts, hiding drink in hollow canes, in specially constructed steel waistcoats, in perambulators, or simply using string to strap the bottle to their legs under their trousers or to suspend it underneath the tail of their jackets.

There was so much profit to be made from the illegal liquor trade that many businessmen got involved, including one Joseph Kennedy, the father of the future President, who made a great deal of the Kennedy family fortune in this way. Drinking became fashionable perhaps because it was illegal, and speakeasies (illegal bars) flourished – in 1928, New York alone had at least 30,000, and although Boston had only 4,000 this was four times higher than the number of legal saloons in Massachusetts before Prohibition. It was clear that hundreds of thousands of people were prepared to defy the law and buy illegal drink, and the very misdemeanours that Prohibition was supposed to curtail flourished, with arrests for drunkenness trebling and deaths from alcoholism increasing by 600 per cent.

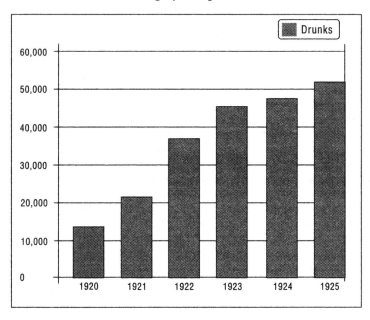

figure 4 arrests for drinking offences in Philadelphia 1920–5 based on figures from the Philadelphia police department

In New York it was possible to buy gin by calling a particular telephone number and for $2 it would be delivered to the door.

Prohibition failed for a number of practical reasons such as low numbers of enforcement personnel and resources, but it also failed because it attempted to force a particular moral viewpoint on the whole of the country with scant regard for immigrant groups such as the Irish, the Germans and the Italians, for whom drinking was an important part of their culture. Prohibition turned ordinary law-abiding citizens who liked the occasional drink into criminals, and increasingly no one took the law seriously. In 1930, a journalist wrote that at a lively party he had attended in Detroit he had spotted the Governor of Michigan, the Chief of Police and four circuit court judges drinking merrily. Opponents of Prohibition came from a wide cross-section of US society, from the brewers and distillers to immigrants and from rich industrialists such as the Du Pont brothers to workers. The tactics they used to persuade the government to repeal prohibition included slogans ('No beer, no work'), the backing of 'wet' candidates and producing anti-Prohibition newspapers, cartoons and pamphlets. The 'great social and economic experiment, noble in motive and far-reaching in purpose' (Herbert Hoover) played a major role in the reduction of respect for the law; it introduced corruption on a vast scale to US society and encouraged the involvement of organized crime in politics and business.

A government report by the Wickersham Commission concluded in 1931 that Prohibition did not work and, following the election of Franklin D. Roosevelt as President in 1933, the law was repealed. The coming of the Depression in 1929 had done much to hasten the end of Prohibition as it was felt that taxing alcohol would raise more taxes which could be spent on lowering the tax burden on the individual and raising money that could be spent on relief. Yet in the end Prohibition failed because it was essentially unworkable.

Gangsters

Bill Bryson notes that it was the more sinister side of Prohibition that gave new meaning to a nineteenth-century word meaning a member of a political gang: in the 1920s this word – gangster – came to mean the member of a criminal gang (Bryson, *Made in America*, 1998). Prohibition took alcohol out of the hands of legitimate businesspeople and let it be exploited by criminals, especially in the cities. Every city had its gangsters and these were almost always of immigrant extraction. Two of the most famous gangsters at this time were in Chicago – John Torrio and Al Capone, both of Italian extraction. However, it would be wrong to think that organized crime at this time was only an Italian-American phenomenon; Irish Americans and Jewish

Americans also played their part. In New York, half of the criminal gangs were Jewish, one-quarter Italian, one-eighth Polish and one-eighth Irish, while in Chicago they were Italian and Irish. During Prohibition, two of the most famous gang bosses in Chicago were Dion O'Banion and John Torrio, the former of Irish extraction and the latter an Italian-American with links to the Mafia.

On the surface O'Banion was a jovial individual who ran a flower shop and sang in the choir of Holy Name Cathedral. Yet he became rich through bootlegging liquor, eventually controlling most of the bootleg business in south Chicago, and he murdered at least 25 people. He was known to carry a rosary in his pocket, have a carnation in his buttonhole, and carry three guns about his person, even on informal occasions. He had his suits especially made with three hideaway pockets to conceal his weapons. If he and 'the lads' went out nights in their tuxedos (he believed in dressing fashionably and in presenting a prosperous image), all chambers were fully loaded.

In total contrast to his gangster activities, O'Banion adored arranging flowers into bouquets, centrepieces and wreaths for special occasions. He worked hard, never missing a day in the shop, arriving promptly at 9 a.m. and not closing until 6 p.m., frequently staying late and coming in on weekends to help balance the books. The shop, Schofield's, naturally became the florist for 'the mob'. Whenever someone was riddled by the typewriter (the nickname for the Thompson sub-machine gun), stabbed, 'taken for a ride' or otherwise disposed of, the funeral flowers naturally came from Schofield's. Capone and Torrio often placed large orders for someone they may have killed but thought deserved a good send-off, and O'Banion always gave them a discount!

O'Banion's sense of humour was legendary, though perhaps best appreciated by those with a criminal mind. One of his more innocent pranks was giving his friend Ex-lax, saying it was chocolate; one of his more dangerous was the shotgun challenge where he would fill the barrels of a shotgun with hard impacted clay and challenge a friend or associate to hit the side of a barn 27.5 m (30 yards) away. In trying to do so, the unfortunate would lose an eye, arm or even part of his face.

John Torrio too was involved in the liquor trade, producing illegal liquor, smuggling in Canadian liquor and opening thousands of speakeasies, in particular in north Chicago. Torrio gained control over Chicago's Mayor, Bill Thompson by offering him huge bribes to turn a blind eye to Torrio's 'business ventures'. When Thompson was defeated in the 1923 election, Torrio and his lieutenant Al 'Scarface' Capone decided to move their centre of operations to a wealthy middle-class suburb of Chicago – Cicero. Here, in the elections of 1924, the gangsters decided to take control of the town council by fielding their own candidates. In spite of appeals by the Cicero voters to the Chicago police, which resulted in a pitched battle in which Capone's brother Frank was killed, the gangsters' candidates were elected. Torrio set about uniting the numerous gangs in Chicago. His plan was to have each gang control a certain area with no interference from neighbouring gangs. Each gang would pay a percentage of profits to Torrio for the sole rights to their own turf. All the gangs were called together to discuss the plan. Most agreed with Torrio's idea – the alternative to agreement was gang warfare and as Torrio was in a commanding position to win any war the prospect was not appealing. There were some who agreed to the plan initially and then reneged on the agreement. One of these gangs was the North Siders led by Dion O'Banion. Following one of O'Banion's 'little jokes', where he set up Torrio to be arrested by the police, Torrio sent for three gangsters from New York – Frank Yale, Albert Anselmi and John Scalise. The three of them shot O'Banion in his flower shop on the morning of 10 November 1924. His North Sider gang had arranged for their beloved leader's body to lay in state for nearly a week in a $10,000 silvery-bronze coffin (rushed by special freight car from Philadelphia) resting on a marble plinth inscribed: 'Suffer the Little Children to Come Unto Me'; thousands of Chicagoans filed past the body. Among the 26 lorry-loads of flowers costing $50,000 was a decorative basket of roses with a card that read, 'Al Brown', Capone's alias.

O'Banion was only the tip of the iceberg. The North Siders gang was taken over by Hymie Weiss and Bugs Moran, who hatched a plot to avenge the murder of O'Banion. Weiss and his boys ambushed Torrio twice but on both occasions he survived. On the first attempt, Torrio walked away from the scene with just two bullet holes in his grey Fedora hat, but his chauffeur and dog were both killed. In the second attempt, Torrio was ambushed outside his apartment block on 24 January 1925. He was hit by shotgun blasts and wounded in the stomach, arm and chest. For a week and a half, Torrio was in hospital guarded day and night by 30 bodyguards.

It was after this close encounter with death that John Torrio passed the organization over to Al Capone. Torrio was 43 years old, a millionaire several times over, and he moved back to Brooklyn, where he retired. In April 1957, at the age of 75, John Torrio suffered a fatal heart attack while at his barber's in Brooklyn.

Capone, known as 'Scarface' following a knife fight, was liked, trusted and obeyed without question by Torrio's 'outfit' by whom he was called 'The Big Fellow'. He quickly proved that he was even better at organization than Torrio, syndicating and expanding the Chicago's vice industry between 1925 and 1930. Capone controlled speakeasies, bookie joints, gambling houses, brothels, horse and racetracks, nightclubs, distilleries and breweries. He was driven around Chicago in an armour-plated Cadillac and became something of a celebrity, with his photograph appearing on the cover of *Time* magazine. Capone was extremely popular both with big business and ordinary citizens because he brought wealth and excitement to Chicago and combined violence with charity. Capone's most notorious killing was the St Valentine's Day Massacre. On February 14 1929, five of Capone's men entered a garage at 2122 N. Clark Street. The building was the main liquor headquarters of bootlegger George 'Bugs' Moran's North Sider gang. Because three of Capone's men were dressed as policemen, Moran's men in the garage thought it was a police raid, dropped their guns and put their hands against the wall. The two men in civilian clothes came in from the corridor and proceeded to open fire with sub-machine guns, firing more than 150 bullets into the victims. The 'policemen' then marched the two 'plain-clothes' killers to the waiting cars, as though arresting them, and drove off. The massacre shocked the USA and led to demands to curtail the gangster menace. Capone seemed to be invincible and the law-enforcing agencies helpless to bring him to justice; judges, police officers and politicians alike were all in the pay of the gangsters and were unable to convict Capone on gangland charges. Eventually a Federal Bureau of Investigation (FBI) team of 'untouchables' led by Eliot Ness collected enough evidence which enabled the federal prosecutors and the US Bureau of Internal Revenue to charge the gangster with tax evasion, demanding millions of dollars in back taxes. Capone's reaction was that they could not claim tax on illegal earnings in line with the popular belief in the 1920s and 1930s that illegal gambling earnings were not taxable income. However, the 1927 Sullivan ruling claimed that illegal profits were in fact taxable. Capone had never filed an income tax return, owned nothing in his own name, and never made a declaration of assets or income. He did all his business through front men so that he was completely anonymous when it came to income. Frank Wilson from the IRS's Special Intelligence Unit was assigned to focus on Capone. Wilson accidentally found a cash receipts ledger that not only showed the operation's net profits for a gambling house but also contained Capone's name; it was a record of Capone's income. In 1931, Capone was indicted for income tax evasion for the years 1925–9. He was also charged with failing to file tax returns for the years 1928 and 1929 and with conspiracy to violate the Prohibition laws from 1922–31. Capone pleaded guilty to all three charges in the belief that he would be able to plea bargain but changed his pleas to not guilty when the judge who presided over the case, Judge James H. Wilkerson, would not make any deals. Capone then tried to bribe the jury but Judge Wilkerson changed the jury panel at the last minute.

Capone was sentenced to a total of ten years in federal prison and one year in the county jail. In addition, Capone had to serve an earlier six-month contempt of court sentence for failing to appear in court. The fines were a cumulative $50,000 and Capone had to pay the prosecution costs of $7,692.29.

In May 1932, Capone was sent to Atlanta; here he took control, obtaining special privileges from the authorities such as a mirror, typewriter, rugs, and a set of the Encyclopaedia Britannica for his cell. The news soon spread that Capone had taken over in Atlanta and he was sent to Alcatraz where there were no other outfit members and where security was so tight that he had no news of the outside world. Unable to control anyone or anything and unable to buy influence or friends, Capone became the ideal prisoner and, in an attempt to earn time off for good behaviour, refused to participate in prisoner rebellions or strikes. After his release on 16 November 1939 Capone spent a short time in the hospital where it was clear that he was suffering from dementia brought about by syphilis. He returned to his home in Palm Island but his mind and body continued to deteriorate and, on January 21 1947, he had an apoplectic stroke. Although he regained consciousness and began to improve, pneumonia set in. Al Capone died on 25 January of a cardiac arrest. Although Capone ordered dozens of deaths and even killed with his own hands, he often treated people fairly and generously. He was the first to open soup kitchens after the 1929 stock market crash, and he ordered merchants to give clothes and food to the needy at his expense.

He opened up clubs and engaged famous artists and jazz musicians such as Duke Ellington and Louis Armstrong. In a television interview, Doc Cheatham, a jazz musician, recalled that Chicago 'lit up overnight…everybody was making money; all this was because of Al Capone'.

The Ku Klux Klan

The first branch of the Ku Klux Klan was established in Pulaski, Tennessee, in May 1866. The name of 'Ku Klux Klan' probably came from the Greek *kuklos* or *kyklos*, which means a circle. However, it has also been suggested that 'Ku Klux' comes from 'the sound of an old-fashioned rifle being cocked'. The word Klan was added to complete the alliteration, and probably originated from the Scottish name for a family, a clan.

Although the Ku Klux Klan was started at the end of the American Civil War in 1864–5, it was reformed in 1915 by William J. Simmons, a preacher influenced by Thomas Dixon's book, *The Ku Klux Klan* (1905) and the film of that book *Birth of a Nation* directed by D. W. Griffith and released in 1915. This film was over three hours long and was filled with powerful, graphic images that made a lasting impression on the audience. It became an immediate sensation and Griffith was hailed as the 'Shakespeare of the screen'. Originally, when Griffith made his adaptation of Thomas Dixon's melodrama, he agreed to pay the author $10,000 for the film rights, but ran short of funds. Dixon very reluctantly accepted $2,500 and 25 per cent of the gross, but this was probably the best deal he had ever made; his proceeds became the largest sum ever received by an author for the rights to a film as *Birth of a Nation* grossed over $18,000,000,

The film may have been a monetary success but it contained many negative stereotypical images of the African-American man which became engrained on the minds of many white Americans. The Jim Crow laws which discriminated against African Americans were endorsed, slavery was romanticized, the Ku Klux Klan was glorified, lynching was condoned; and African Americans were represented as simple-minded beasts driven primarily by lust and envy. Many Southern whites were elated. On Thanksgiving night in 1915, 25,000 Klansmen paraded through the streets of Atlanta, Georgia, to celebrate the opening of the movie. *Birth of a Nation* with its distorted version of history, was idolized by the Ku Klux Klan and was interpreted as an endorsement of Klan values because of its presentation of the Ku Klux Klan as heroes and southern African Americans as villains.

The 1920s became the golden age of the Klan, with various marches, public speeches and open recruitment. By 1920 the Klan had over 100,000 members: by 1925 this number had grown to an estimated 5 million. Many of the citizens of the USA were easy targets for Klan propaganda, as the rising immigration numbers had caused them concern. The Ku Klux Klan became extremely hostile to Jews, Roman Catholics, socialists communists and anybody they identified as foreigners. The Klan believed the USA was being legally invaded by different nationalities and that its duty was to protect the WASPs and to fight for 'native white Protestant supremacy' while protecting decent American values. In the years following the First World War there were riots in many northern towns, the worst being in Chicago where 33 people died in the first week of the riots. The Klan used the riots to stir up racial hatred; in the southern states the Klan was vehemently anti-African American while elsewhere it was more anti-Catholic and anti-Semitic with members swearing an oath of loyalty to the USA and promising to oppose 'any cause, government, people, sect or ruler that is foreign to the USA'.

In November 1922, Hiram Wesley Evans became the Klan's leader or Imperial Wizard. Under his leadership the organization grew rapidly and, in the 1920s, Klansmen were elected to positions of political power and included state officials in Texas, Oklahoma, Indiana, Oregon and Maine. Even on the rare occasions they were arrested for serious crimes, Klansmen were unlikely to be convicted by local southern juries. In Indiana, the movement was so strong that its leader, D. C. Stephenson, was able to say with confidence 'I am the law in Indiana' since he controlled many of the state's politicians through bribes and blackmail. Not content with this control, Stephenson decided to run as a candidate for the Senate and expressed his ambition to be President someday.

Lynching became more and more commonplace in the southern states and was used as a means of keeping African Americans and other non-WASP groups under control. Lynching was incredibly violent and often included humiliation, torture, burning, dismemberment and castration of the unfortunate victim before hanging. Victims were beaten and whipped, many times in front of large crowds that sometimes numbered thousands. Onlookers sometimes fired rifles and handguns into the corpse while people cheered, and children played during the proceedings; even pieces of the corpse were taken by onlookers as souvenirs of the event. In many photos of lynching parties, onlookers and members of the mob can be seen smiling and posing for the camera unafraid of prosecution or reprisal since few white men were punished for a lynching; the events were even announced in the newspapers beforehand, indicating a link with local law enforcement.

In 1909, Ida Wells, W. E. B. Du Bois and dozens of other prominent African Americans and whites formed an organization – the National Association for the Advancement of Coloured People (NAACP). This pressure group became the main opponent of the Ku Klux Klan. After their first conference, the NAACP launched an anti-lynching campaign that would span 30 years. The group put pressure on local and federal politicians and lobbied Washington to declare publicly that lynching was a clear violation of the Constitution. In 1915, NAACP organized a nationwide boycott of D. W. Griffith's racist film, and to show that the members of the organization would not be intimidated, it held its 1920 annual conference in Atlanta, considered at the time to be one of the most active Ku Klux Klan areas in the USA. In New York, NAACP hung a large banner outside its headquarters announcing every time a man was lynched. Public outrage grew. As time passed, lynching steadily decreased in spite of indifference from Washington as the Supreme Court preferred to let the individual states handle the lynching crisis since the Court saw them as a local problem. In 1925, a 'scandal' rocked the Klan when the 'Grand Dragon' (leader) of the Klan in Indiana, D. C. Stephenson, was put on trial for kidnapping, raping and mutilating a female assistant, Madge Oberholzer. It was said that her body was covered in vicious bite marks made by human teeth, and so frightened was she by this abuse that she took poison and was left to die by Stephenson. Madge Oberholzer gave evidence against Stephenson from her deathbed. He was arrested, tried and convicted; instead of going to the Senate, he went to prison for life.

After the conviction of Stephenson, for second-degree murder, and evidence of corruption by other members such as the Governor of Indiana and the Mayor of Indianapolis, membership of the Klan fell to around 30,000. In the late 1920s the Klan started to fade. In 1924 it still had about 40,000 members, but the number suddenly dropped to 35,000 by 1930. This trend continued during the Great Depression and the

Second World War, and in 1944 the organization was disbanded but did not die out altogether.

Social changes

During the 1920s, the transformation of US society was accompanied by a growing division between rural and urban USA, with many country people becoming increasingly worried by the changes in social attitudes that they saw around them. The emphasis on consumer goods was tantamount to greed and self-indulgence in their eyes, provocative dancing led to promiscuity, and the temptations of city life were luring their children away from traditional US values, hard work, thrift and family life. The numbers attending church in the southern and mid-western states remained high and this area became known as the 'Bible Belt'. Here, Christian fundamentalists, who believed that everything in the Bible was true, held sway and endeavoured to prevent the spread of urban vice by passing laws to maintain traditional values. These laws included the banning of wearing 'indecent' bathing costumes, gambling on the Sabbath, 'petting', and the giving of advice on contraception, and they were staunch supporters of Prohibition. Some states also banned the teaching of the theory of evolution as outlined in Charles Darwin's book *The Origin of the Species*. According to the Bible, God had created heaven and earth in six days and then rested on the seventh; according to Darwin life on earth evolved gradually over millions of years and human beings are descended from apes.

On 4 May 1925 the following advertisement appeared in the *Daily Times*.

> We are looking for a Tennessee teacher who is willing to accept our services in testing this law in the courts.

It had been placed by the American Civil Liberties Union which had been established to fight for freedom of speech and minority rights. The law the advertisement referred to was the Butler Act (1925) – an anti-evolution law in Tennessee which had been passed in 1925 and forbade the teaching in public schools of any evolutionary theory that questioned the book of Genesis' version of the creation. The teacher that replied to this advertisement was John T. Scopes, a science teacher in Dayton, who allowed himself to be caught teaching the theory of evolution and was taken to court.

The 'Monkey Trial' in July 1925 was a media sensation and the first US trial to be broadcast on the radio. Scopes was defended by Clarence Darrow, a famous criminal lawyer, and the prosecution was led by William Jennings Bryan. Both sides tried to influence public opinion and the trial was billed as a battle between science and religion. Scopes had broken the law, of that there was no doubt, and he was fined $100 as a result, but it was the arguments for and against the theory of evolution that the prosecution and defence concentrated upon. In the end, although Scopes was found guilty, the outcome of the trial was generally regarded as a victory for Darrow and a blow to the fundamentalists trying to censor education.

Prohibition and anti-evolution were part of a greater national movement which attempted to enforce moral and social conformity by using the law. There was strict censorship of books, plays and films, the latter regulated by the film industry itself when it set up its own guidelines and censorship board in 1922. Many of the older generation were horrified by society's seeming obsession with sex, and many blamed the advent of jazz which was denounced as degenerate. God-fearing people such as the Reverend Burke Culpepper railed against jazz music and the new dance forms it generated: 'Dancing is a divorce feeder. It is heathen, animalistic and damnable. It degrades womanhood and manhood.' Magazine articles such as 'Does Jazz put the Sin in syncopation?' (*Ladies' Home Journal*, 1921) claimed that, 'Jazz stimulates to extreme deeds, to a breaking away from all the rules and conventions; it is harmful and dangerous, and its influence is wholly bad.' To many, the appearance of the 'flapper' epitomized the changes in US society and no other person better fitted the description of a flapper than the film star Clara Bow – the 'It Girl'. F. Scott Fitzgerald believed her to be 'the quintessence of what a flapper signifies: pretty, impudent, superbly assured, worldly wise and briefly clad' (*Tales of the Jazz Age*, 1922)! Certainly women's lives changed during the 1920s: no longer were women exclusively confined to homemaking and childrearing but had opportunities to find employment and follow a more independent lifestyle than ever before. By the end of the 1920s there were over 10 million women working, helped by the fact that they were cheaper to employ than men. Women threw off their restrictive corsets, bobbed their hair and wore short skirts and make-up – items previously associated with prostitutes. They were seen out and about, unaccompanied by chaperones, drinking, smoking and driving all of which would have been frowned upon before the war. Middle-class women found that the new domestic appliances available on the market gave them more free time, and the car meant that they had a freedom not experienced by their mother's generation. Yet not every woman found the 1920s to be a life-changing experience; for thousands of women in rural areas life continued in the same way, and the difference between middle-class women and working-class women was significant, the latter having fewer labour-saving devices and having to work outside the home in order to make ends meet. Millions of immigrant women clung to the tradition that put the man firmly at the head of the family; farmers' wives struggled to make ends meet in a world of ever-decreasing prices for farm produce.

Women's primary responsibilities remained in the home. In politics, although the fourteenth amendment had given women the vote, few held political office; in the workplace there was little progress towards equality with men – most women doing menial jobs earned far less than men, and few women gained managerial positions or professional jobs. However, women's roles had changed. The fact that advertising was aimed specifically at women shows that advertisers at least believed that it was the women who took most of the spending decisions in the family, and it has been suggested that even Henry Ford bowed to this belief when he abandoned his 'black only' policy for cars because women wanted coloured cars!

05

politics and the economy in the 1920s

This chapter will cover:

- the economic boom and the role of the Republican Presidents
- Henry Ford and mass production
- the 'Roaring Twenties' – did everyone benefit?

Politics during the 1920s was dominated by the Republican Party and the belief that it was not the function of government to intervene in the domestic economy or people's lives unless the USA's vital interests were under threat. Business was left alone to organize its own affairs and there were few attempts at social reform during these years. However, the government did intervene in foreign trade by introducing an element of protectionism, that is, protecting domestic industry against competition from abroad by setting tariffs or import duties on foreign imports. The government also intervened in certain moral and social issues such as censorship of Hollywood films, the imposition of Prohibition and the banning of the teaching of evolution in schools following the 'Monkey Trial'.

Warren G. Harding was the twenty-ninth President of the USA but not one that has gone down in history as an illustrious leader. One historian has even gone so far as to claim that whenever the past Presidents of the USA are placed in rank order, Harding always fills last place. Harding had been a compromise candidate – the best of the second raters, as one delegate to the Republican convention described his nomination in 1920, yet his desire to return to 'normalcy' in the years following the First World War struck a chord with middle America. His policies of higher tariffs, lower taxes, fewer immigrants, more aid for the farmers and less involvement in foreign affairs accurately reflected the mood of the country. Harding was an amiable rogue who liked pretty girls, parties and giving key posts to his 'Ohio Gang' of friends. He found many government issues to be too complex for him and in order to ensure that his policies were implemented effectively, he delegated much of his presidential authority to the more able leaders of his government departments such as Charles Evans Hughes (Secretary of State), Herbert Hoover (Secretary of Commerce) and Andrew Mellon (Secretary of the Treasury). Harding's term in office saw a return to laissez-faire politics where government intervention in the economy was kept to a minimum; in his words 'we want less government in business and more business in government'. The progressive policies of previous administrations were reversed as taxes were reduced, high tariffs returned, anti-trust laws were ignored and workers neglected in favour of employers. Two important pieces of legislation passed at this time were the Quota Act (1921), which limited the number of immigrants to 3 per cent of the population of the respective ethnic groups living in the USA in 1910, and the Fordney-McCumber tariff (1922) which raised import duties on foreign-made goods sold in the USA, thus making US goods cheaper.

It was not long before corruption in high places within Harding's administration became apparent; the Alien Property Custodian had accepted bribes, the head of the Veteran's Bureau had 'wasted' $250 million, Harding's friend Jesse Smith was found to be selling pardon's to law-breakers, but the most famous scandal was that of the 'Teapot Dome'. In 1922, Albert T. Fall, the Secretary of State for the Interior, was accused of secretly leasing government land in the Teapot Dome oilfields in Wyoming and Elk Hills, California, to oil companies in return for huge 'loans'. Fall was convicted of receiving bribes and sentenced to imprisonment for a year. Harding refused to believe that his cronies were dishonest and at one point declared: 'If Fall is not honest then I'm not fit to be President.' Recent research suggests that Harding was not personally involved in any of the corrupt activities but the revelations of the dishonesty of his associates, made public after his death in office on 2 August 1923, overshadowed his presidency.

President Calvin Coolidge 1923–9

Calvin Coolidge, Harding's Vice-President, was quickly sworn in as the new President in an emergency ceremony which was held in a Vermont farmhouse by the light of a kerosene lamp. Coolidge was quiet and reserved and known as 'Silent Cal' because he refused to engage in small talk; when teased by a White House guest who had bet that she could make him say three words, he replied curtly 'You lose.' A firm believer in laissez-faire, Coolidge insisted on 12 hours' sleep and an afternoon nap every day. He believed that 'the business of America is business' and proceeded to give as much help to businesspeople as possible by lowering taxes in the Revenue Act (1925). This encouraged consumer spending and business investment, which in turn led to the economic prosperity known as the 'Roaring Twenties'. Coolidge refused to stand in the presidential election of 1928 and in his place the party chose Herbert Hoover. When Coolidge died in 1933, Dorothy Parker asked: 'How can they tell?', but to the majority of Americans he embodied the traditional values threatened by the forces of change in society.

The economic boom

The USA economy suffered a short depression following the end of the First World War. Four million demobilized soldiers came back to the country, together with many immigrants from war-torn Europe, making jobs scarce, especially as many industries were laying off workers since there was no longer any need for the same high level of production once the war had ended. Prices had doubled since 1914 and wages had barely risen, but with the increase in unemployment many employers knew they were in a strong bargaining position, and refused to increase wages. This resulted in a wave of strikes, some violent, throughout 1919. However, the depression was short lived, and by the early 1920s, the country was booming as the economy grew rapidly and, by 1926, Americans were officially the richest people in the world as their standard of living reached new heights. According to the historian, Maldwyn Jones, 'business made huge profits, jobs were generally easy to find, standards of living rose appreciatively' (*The Limits of Liberty*, OUP, 1995). There was a general air of prosperity and a 'feel-good factor' which gave Americans confidence in the idea that anyone could be successful if they worked hard enough.

Why was there a boom in the 1920s?

American prosperity was based on a firm foundation. The country had vast amounts of natural resources including oil, coal, minerals and land; the war had enabled the US economy to expand by providing the country with new markets and speeding up technological change; technological developments such as electricity, automation and plastics helped modernize existing industries and create new ones; new production techniques such as the assembly line made mass production possible, and this in its turn speeded up the production of goods and drove down prices so that more people could afford them and more were sold. More and more people lived in towns and cities, and the rising population led to a rising demand for consumer goods which new technology and production methods provided in ever increasing quantities. This increased consumer demand was one of the keystones of economic prosperity, especially when coupled with advertising on billboard posters, in magazines and on the radio. The development of advertising encouraged people to buy these goods, and the existence of credit facilitated purchases in cases where cash was not available immediately. People frequently purchased goods from mail-order catalogues such as Sears, Roebuck and Co., and paid for them in easy monthly instalments. Even people in remote rural areas could buy anything from these catalogues, from farm machinery to clothes and household goods, since the improvement in transport and the road system meant goods could be delivered more easily. Most of all, the feel-good factor gave the American people confidence to buy goods, invest in industry and to be open to new ideas. The three Republican Presidents during the 1920s encouraged business through their *laissez-faire* policies. Lower taxes meant more money was invested and people had more disposable income to spend on manufactured goods. The government's tariff policies protected the home industries from foreign competition by placing import duties on foreign goods.

New industries

New industries such as electricity and electrical goods, chemicals and cars, dominated the economic boom. Electricity not only lit people's homes it also powered the factories and led to the development of a whole range of electrical appliances for the home. The chemical industry helped to increase agricultural yield through fertilizers and created plastics and man-made fibres with a wide variety of uses. Cars were mass produced so that prices fell to such a low level that most families could afford to buy one, particularly with credit being readily available. In addition, the motor industry had a knock-on effect, creating a demand for glass, rubber, steel, roads, petrol stations and skilled mechanics. As confidence in the US economy grew, so too did the skyscrapers as big companies tried to demonstrate their power, prestige and market superiority by building higher and more extravagant edifices. Architects William Van Alen and H. Craig Severance were employed to design a building at 40 Wall Street in Manhattan's financial district. When the partners split acrimoniously during the project's construction, Van Alen left the firm and went uptown to work on the new Chrysler skyscraper. Their competitiveness reached upwards into the heavens; to begin with Severance secretly had a lantern and flagpole added to the top of 40 Wall Street to make his tower the tallest. When Van Alen found out about this trick, he replied by building a secret spire in the elevator shaft of the Chrysler building's crown. Once Severance's tower had been completely finished and 'topped off' (in November 1929), Van Alen had the spire hoisted into place. Severance's 40 Wall Street had been the world's tallest building for about 90 minutes but that title remained with the Chrysler building for a much longer period of time!

During the 1920s, the construction industry was busier than it had ever been building factories, offices, banks, hospitals, schools, public buildings and homes in the suburbs – easily accessible thanks to the advent of the motor car.

Henry Ford

One name is inextricably linked to the motor industry, that of Henry Ford. He became a symbol for the USA's enterprise and prosperity and had a major impact on both industrial production and society. He believed that it was better to sell a large number of cars on a small profit margin rather than few cars with a higher profit margin. In order to do this he pioneered a new method of making cars using an assembly line: workers were responsible for the assembly of just one component and stood in one place as the conveyor belt moved the car to each in turn. This speeded up the assembly of cars; in 1913 one car was produced every three minutes, by the 1920s one car was completed every ten seconds. The work was monotonous and many workers left their jobs after a few months because of boredom and exhaustion. In order to stem the flow of labour, Ford announced a daily wage of $5 – far more than most employers were offering at the time – small wonder the workers flocked to Detroit to look for work!

However, not all Ford employees were happy with their lot. Mike Widman, who worked in the River Rouge plant in Detroit, recalled that the gates were locked at 8 a.m., that there were men in plain clothes keeping the workers under surveillance and that the workers had to ask permission to go to the toilet. Indeed, Ford himself ordered that the factory conveyor belt be secretly speeded up so that workers had to do their work more quickly without realizing! Yet in Alistair Cooke's opinion, 'Ford's original labour policies made him the American god to employees...in 1914 the national wage was $2.40 a day. Ford paid a minimum of $5.00...By 1926...he had quadrupled the average wage to nearly $10' (Alistair Cooke, BBC series, America, 1973). Ford took an interest in his workers whom he was convinced were 'not living as they should...Their homes are crowded and unsanitary.' He created the Ford Sociological Department with 50 inspectors who made spot-checks on the homes of Ford employees. They checked cleanliness, health and diet, and if families did not keep these to a certain standard half of the take-home pay that came as part of the profit-sharing bonus could be withheld. Yet Ford also recognized the need for leisure time and relaxation. He organized dances and social functions for his workers and allowed them to buy Ford cars at a discount. Ironically, Ford himself never had a driver's licence!

Ford's car, the Model T Ford, or Tin Lizzy as it came to be known was unique and extremely popular. It had huge rear springs which made it wobble but which enabled it to run on unmade roads and tracks. It was possible to take off the rear wheel and connect the hub, via a belt, to a circular saw or farm machinery, and could be easily repaired by people with a modicum of mechanical knowledge. The car was the saviour of rural farmers, enabling them to get into town faster and more easily, thus ending their isolation. As one farmer's wife wrote to Ford in 1918, 'your car has lifted us out of the mud. It brought joy to our lives'. By the mid-1920s one out of every two cars sold was a Model T Ford.

Although Henry Ford famously told customers that they could have a Model-T in any colour, as long as it was black, Enzo Ferrari insisted on having his sporty cars painted with vibrant colours. Ferrari did make one notable exception, however, when he presented a black Ferrari as a gift to Henry Ford's son. It was not until 1925 that Ford finally introduced two new colours: green and maroon.

Henry Ford was once amused to receive a letter from an unlikely fan, 'While I still have got breath in my lungs,' it read, 'I will tell you what a dandy car you make...I have drove Fords exclusively when I could get away with one'.

The author of this glowing tribute? The notorious killer Clyde Barrow of Bonnie and Clyde fame. Barrow was later killed in an ambush in the last Ford he ever stole.

The 'Roaring Twenties'

The term the 'Roaring Twenties' has been coined to describe the period because it seemed to describe it perfectly, portraying the decade as an era of adventure and prosperity. This was the decade when Charles A. Lindbergh flew the Atlantic – non-stop from the USA to Paris – becoming a hero who personified the

USA's hopes and ambitions in the process. Skyscrapers soared to new heights; strange crazes such as flagpole sitting, dance marathons and Mah Jong took hold of people and then disappeared; the Charleston and the Black Bottom dances were condemned by many as being immoral. Young women called 'flappers' drank cocktails, smoked, drove cars, flew airplanes wore short skirts or trousers, lots of make-up and cut their hair short in a bob – they felt free to behave as they pleased, and were criticized for their promiscuity by people with a more traditional view of a woman's role. F. Scott Fitzgerald summed up the 1920s succinctly when he wrote: '...parties were bigger, the pace was faster, the shows were broader, the buildings were higher, the morals were looser and the liquor was cheaper' (*Echoes of the Jazz Age*, 1931).

Jazz music

The 1920s gained the nickname of the 'Jazz Age' from the rise of jazz, a type of music associated with African-American culture. Its origins were in the Deep South, but as many African Americans moved to the northern states, jazz developed into an urban-based, northern brand of music with African-American musicians such as Duke Ellington, Louis Armstrong, Fats Waller and Bessie Smith dominating the scene.

Literature

The writers of the 1920s have sometimes been called 'The Lost Generation', referring to the self-exiled expatriates who lived and wrote in Paris between the wars. These writers, looking for freedom of thought and action, changed the face of modern writing. Realistic and rebellious, they wrote what they wanted and fought censorship for profanity and sexuality. They incorporated Freudian ideas into their characters and styles. The group included Ernest Hemingway and F. Scott Fitzgerald, whose writing displays disillusionment with the society of the 1920s. Fitzgerald's novel *The Great Gatsby* (1925) describes many of the material excesses associated with the Roaring Twenties, while Hemingway's *A Farewell to Arms* (1929) deals with people damaged by the war. Sinclair Lewis wrote critically about small town America in his book *Main Street* (1920) and about middle-class life in *Babbit* (1922). An African-American cultural renaissance, centred on Harlem in New York, took place during the decade as talented African-American writers and artists collected together under the leadership of the poet

Weldon Johnson to make white people more aware of the 'black experience' via their work. In his poem 'Silhouette' (1926), Langston Hughes touches on the African-American experience of lynching in the southern states, and Richard Wright, in his novel *Native Son*, set new standards for African-American literature with his moving attack on white racism.

The media

During this era there emerged a plethora of magazines, newspapers and radio shows which heralded the advent of the media age. Magazines before the war had been muck-raking journals like *McClure's*, which had a wide readership because of its exposure of corruption and greed in business and politics; post war the theme of reform was dropped and the culture of consumerism picked up. *Ladies' Home Journal* and *The Saturday Evening Post*, featuring Norman Rockwell's paintings on its cover, became commonplace in middle-class homes all around the country. Hoping to attract serious newsreaders, Henry Luce began publishing *Time* in 1923, and new tabloid newspapers launched after the war like the *New York Daily News* achieved large circulation by covering crime, sports and scandals. Advertisers, who now reached millions of consumers on a daily or weekly basis, hired movie stars and sports figures to persuade Americans to buy all types of products, from coffee to tobacco products.

The first radio broadcasting station was opened in Pittsburgh in 1920, and the first national radio network, the National Broadcasting Company (NBC), in 1926 closely followed by Columbia Broadcasting System (CBS) in 1928. In ten years radio had grown into a billion dollar industry buoyed up by the discovery that advertising on the radio could boost sales of cars, soap or soft drinks. It is estimated that by the end of the decade 40 per cent of all homes owned a radio set. The radio gave Americans a new leisure activity, offering them access to music such as jazz or dance bands, to educational programmes, to soap operas and sporting events. The popularity of spectator sports was increased by the ability of radio to reach even those who could not be present at the event, and the media helped to turn sporting stars such as Jack Dempsey (the Manassa mauler), Babe Ruth (the Sultan of Swat), Bobby Jones (the golfer) and Harold 'Red' Grange (American Footballer) into national heroes.

Radio also reported the flight of Charles A. Lindbergh in his plane, the *Spirit of St Louis* across the Atlantic. On 20 May 1927, Lindbergh took up the challenge offered by a New York businessman to fly non-stop from New York to Paris. His plane was a single engine monoplane; he had no radio, no map, no parachute, yet he was able to complete the flight of 5,760 km (3,579 miles) in 33.5 hours with only a few sandwiches and 1.1 litres of water to sustain him! The reaction of the American people was one of immense pride and enthusiasm; as Lindbergh's ship back from France approached the American coast, four destroyers and 40 aeroplanes went out to greet him; New York gave him a tickertape parade with over 1,800 tonnes of tickertape being thrown from the buildings as he passed. 'Lucky Lindy', as he was known, seemed to personify the American Dream – embodying all the qualities Americans claimed as their own, courage, perseverance and rugged individualism. Lindbergh's prize for this feat was $25,000 and a fame which endures to this day, although his fame was not a blessing. In 1932, Lindbergh's baby son was kidnapped and a ransom note demanded:

Dear Sir,

Have 50,000$ redy 25000$ in 20$ bills 15000$ in 10$ bills and 10000$ in 5$ bills. After 2–4 days will inform you were to deliver the Mony.

We warn you for making anyding public or for notify the Polise the child is in gut care. Indication for all letters are singnature and 3 holds.

(Bruno Richard Hauptman)

The ransom was paid but the baby not returned. Then, on May 12 1932, 72 days after the kidnapping, the decomposed body of a baby was found in the woods near the Lindbergh house. The child had died from a fractured skull and had been dead, in all likelihood, since the night of the kidnapping. Two days later Charles Lindbergh identified his son's body by examining its teeth. The kidnapping investigation was now a murder investigation. Finally, on September 19 1934, police arrested Bruno Richard Hauptmann, a German-born carpenter. A search of Hauptmann's home revealed $14,000 of the Lindbergh ransom which he claimed to be holding for a friend, Isidore Fisch, who had just died. Despite his plea of innocence, Hauptmann was found guilty of the murder of Charles Lindbergh Jr.

The film industry

By the early 1920s, Hollywood in California had become the film capital of the world – its clean air, sunny climate and close proximity to both desert and mountain scenery made it an ideal location for a wide variety of films. In this suburb of Los Angeles, the studios made Westerns, thrillers, comedies, religious and historical epics, sentimental tear jerkers and romantic escapades. Generally the films were made to a formula and their very predictability made them extremely popular with the film-going public. The industry provided millions with a cheap form of entertainment where they could lose themselves in a fantasy world of luxury and adventure for a few cents before going back to reality. The Hollywood stars provided the public with a vicarious taste of high society and the kind of lifestyle they could only aspire to. People wanted to know what fashions their favourite stars were wearing and what they were doing so that they might copy them in their own lives. The studios employed agents to ensure that the public got plenty of suitable publicity and to keep any hint of scandal under lock and key. Many older Americans were shocked by the morality (or lack of it) in Hollywood films. Often highly suggestive language and sex symbols such as Clara Bow (the 'It Girl') and Rudolph Valentino were used in the adverts for films. The private lives of some Hollywood stars were shocking to many and several scandals were hushed up by the studios. When Gloria Swanson got married at the age of 25 to a member of the European nobility, her fans rejoiced that she had met her 'prince' not knowing that she was already pregnant. Swanson herself realized that had her public known about her pregnancy, her career would have been finished. Some scandals did come into the public domain, such as the mysterious death of a young girl at a party given by Fatty Arbuckle, and there were calls for the government to introduce censorship of the movie industry. In order to prevent this, Hollywood introduced the Hays code of conduct which insisted that no film be produced in Hollywood that might 'lower the moral standards of those who see it'. The code demanded that screen kisses run for no longer than 3 m (10 ft) of film, that there be no nudity and that the sympathy of the audience be kept away from the side of 'crime, wrong-doing, evil or sin'.

Silent movies

The early 1920s was the period of the silent movies with 'in-house' piano players providing the background music during the films. Stars such as Rudolph Valentino, Mary Pickford, Clara Bow, Harold Lloyd, Charlie Chaplin, Buster Keaton, Laurel and Hardy, Gloria Swanson and Theda Bara graced the silent screen, bringing romance, comedy and adventure into the lives of ordinary Americans. In 1927, an average of 60 million people went to the cinema each week, but by 1929 this had risen to 110 million because of the birth of the 'talkies'. Hollywood studios competed with each other to produce the most expensive star-studded films such as *Beyond the Rocks* (1922) starring Gloria Swanson and Rudolph Valentino. This told the story of a poor but noble English girl who marries an elderly millionaire only to meet the man of her dreams (Valentino) on the honeymoon. Rudolph Valentino was marketed on his sex appeal, with magazines reporting women fans fainting when they saw him. He popularized bellbottom trousers, revolutionized the technique of movie love-making, and boosted the sale of Vaseline (for hair grooming). In 1926, Valentino died tragically of complications following appendicitis – he was only 31. The streets outside the funeral parlour where his body lay were crowded with thousands of people and it is estimated that over 100,000 people filed past his corpse to pay their respects. So great was the hysteria surrounding his death that 100 mourners were injured in the crush to gain admittance to view the body, and there were reports of female fans committing suicide as they could not face life without him. For many years on the anniversary of Valentino's death, a mysterious woman dressed in black would appear to lay a wreath of flowers on his grave. Her identity has never been established.

Hollywood was not all sex and romance and the silent film comedies of the era remain perennial classics. The comic greats such as Buster Keaton, Harold Lloyd and Charlie Chaplin made films which the public flocked to see.

By the end of the decade, the Hollywood film stars found themselves in competition with cartoon characters, such as Mickey Mouse, Pluto, Goofy and Donald Duck, created by Walt Disney. The first full length talking movie, *The Jazz Singer* starring Al Jolson, was completed in 1927 and this, together with the arrival of colour films at the end of the 1920s, marked the beginning of mass cinema audiences as the 1930s saw the dawn of the 'golden age' of Hollywood. The arrival of sound created an upheaval in the film industry, and studios faced many problems. Many Hollywood actors and actresses lacked good voices and stage experience, and their marketability decreased.

As many stars of the silent era had heavy accents and harsh voices, the arrival of the 'talkies' saw their careers shattered, as was the case for Polish-accented Pola Negri and Clara Bow. Others like Joan Crawford, Greta Garbo, Ronald Colman, Lon Chaney and Gloria Swanson survived the transition but elocution lessons from diction coaches became a necessity. Other silent stars, such as Mary Pickford, failed to make the transition to talkies and retired in the 1930s. Silent film studios became obsolete, and new investments had to be made for expensive new equipment, technological innovations, and soundproofed stages. Films that began production as 'silents' were quickly transformed into sound films; by 1930 the silent movie had practically disappeared.

The economy in 1928

Most historians seem to agree that the economic problems which seemed to begin with the Wall Street crash in 1929, and which developed into the Great Depression of the 1930s went beyond the stock market and were apparent before 1929. As early as 1926, the Florida land boom had encouraged speculators to buy land in Florida in the hope of selling it on and making a quick profit. Over 90 per cent of the buyers had no intention of ever occupying the property. Many speculators bought with a 10 per cent deposit or 'binder' and then sold quickly at a profit to avoid having to pay the full amount. Many did indeed make a fat profit as house prices in Florida rose to unprecedented heights, but many of the building plots were worthless – the land was swampy or too far from the beach – and, as buyers realized their mistakes, prices plunged and individuals, builders and even banks went bankrupt. The final *coups de grâce* were two hurricanes which ravaged Florida in 1926, killing hundreds and leaving thousands of building plots under water. The housing market collapsed and many people found themselves in a position of negative equity with their houses and property hugely overpriced. Yet the nation remained confident in its economic prosperity and Hoover's platform for the 1928 election promised: 'A chicken in every pot and a car in every garage' and: 'We shall soon with the help of God be in sight of the day when poverty will be banished from this nation.' No wonder Hoover's polled over 21 million votes to his rival's 15 million. In spite of his brave words, his presidency was doomed from the start; within six months of his inauguration the Wall Street crash plunged the USA into a deep economic depression. However, in 1928 there was little sign of the impending disaster as the President of General Motors claimed, 'our general economic and industrial situation is thoroughly sound,' and most other leaders of industry agreed with him. Company profits were still increasing, the stock market was booming, speculators were still making fortunes, sales of motor cars had reached nearly 4.5 million, and the easy availability of credit meant that consumers were still spending. Underneath this superficial prosperity, the reality was very different. Not all Americans were prosperous and many could not afford to buy consumer goods such as cars and refrigerators. An estimated 4.2 per cent of the population was living below the poverty line, small farmers, new immigrants, African Americans and workers in the old industries such as coal and cotton made little economic headway and some saw their standards of living fall during this time. Since US economic prosperity had been built on the principle of mass production, having such a limited market for manufactured goods was precarious. There was little demand for US goods from overseas markets either; in order to buy US goods other nations needed to sell their goods to US firms to get the currency to buy US goods. Since the government had placed such high tariffs on imported manufactured goods they were too expensive for Americans to buy. In retaliation, foreign countries placed duties on US goods, thus ensuring that overseas markets for US manufactured goods contracted. With less demand at home and abroad it soon became apparent that there were too many goods being produced, and some manufacturers began to cut back on staff and production. By 1928 2 million people were unemployed. There was also overproduction in agriculture too as farmers produced too much, food prices fell and many defaulted on their mortgages or rent.

By the late 1920s many hundreds of thousands of Americans were in debt, lured by easy credit and the prospect of getting rich quick by speculating in stocks and shares. Most companies had been doing well and the people who had bought shares in the companies that were prospering were paid good dividends on their investment. More and more people wanted to share in this prosperity and bought shares. Indeed, the 1920s had seen a frenzy of gambling on the Stock Exchange by ordinary Americans attracted by newspaper stories of millions of dollars being made overnight. One writer, Cecil Roberts, recalled going to his barbers and being advised to buy shares in Standard Gas! Many invested their lifesavings, others borrowed money to buy the shares and some even bought shares 'on the margin' – a type of hire purchase of shares where the broker would accept a 10 per cent deposit called a 'margin' for shares, which could then be sold before the rest of the payment had to be made. In this way, large profits could be made for very little initial outlay. Billions of dollars were invested and this forced up the price of shares way beyond their true value. Amateur investors did not really understand the stock market but tended to gamble on tips, hunches or simply by following the herd; they failed to appreciate that sometimes markets can fall suddenly because they were so confident that share prices would continue to rise. Once this confidence evaporated, the bubble of speculation would burst, prices would collapse and banks would demand repayment of loans in cash.

06

the Depression years

This chapter will cover:
- the Wall Street crash
- the effect of the Depression on American society
- government action or inaction?

They roared like lions. They hollered and screamed, clawed at one another's collars. It was a bunch of crazy men. Every once in a while, when shares in Radio or Steel took another tumble, you'd see some poor devil collapse and fall to the floor.

So wrote a reporter on the Stock Exchange Guardian on 30th October 1929. What had caused grown men to behave in this way? Why did a fall in the price of shares cause some brokers to jump from their office windows, pensioners to take their lives, families to live in cardboard shacks, and a whole decade to be named the years of Depression?

The Wall Street crash

By the summer of 1929, many factory warehouses had stockpiles of unsold goods and had begun to lay off workers, and many richer investors had begun to sell their shares amid rumours that company profits were declining fast. Share prices began to fall in September and some financial advisers gave warnings of a disaster ahead.

'Sooner or later, a crash is coming and it may be terrific,' said Roger Babson, a financial expert in September 1929. It was a self-fulfilling prophecy; a few took head of his words and began to sell their shares, resulting in a fall in prices and a feeling of nervousness replacing the confidence previously seen in financial circles. On the 19 October, a number of nervous dealers sold large blocks of shares and, on 24 October, panic hit Wall Street as soon as the gong marking the start of trading sounded at 10 a.m. The rush began. More than 12 million shares were sold on the 'day the dam burst' and millions more were offered for sale but failed to find buyers. In an attempt to calm the market, six bankers in New York hatched a plan to reassure investors by buying up some of the shares; six of their employees were sent to spend $240 million on a selection of shares in an attempt to restore confidence. It seemed at first that this daring plan had succeeded; by 25 October prices steadied at a lower level and although they remained low, they had stopped falling. Following the weekend there was more panic selling, 9 million shares traded on 28 October and prices fell steeply but this was nothing compared to the selling that took place on Tuesday 29 October. Black Tuesday, or Terrifying Tuesday, saw 16 million shares offered for sale, the average share price falling some 40 points and investors losing $8,000 million. In one day the shares in Union Cigar fell from $113 each to $4 – the president of the company committed suicide by jumping from a window ledge. Hundreds of thousands of investors were ruined, including ordinary people who had invested their lifesavings in stocks and shares. Luigi Barzini recalled that, 'an old couple who lived not far from us lost everything in the crash. It was too late for them to start life again so they committed suicide' (*O America: A memoir of the 1920s*, 1977). It was not only individuals who lost everything, many banks made heavy losses. As they were unable to recover loans from borrowers who had gone bankrupt, and with frantic depositors hammering on their doors to get their hands on the savings they had deposited with the banks, many banking establishments went bust. This affected more ordinary citizens who had perhaps resisted the urge to get rich quick but had carefully put aside their hard-earned cash 'for a rainy day'. That rainy day had come, but their savings had disappeared. Without bank loans to tide them over, many businesses were forced to close, creating a sharp rise in unemployment. Thus began a vicious circle; unemployed people had less to spend, fewer goods were bought and factories were forced to lay off more workers; banks were affected as more people and businesses defaulted on their loan agreements, they were forced to close and the cycle began again. The high unemployment was the most tragic consequence of the Wall Street crash and it led to the most horrific poverty all over the USA. In every town and city queues of shabbily dressed men walked the streets searching for a job; begging from passers by; queuing for food at soup kitchens such as the one set up by Al Capone in Chicago where 40 per cent of the working population was out of work.

The reality of unemployment

The arrival of the Depression devastated the lives of millions of Americans. At its height there were 13 million unemployed, but in order to take account of the real numbers who suffered one also needs to count wives, children, pensioners, annuitants and thousands of other people who were not considered unemployed but were directly affected by the crash and the Depression which followed. Since no form of government assistance or unemployment benefits existed, starvation was a real threat to many and it was usual to see people scavenging on rubbish heaps. The *New Republic* magazine reported in 1933 that in Chicago, 'A widow fed herself and her 14-year-old son on garbage. Before she picked up the meat, she would always take off her glasses, so that she could not see the maggots.'

More and more people depended on private charities, queuing for hand-outs of bread and soup, but it soon became apparent that charities simply could not cope with the vastly increased demands for their services. By 1932, the Red Cross could only afford to give needy families 75 cents a week and visiting nurses in New York found children constantly famished. As unemployment struck, many families were unable to keep up the mortgage repayments and found themselves homeless, resorting to building themselves shacks of canvas, wood or tin in shanty towns, or 'Hoovervilles', others lived out of old rusted car bodies. One typical Hooverville 'development' was described as being made up of around 100 dwellings about the size of a dog house or chicken coop, and made from wooden boxes, metal cans, strips of cardboard or old tar paper.

The Great Depression did not affect everyone in the same way. Up to 40 per cent of the country never faced real hardship during those years and many rich people felt no impact at all and were oblivious to the suffering of others. By 1933, the unemployment rate hovered close to 25 per cent and although it fluctuated during the 1930s, it never fell below 14.3 per cent until 1941.

The effect of the Depression on the family

Families suffered a dramatic loss of income during Herbert Hoover's term in office, and this put a great deal of strain on family life. Some reacted by pulling together, making do or relying on family and friends for help, and only after exhausting all possibilities would they look to the government for help. The Depression changed family life in dramatic ways; many couples delayed marriage for lack of funds; the divorce rate dropped sharply as it was too expensive to pay the legal fees and support two households; birth rates dropped below the replacement level. Traditional roles within the family also changed during the 1930s. Unemployed men now had to rely on their wives and children to help make ends meet and many did not take this change in their status within the family unit at all well. Many men stopped looking for work completely, paralysed by their bleak outlook and loss of self-respect; others became so frustrated that they

walked out on their families. A survey in 1940 revealed th[...]
million married women had been abandoned by their husbands.

On the other hand, women found their role within the family enhanced. They had little alternative but to go against the traditional opposition to married women working outside the home in order to help support their families. African-American women found it easier to obtain work than their husbands, and took up work as domestic servants, clerks, textiles workers and other occupations, employment which increased their status and power in the home, and won them a new voice in domestic decisions.

The Depression in the countryside

Life became even harder for the USA's farmers, many of whom were ironically producing too much food. Farmers could not even afford to harvest their crops so low had the prices fallen; as food rotted in the countryside, people in the towns who could not afford to buy it, starved. As their income fell, increasing numbers of farmers were unable to pay their mortgages, but the banks were unsympathetic and merely sent bailiffs to evict them and repossess the land. Rural poverty was every bit as squalid as urban poverty; a reporter for the *New York Post* described a six-year-old boy suffering from malnutrition, anaemia and rickets, his stomach swollen several times its normal size, licking the paper bag some meat and cornmeal had been carried in so desperate was he for food, while his younger sibling, not more than a year old, 'suckled the dry teats of a mongrel bitch'.

The situation worsened still further between 1931 and 1936 when there was a serious drought in the South and Mid-West. This area had once been fertile grazing land but during the war there was more money to be made from growing crops and, therefore, farmers were persuaded by the banks to change to growing crops. The top soil, exposed to the elements once the grass had been removed to grow these crops, became dust in the hot summers with their fierce winds and little rainfall and over 20 million hectares (49.5 million acres) of land became little more than desert. This area was known as the 'Dust Bowl' because the wind would whip up the dusty soil into vast dust clouds which suffocated everything in sight.

By 1935, winds reaching 96.5 km (60 miles) per hour had been recorded and these whipped the dry soil into gigantic clouds, as

ı (1,000 ft), which blocked the sun. Dust even
President's desk in Washington and was also
y ships 805 km (500 miles) out to sea. Dust storms
d highways in impenetrable clouds, and stranded
ısts. With the land blown away literally, farmers left the
. By the end of the decade almost half the population, an
ımated 300,000 from Oklahoma alone, had migrated.

Many farmers, in particular from Arkansas and Oklahoma, fled
to the West Coast and California where they hoped to find work
such as fruit picking and a better life. John Steinbeck in his book
The Grapes of Wrath (1939) described the experiences of these
'Okies' and 'Arkies' as they were known, and the lack of a
welcome they found waiting for them in the 'land of plenty'.
Photographers like Dorothea Lange and Walker Evans captured
the plight of the migrant farm workers in California and the
Dust Bowl that they had left behind, each picture telling a story
with simple dignity. With all this firsthand information of the
fate of the urban and rural poor, what action did the
government of Herbert Hoover take?

Herbert Hoover and government action

We'd like to thank you, Herbert Hoover,
For really showing us the way,
You dirty rat, you bureaucrat,
You made us what we are today.

This chorus comes from the Broadway show (and later
Hollywood film) *Annie* which was set in the USA in 1932. In the
show, the chorus is sung by homeless people in New York City.
Although written some time after the 1930s, the song sums up
what many Americans in the early 1930s thought of their
President.

The economist J. K. Galbraith is very critical of the failure of the
Republican administrations of the 1920s to regulate business
and the Stock Exchange more effectively but the Republican
policy of laissez-faire was a policy which most Western
governments followed at the time.

Herbert Hoover, the thirty-first President of the USA (1929–33),
did not completely favour this traditional laissez-faire approach
but nor did he believe in government intervention. He favoured
a 'rugged individualism' where people achieved success by their

own hard work and effort, and where the role of the government was to support private initiative. This voluntary co-operation can be seen in Hoover's efforts to deal with the economic crisis when he urged business to maintain production and wage levels and state governments to continue spending on public works. For the deep depression facing the USA, this was not enough and Hoover was forced to increase the spending of the federal government on public works and provide government loans to business, but he refused to introduce unemployment benefit. His introduction of the Hawley-Smoot tariffs (1930) to protect US industry merely made European countries increase their tariffs on US imports. The numbers of unemployed, hungry and homeless Americans grew and it was clear that Hoover's attempts to find a middle way between laissez-faire and state intervention had failed.

According to many historians, Hoover did too little too late, and to the people of 1930s America he was a figure of hatred or ridicule. His President's Organization for Unemployment Relief did not spend government money on relieving unemployment but used money donated by charities. The falling prices for farm produce had led to a huge number of agriculture bankruptcies in the 1920s which increased in the 1930s, yet all Hoover could suggest was that farmers should grow fewer crops. His attitude towards the Bonus marchers in 1932 led the homeless to name their cardboard shanty towns 'Hoovervilles', and a newspaper covering a homeless person was called a 'Hoover blanket'. Hoover's reputation was completely shattered by the Bonus army affair of 1932.

The Bonus army

In 1924, a grateful Congress had voted to give a bonus to First World War veterans – $1.25 for each day served overseas and $1 for each day served in the USA. However, the bonus payment would not be made until 1945. By 1932, the Depression had begun to bite and many of the veterans, now unemployed, wanted their money immediately. In May 1932, some 15,000 veterans, many unemployed and destitute, descended on Washington DC to demand immediate payment of their bonus. They called themselves the 'Bonus Expeditionary Force' (BEF) mirroring the title given to the US forces in 1917 – the public dubbed them the 'Bonus Army'. All around the city the Bonus army, accompanied by their families, set up ramshackle shanty towns and tents, the largest of these being at Anacostia Flats just across the river from the Capitol. Here, approximately 10,000 people, veterans and their families, lived in the shelters they had built from materials dragged out of a nearby rubbish dump – old packing boxes and scrap tin covered with straw roofs. Discipline in the camp was good; streets were laid out, latrines dug, and drills held daily. Newcomers to the camp had to register and prove they were bona fide veterans who had been honourably discharged before they were allowed to stay.

On 17 June, the Senate voted on the bill already passed by the House to give the veterans their bonus money immediately. At dusk, 10,000 marchers crowded the Capitol grounds waiting for the Senate's decision. Walter Waters, the leader of the BEF, had bad news for them; the Senate had defeated the bill by a vote of 62 to 18. The crowd were stunned into silence. 'Sing "America" and go back to your billets,' Waters ordered the crowd, and they obeyed. On 28 July, Attorney General Mitchell ordered that the veterans be cleared from all government property by the Washington police. The police met with resistance, shots were fired and two marchers were killed. On hearing of this incident President Hoover ordered the army to clear out the veterans. Infantry, cavalry and six tanks were dispatched to do the job under the command of General Douglas MacArthur. The troops assembled on Pennsylvania Avenue below the Capitol, and thousands of civil service employees leaving work lined the streets to watch. The veterans, assuming the military display was in their honour, cheered the soldiers but suddenly the cavalry turned and charged; soldiers with fixed bayonets followed, hurling tear gas into the crowd. The spectators were horrified.

By nightfall the veterans had retreated across the Anacostia River where Hoover ordered MacArthur to stop but, as he was to do again in the Korean War in the 1950s, MacArthur ignored the command and led his infantry to the main camp. By early morning, the 10,000 inhabitants had been dispersed and the camp was in flames. Two babies died and nearby hospitals were overwhelmed with casualties. Eisenhower later wrote, 'The whole scene was pitiful. The veterans were ragged, ill-fed, and felt themselves badly abused. To suddenly see the whole encampment going up in flames just added to the pity.' Yet MacArthur justified his actions claiming that the veterans were little more than a revolutionary mob and that the very institutions of the government had been threatened by them. Many Americans did not agree with him, their sympathies lay with the Bonus marchers; Hoover's name was despised and some cinemas even refused to show newsreels in which Hoover appeared. Nonetheless, Hoover's office did not receive a flood of letters condemning his action, and there were no mass demonstrations against government action. Possibly this was because the BEF was dismissed by the President as 'thugs, hoodlums and communists'; by raising the spectre of revolution Hoover retained control but at the cost of his own reputation as President.

Hoover was condemned for his cold-heartedness and indifference but he did try, within the limits of his beliefs and power, to soften the effects of the Depression. He intervened in the economy far more than any of his predecessors had done and his efforts to break the vicious downward spiral of deflation seemed, in 1930, to be having some success. He had created the Federal Farm Board to bolster agricultural prices and urged state governments to spend on capital projects which would create work. As the Depression deepened during 1931–2, he set up the Reconstruction Finance Corporation (RFC) to lend money to financial institutions that were experiencing difficulties, and he passed acts to expand credit and empower the RFC to spend on public works. Indeed, few politicians advocated more radical measures than Hoover but he was obstructed by a Democrat dominated Congress obsessed by the vision of a balanced budget, and his efforts came to nought.

The 1932 presidential election

To the people of America, the presidential election of 1932 presented a clear choice. On the one hand they could vote for Herbert Hoover on his past record, with his promises of prosperity 'just around the corner' and his attempts to instil confidence in the economy, caricatured on a Democratic election poster by a very sarcastic cartoon by Harry Cornell Greening in which Hoover urged the electorate to 'Smile away the Depression'.

On the other hand they could vote for the Democrat candidate, Franklin Delano Roosevelt (FDR), who radiated a jaunty optimism and energy, whose campaign song asserted that 'Happy days are here again', who promised a 'New Deal for the American people', and whose platform promised government intervention to provide jobs, revive industry and agriculture and

figure 5 cartoon of the smilette – a democrat election poster making fun of Hoover's approach to solving the depression. By Harry Cornell Greening.

help for the poor and unemployed. In particular, FDR promised government action for the 'forgotten man at the bottom of the economic pyramid'. FDR was an excellent public speaker and did not hesitate to take his message to the US people, travelling all over the country talking directly to the people about the problems they faced – all this in spite of the fact that he had lost the use of his legs after having contracted polio in 1921. Conversely, Hoover dared not go out in public for fear he be attacked!

The result of the 1932 election was a landslide for FDR who gained 22.8 million votes to Hoover's 15.7 million. Between

Roosevelt's election victory in November 1932 and his inauguration in March 1933, the Depression was at its height and the US people awaited Roosevelt's proposals anxiously. First the outgoing President had to hand over to his successor. It was a different Herbert Hoover who stood beside the new President at the latter's inauguration in Washington on 3 March 1933 – his eyes were red, his voice was hoarse and his hands were trembling, he swayed on the platform and looked physically and mentally exhausted. Only five years earlier he had been confident in his election speeches, but the Wall Street crash and the Depression which followed in its wake shattered this confidence and ridiculed the 1928 election promises. In complete contrast to this image of exhaustion was Roosevelt's first speech as President which has been described by the historian Hugh Brogan as: 'one of the turning points of American history' (*History of the United States of America*, 1985). Roosevelt assured the American public that the only thing they had to fear was fear itself, and he proposed a 'New Deal' to rebuild the US economy and called for sweeping powers to be given to him so that he might meet the economic crisis. These powers were needed quickly – the day before the inaugural ceremony two major banks had stopped trading, people rushed to withdraw their savings and there was a fear that more banks would go 'bust', thus beginning a new economic crisis. Could FDR, newly inaugurated as President, nip this crisis in the bud?

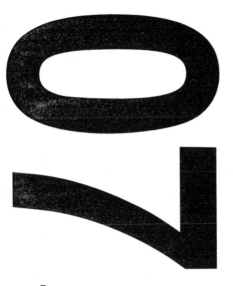

07

Franklin D. Roosevelt and the New Deal

This chapter will cover:
- the New Deal – policies for the 'forgotten man'
- how successful was the New Deal?
- did all sectors of society benefit from the New Deal?

Let me first of all assert my firm belief that the only thing we have to fear is fear itself. Nameless, unreasoning, unjustified terror which paralyses efforts to convert retreat into advance. This is no insolvable problem. This nation asks for action and action now.

This speech extract is no 'call to arms' against a foreign enemy or terrorist threat but part of Franklin D. Roosevelt's 1933 inaugural speech. Yet in a way it was a 'call to arms', it was a plea to all Americans to unite in the war against unemployment, poverty and want. In keeping with this image, Roosevelt proposed to make use of legislation granted to the President during the First World War; the Trading with the Enemy Act allowed the President to take extraordinary action without having to ask Congress to ratify that action so that, in an emergency, the President could take immediate action to address the situation.

His promise of 'action now' was acted upon two days after his inauguration when Roosevelt ordered all the banks to close for a four-day 'Bank Holiday' so that he could review the situation and develop a strategy to put the banks on a secure footing and restore faith in the economy. He then asked Congress to pass the Emergency Banking Act which allowed government officials to inspect the accounts of the country's banks; only those with sufficient cash reserves and those which were properly managed would be allowed to reopen. The government would guarantee the savers' money. Roosevelt followed this up with one of his 'fireside chats' – he addressed the nation on the radio and shared his vision with the people of the USA. He spoke about the banking crisis and reassured the people: 'It is the government's job to straighten out this situation and do it as quickly as possible. We must have faith; you must not be stampeded by rumours. Together we cannot fail.'

Roosevelt's 'pep talk' worked. The banks reopened on Monday 13 March but there was no panic, in fact over $300 million of gold deposits were returned to the banks and, overall, more money was deposited than was withdrawn. The USA had placed its trust in Roosevelt.

The Hundred Days

The period from 4 March to 16 June 1933 is known as the 'Hundred Days', a period when Roosevelt used his powers under the Trading with the Enemy Act to face the nation's problems and attempt to solve them. The banking crisis dealt with, Roosevelt turned his attention elsewhere. On 15 March, the Economy Act was passed which cut government budgets and the wages of the armed forces and government employees by 25 per cent and 15 per cent respectively. This enabled the government to amass nearly $1 billion to spend in other areas such as poverty and unemployment. In a surprising but very popular move, on 20 March the Beer Act swept aside Prohibition and facilitated the creation of new jobs while at the same time bringing the government extra revenue from the tax on alcohol.

figure 6 cartoon commenting on Roosevelt and prohibiton

(Source: Bring him in! By W. J. Enright. *The Chicago Herald & Examiner* 18 March 1933. FDR Cartoon Archive/Niskayuna High School.)

The New Deal

Roosevelt had spoken of his 'New Deal' during his electoral campaign but, at that time, had no blueprint as to what this actually was. With the aid of a 'brains trust', a collection of academics who thought up ways to combat unemployment, the New Deal took shape. Put simply, it consisted of policies which put into action the principles of 'the 3 Rs': relief, recovery and reform.

Relief from the effects of the depression was needed for the millions of poor and unemployed. Recovery from the economic depression could be achieved by getting the unemployed back to work and by 'priming the pump', that is, once the people started to earn wages they would start spending and this in turn would stimulate the economy and create more jobs. Reform of financial and governmental institutions was needed to ensure that the economic chaos of 1929–33 never happened again.

At the very heart of the New Deal were the 'alphabet agencies' – government agencies (known by their initials) funded by the taxpayer and designed to give the US people help and support in all aspects of their life.

The alphabet agencies

In 1933 the emphasis was on getting the USA back to work and tackling some of the causes and effects of the terrible poverty experienced by millions. The needy were helped by two main agencies: the Federal Emergency Relief Administration (FERA) which provided emergency relief; and the Home Owners Loan Corporation (HOLC) which loaned money at low interest rates to more than a million people who were behind with their mortgage repayments so that they would not be made homeless.

The FERA provided $500 million to state governments so that they might provide emergency relief in the shape of soup kitchens, clothing, and schools for those who were homeless, impoverished and on the verge of starvation. Harry Hopkins was put in charge of FERA and his ideas can be seen in much of the ideology of not only this agency but other aspects of the New Deal as well. He was opposed to the idea of 'dole' and firmly believed that the unemployed needed work rather than hand-outs since it would give them back their self-respect, raise their morale, and at the same time the work they did would improve their surroundings and be socially useful.

Work for the unemployed was the priority of three agencies: the Civil Works Administration (CWA) was a short-term scheme which aimed to provide as many people as possible (over 4 million) with jobs during the harsh winter months; the Civilian Conservation Corps (CCC) which provided six months of labouring work on mainly conservation projects for unemployed men aged between 18 and 25; the Public Works Administration (PWA) which aimed to provide public works to benefit society as a whole such as building dams, sewers, bridges, schools, hospitals and houses, and had a budget of $3.3 billion. The CWA spent $1 billion on short-term projects for the unemployed such as building or improving roads, public buildings and airports. The workers were paid 40 cents an hour if unskilled, and $1 an hour if skilled. Unfortunately not everyone agreed with the work created by the CWA, claiming that many of the tasks were bogus, calling them 'boondoggles' a word meaning an unnecessary or wasteful project or activity. In Hopkins' view though, the CWA got money circulating in the economy and helped many to survive the winter months.

The CCC proved to be one of the great symbols of the New Deal; Roosevelt himself expressed his regret that he was unable to participate in one of the camps combining as they did physical work with outdoor living and military-style discipline. Indeed, he found time to visit many of the camps, although as Frances Perkins (head of the National Recovery Administration (NRA)) said, Roosevelt had no real idea of what was involved in setting up the schemes, and tended to exaggerate their importance.

The PWA was part of the National Industrial Recovery Act (NIRA) whose aim was to provide jobs and stimulate the economy. Harold Ickes who ran the PWA was extremely careful not to be accused of passing off 'boondoggles' as work, to such an extent that he took a great deal of time to make decisions and was always anxious that the work gave good value for the government's money. The PWA was intended only to create work for skilled workers, which still left many unskilled workers without work, and because of Ickes' attention to minutiae the money was very slow to trickle into the economy. The other wing of the NIRA was the NRA, an organization which aimed to increase workers' wages (so that they could spend more on goods), improve their working conditions and increase the prices of factory goods to enable factory owners to make more profit and thus employ more staff. The companies who signed up to voluntary codes which fixed fair prices and wages received the right to use the Blue Eagle logo when selling their goods, and the public was encouraged to buy these branded goods by forceful publicity campaigns.

The plight of the farmers did not go unnoticed and two agencies were created specifically for them: the Farm Credit Administration (FCA) refinanced 20 per cent of farm mortgages at lower rates of interest and saved many from being evicted; and the Agricultural Adjustment Administration (AAA) was more controversial as it aimed to raise farm prices by reducing surpluses. Farmers were paid to produce less, to take land out of cultivation, to plough up their cotton or tobacco crops and to slaughter their livestock (some of the meat was used for feeding the poor, but 90 per cent was destroyed). Farm incomes rose by 50 per cent as a result, but ironically tenant farmers and sharecroppers actually suffered from the AAA's policies. They were evicted by their landowners and replaced by machinery bought with money from the government. In addition, the AAA came increasingly under the control of the larger and wealthier farmers who then benefited most as they claimed compensation for cutting production. The AAA did next to nothing to help millions of farm workers and sharecroppers, many of them African Americans, who continued to suffer from extreme poverty.

The Tennessee Valley Authority (TVA) was set up to develop a huge area covering seven states. This region had been farmed intensively and had suffered from soil erosion, dust damage and flooding. The area had very little industry and high unemployment, and the aims of the TVA were to revive both agriculture and industry in one vast programme. Thirty-three dams were built to regulate the Tennessee River and some were used to provide cheap electricity for farmers, domestic consumers and the light industry firms which moved into the area to take advantage of the cheap electricity. The river had locks built along it, creating a 1046-km (650-mile) long waterway on which materials could be imported to the area and produce exported. Farmers were encouraged to improve the soil by planting trees to stop soil erosion and by using fertilizers to regenerate the land. Thousands of jobs were created, agricultural land was improved and living standards rose in one of the worst hit areas of the Depression. Nevertheless, this agency too had its share of critics; the private electric companies believed that the TVA's electricity prices competed unfairly with their own; supporters of laissez-faire economic policies saw socialist tendencies and state planning at work in the TVA; many aspects of the TVA's work were racist, for example, when the new town of Norris was built in the Tennessee Valley, no African Americans were allowed to live there. In spite of these shortcomings, there is considerable evidence to suggest that the TVA was one of the most successful agencies of the New Deal.

But what of the financial institution which had been one of the major causes of the Depression? In 1934, the Securities and Exchange Commission (SEC) was set up to regulate the Stock

Exchange in a variety of ways including measures to ensure that 'buying on the margin' would not cause the chaos it had in 1929; henceforth a down-payment of 50–60 per cent was required when buying shares.

The Second New Deal

In January 1935, Roosevelt used the occasion of his State of the Union speech to announce his intention to broaden the remit of the New Deal and the policies which followed this speech are often referred to as the 'Second New Deal'. The emphasis of this new departure was on government intervention to provide welfare for those affected by the Depression by introducing some social security benefits, to offer more protection to workers, and to replace those policies and agencies that the Supreme Court had ruled to be unconstitutional.

The Social Security Act of 1935 introduced a compulsory system of old-age pensions, unemployment and sick pay funded jointly by federal and state governments. The benefits were hardly generous and, as the schemes were paid for by contributions of 3 per cent by both employer and employee, no payments were forthcoming until 1942. Then the unemployment benefits were calculated as a percentage of what the person earned while employed, not what they actually needed to survive on when unemployed. Farm labourers, casual labour and servants, groups who were often in the direst need of aid, were not eligible for the pensions or the benefits.

Although the Act provided very basic benefits, there was much opposition to it from conservative Republicans who saw the spectre of socialism in this interference by the state in the lives of the American people. In spite of the Republican opposition to this erosion of what they considered to be the traditional values of US society, the Act was probably the most radical and potentially most important of all the laws passed by the New Deal.

In 1935, the Works Progress Administration (WPA), perhaps the most famous public works agency, was set up to employ people on projects valuable to the community. This new agency took over the work of the CWA and the PWA and was run by the former head of the CWA, Harry Hopkins. It became the country's largest employer, providing work for over 8.5 million people on over 1.5 million projects which included building roads, public buildings, schools, airports, bridges, sewers and tunnels. The WPA even allocated 7 per cent of the budget to hire writers to record the experiences of the American people and to write tourist guides as part of the Federal Writers' Project. As part of the Federal Arts Project, artists painted murals in public buildings and produced sculptures to be displayed in public spaces. Actors were sent out to tour the nation and perform plays and shows as part of the Federal Theatre Project, and film stars such as Orson Welles and John Huston benefited from WPA money to finance their productions. The photography of people like Dorothea Lange and Walker Evans recorded the state of America in the 1930s, once again thanks to payments by the WPA. The psychological impact of these arts projects should not be underestimated. Although criticized by many, they ensured that Americans were aware of their history, culture and traditions; they lifted spirits in communities devastated by the Depression; and transformed the appearance of many down-at-heel areas in the cities. Just as Roosevelt had hoped, the WPA preserved the 'self-respect...self-confidence and courage and determination' of the unemployed.

Industrial problems continued to manifest themselves throughout the Depression years. Trade unionism in the USA was weak and workers who tried to improve their wages and working conditions found it difficult for a variety of reasons. The federal nature of the USA restricted nationwide union activity, thus reducing the effectiveness of the unions; immigration had resulted in a plentiful supply of cheap labour which drove down wages; the federal courts tended to side with employers in cases concerning freedom of contract; many employers were determined to prevent union activity in their businesses and dismissed or used violence against workers who complained about wages and conditions or tried to engage in collective bargaining.

The National Labour Relations Act of 1935, or Wagner Act (named after its creator, Robert Wagner, chairman of the NRA), aimed to establish the rights of workers to join unions without fear, to choose their own representatives rather than having them chosen for them by their employers, and to bargain collectively rather than negotiating individually with their employers. With the legal protection afforded them by this Act, workers began to join unions and membership rose from 3 million in 1933 to 9 million in 1939. With the backing of the National Labour Relations Board (NLRB), which could not only bargain on behalf of the workers but could also prevent companies from using blacklists and company unions, the power and confidence of the unions grew. In 1936, many separate unions were amalgamated into the Congress of Industrial Organizations (CIO) which was big enough to bargain with major employers. Yet many employers were unwilling to negotiate with the unions. Ford, for example, had 'goon squads' – about 800 individuals who used violence to keep the workers in line – and a network of spies who kept him informed of workers who tried to form unions. The steel industry was also generally unwilling to recognize the unions; some steel companies had signed contracts recognizing basic hours and wages but others were determined to break the strikes organized by the CIO. This resulted in the Chicago 'Memorial Day Massacre' in 1937 where striking workers from the Republic Steel Company, together with their families, were attacked by 500 armed Chicago police, resulting in ten strikers being killed and 90 injured.

In spite of setbacks such as these there were successes too. Following a Christmas sit-in in the General Motors plant in Flint, Michigan, the head of the company, Mr Knudsen, was forced to recognize the Union of Auto Workers.

The AAA had helped many farm owners but, as previously mentioned, had largely ignored the plight of sharecroppers and tenant farmers. The Resettlement Administration (RA), set up in 1935, aimed to help those who had been evicted when their land had been taken out of production by trying to move 500,000 of them to be settled in new areas where they would also be encouraged to develop better farming skills. In the end, only 5,000 were resettled because of the huge cost involved in this and because, surprisingly, few wanted to move. The Farm Security Administration (FSA) of 1937 gave loans to sharecroppers and tenant farmers to buy their own land, and it also established labour camps for migrant farm workers like those described by John Steinbeck in *The Grapes of Wrath* (1939). Steinbeck describes the experiences of a migrant family as they move from camp to camp finally arriving at a government camp which has wash tubs, running water, five sanitary units and a nurse who comes to teach the children. Steinbeck's character exclaims, 'Well for Christ's sake! Why ain't they (sic) more places like this?'

The Supreme Court had cancelled the AAA in 1936 but another Act was immediately passed by Congress: the Soil Conservation Act (1936) made grants to those farmers who took measures to improve and conserve the soil on their land and, by 1940, over 6 million farmers who had joined the scheme were receiving subsidies of, on average, $100 a year. The popularity and success of the Second New Deal was soon placed under scrutiny by the electorate during the election of 1936. Had Roosevelt gained the confidence of the nation sufficiently to be elected for a second term in office?

The 1936 presidential election

Roosevelt was unanimously re-nominated by the Democrats as their candidate in the 1936 election while the Republicans chose Alfred Landon. As expected, Roosevelt was criticized for wasting money, for failing to balance the federal budget and for giving too much power to the unions. Even the newspapers opposed Roosevelt. For his part, Roosevelt portrayed himself and the Democrats as siding with 'the forgotten man, the little man, the man nobody knew much about' against big business and the rich. He was touched when, while campaigning around the country, thousands of people would turn up to catch a glimpse of the President and shout out things such as, 'he saved my home' or 'he gave me a job', and he received thousands of letters telling of how he had made a difference to people's lives. To the people it seemed he could do no wrong, and when the result of the election came he gained a landslide victory with a majority of 8 million votes. Only two states failed to support him, Maine and Vermont.

Roosevelt's second term was beset by a number of problems. In late 1937 came a period of economic recession when Roosevelt had cut back on his spending programmes which resulted in problems for several industries. By 1938, Roosevelt had become preoccupied with overseas problems caused by the rise of the fascist dictatorship in Italy and the Nazi dictatorship in Germany.

Opposition to the New Deal

In spite of the landslide result in 1936 which showed the majority of Americans supported Roosevelt, many remained unconvinced by the New Deal and staunchly opposed the departure from the traditional principles of self-reliance, rugged individualism and minimal government interference in the lives of the people.

Some Republicans believed the New Deal was dangerously close to socialism, even communism, with the TVA being compared to the economic planning seen in Communist Russia. As the Republican Frank Knox claimed, 'The New Deal candidate has been leading us towards Moscow.' These Republicans claimed that money was being wasted on pointless jobs which were only temporary, and that government expenditure was obstructing a balanced budget. Roosevelt was personally criticized for acting in a dictatorial manner and for making the federal government over-powerful. As the Republican Party was the party of big business, it was natural that the policies which intervened in the economy and supported the unions would come under a considerable amount of criticism.

So incensed were some wealthy businesspeople that they formed the American Liberty League to preserve individual liberty and oppose the New Deal. Surprisingly, some Democrat politicians, mainly from the southern farming areas, joined the League fearful of the Wagner Act and other aspects which supported trade unionism.

Many wealthy Americans resented paying higher income tax to pay for the New Deal agencies. *Harpers* magazine ran an article called 'They Hate Roosevelt' which told of one wealthy resident of Park Avenue who had been imprisoned for threatening Roosevelt with violence. Others believed the President had betrayed his own class.

On the other hand, some individuals claimed the New Deal did not go far enough since there were still 9 million unemployed in 1936. Senator Huey 'Kingfish' Long had once supported the New Deal but he became increasingly convinced that it was insufficiently radical. He proposed a 'Share Our Wealth' scheme which was certainly more radical and which proposed to confiscate all personal wealth over $3 million and share out the money so that each American family would have $4,000–5,000. Free education and old-age pensions, cheap food and a minimum wage were some of his other proposals. He was assassinated in 1935 by a young doctor.

Dr Francis Townsend also had plans to improve the New Deal. He proposed that everyone over the age of 60 should receive $200 a month provided they gave up their jobs and spent all of the money each month. This would create new jobs for younger people and stimulate the economy, in addition to giving older people the recognition they deserved.

Father Coughlin, the 'radio priest', broadcast his ideas to the nation every Sunday evening during the 'Golden Hour of the Little Flower' and reached an audience of 40 million – even larger than those who listened to Roosevelt's fireside chats. He criticized Roosevelt for failing to tackle the problems of the poor and set up the National Union for Social Justice, promising work and fair wages for all.

Although these individuals had very many followers, their attacks on the New Deal did not lead to a corresponding loss of votes for Roosevelt and were therefore less of a threat to him and his policies than the Supreme Court.

One of the roles of the Supreme Court is to decide whether the laws passed by Congress are constitutional, and if the Court decides the laws are contrary to the Constitution it can block them. Supreme Court judges are nominated by the President who tends to choose judges who reflect his own political beliefs. During the 1930s, the Supreme Court judges had been appointed mainly by Republican Presidents; of the nine judges in the Supreme Court, six were over 70. These judges believed the New Deal was undermining one of the main purposes of the American Constitution – to defend the freedom of the individual against excessive government control.

In 1935, following the 'Sick Chicken' case the Supreme Court ruled that the NRA codes on fair trading were unconstitutional. The Schechter Poultry Corporation had signed up to the NRA codes on fair trading but had broken them on several occasions, for example, when they sold an 'unfit chicken' to a butcher. When the corporation appealed to the Supreme Court against the verdict that they had broken the codes, it decided that the agencies could not interfere in matters of trade within a state. The NRA code was declared illegal and a further 750 codes scrapped.

In 1936 in The United States v. Butler et al case, the Court ruled that the AAA was illegal because the responsibility for aid to farmers lay with the state governments not the federal government.

In all, out of the 16 cases concerning the 'alphabet agencies' that came before the Court, it was ruled that Roosevelt and the Congress had acted unconstitutionally in 11 of them.

Roosevelt was determined to reform the Supreme Court and proposed to forcibly retire the six judges who were over 70 and replace them with judges who would be sympathetic to his policies and to the New Deal. This attempt to 'pack' the court with his sympathizers caused great apprehension in American society and even amongst his own supporters – could Roosevelt be turning into a dictator? His plan was swiftly rejected, but it had the desired effect. In April 1937, the Court reversed the 'Sick Chicken' verdict and, on review, declared legal several aspects of the Social Security Act including old-age pensions and unemployment insurance. Several of the judges retired soon after this and Roosevelt was able to appoint his own judges to fill the vacancies. However, some damage had been done to Roosevelt's reputation as an honest politician, and the whole episode earned him more enemies.

Did all Americans benefit from the New Deal?

Most minorities benefited little from FDR's New Deal programme. Minorities who had habitually been the 'last hired, first fired' even before the Depression, were the first ones to be affected by the job lay-offs. Most of the programmes targeted unemployed white males in an attempt to keep the Democratic Party united and pass New Deal legislation through a southern-dominated Congress. African-American males were either excluded from programmes or had to settle for separate and lower pay scales. The emphasis on getting white males back to work can be seen in the South West where a shortage of jobs led to the illegal deportation of 400,000 Mexican Americans in order that whites could get more jobs or government relief.

The Depression had made the working lives of African Americans more difficult than before as many found themselves competing with white Americans who had previously scorned unskilled labour and menial work as suitable only for African Americans, but who now were desperate for any kind of work themselves. The New Deal did little for unskilled workers and consequently had less impact on the African-American population. In the South there was widespread racism and segregation which was continued in the New Deal. African Americans were segregated in the CCC camps as W. L. Katz recalls: 'The coloured from several buses were herded together; and stood in line until after the white boys had been registered and taken to their tents' (*Eyewitness: the Negro in American History*, 1967). As previously mentioned, in the Tennessee Valley the new town of Norris excluded African Americans from living there. African Americans found it difficult to get work and by

1935 around 30 per cent were living on relief. However, approximately 200,000 African-Americans took part in the CCC programme and many benefited from the slum clearance programmes of the New Deal. Mary MacLeod Bethune scored a double victory when she became the head of the National Youth Administration (NYA); she was the highest ranking African-American appointee in the Roosevelt administration and she was a woman.

Lynchings and injustice increased during the Depression years, but Roosevelt refused to support a proposed law against lynching for fear he lose the support of southern Democrats. Eleanor Roosevelt, however, did support groups opposed to racism and publicly denounced segregation. When she attended a conference in Alabama in 1938 and found that black and white delegates were segregated, she moved her chair to sit firmly between the two groups.

Native American Indians did benefit from the New Deal. The 1934 Indian Reorganization Act provided money to buy reservation land so that tribes could own it and the amount of land owned by them increased from 19 million hectares (47 million acres) to 20 million hectares (50 million acres). The Act also gave Native American women formal political rights and encouraged them to get an education providing training as seamstresses and domestic workers. The 1934 Act also encouraged the Native Americans to pursue their cultural and religious traditions and gave them the right to set up their own courts of law.

In spite of high profile members of the Roosevelt administration being female, women generally did not benefit greatly from the New Deal. There was a great deal of resentment of women working during the Depression and many believed, erroneously, that women were taking jobs for 'pin-money' or that they were keeping men out of work. Male trade unionists tended to be of the opinion that a married woman's place was in the home. Yet in some industries the idea of 'same work, same pay' was beginning to take root, although the gap between the earnings of men and women continued and not just within the industrial sector; a female school teacher still earned 20 per cent less than her male counterparts in 1939.

As many of the New Deal programmes revolved around construction and manual labour, few women benefited from them: only 8,000 women were employed in the CCC between 1933 and 1941, compared to 3 million men. The Social Security

Act included Aid to Dependent Children which was particularly useful to women with young families who were unable to go out to work, yet a number of states tried to avoid paying this by introducing conditions such as only married women being able to claim, or it only being available to white families.

The New Deal did, however, provide women with role models. Eleanor Roosevelt, the President's wife, became actively involved in a number of organizations which were trying to improve the position of women for example, the Women's Trade Union League. She became a symbol of social justice and acquired her own 'fan club' through her daily newspaper diary, regular broadcasts, speeches and tours. Frances Perkins became the first woman to hold a cabinet post when she was appointed Labor Secretary in 1933. Mary MacLeod Bethune, the daughter of former slaves, was appointed Director of Negro Affairs. Frances Allen became the first woman judge on the US Court of Appeals. Grace Abbott established the Children's Bureau to aid homeless and neglected children, and Nellie Taylor Ross became the first woman Director of the Mint.

The new slump

By 1937, Roosevelt began to have doubts about 'deficit financing', that is, borrowing money to meet the emergency conditions of the 1930s, intending to pay it back later once tax receipts had increased as more and more people found work. He did not believe that this could continue indefinitely but that it would eventually become imperative to 'balance the budget' and spend only what was returned in taxes. In 1937 the government's debt had reached $4 billion, and although the British economist John Maynard Keynes urged Roosevelt to increase government spending further, the President substantially reduced public spending. The result was a repetition of the economic downward spiral seen in the early 1930s which, in spite of Roosevelt's reversal of the cutbacks, continued until April 1938. This period was known as 'Roosevelt's Recession', a time of increasing unemployment with 10 million people out of work by 1938. The rising unemployment was only halted by the huge government spending which took place with the advent of the Second World War. Even so, as late as 1941 there were still 6 million unemployed, and it was not until 1943 that unemployment ceased to be of major concern.

Roosevelt's achievements

It is difficult to be completely objective about Roosevelt's policies since his New Deal inspired a great deal of controversy both at the time and amongst historians attempting to assess the programme's effectiveness. To some, Roosevelt had made the federal government too powerful, and he had crushed the qualities such as self-reliance and rugged individualism which they believed had made the USA great. To others, he had successfully steered the USA through the worst Depression of the twentieth century, and had prevented the rise of those extreme forces which manifested themselves in Europe at this time – fascism and communism.

Roosevelt failed to beat high unemployment which remained at 17 per cent of the working population in 1939. Certain groups were discriminated against by the New Deal policies; although more Catholics, Jews and African Americans worked on federal projects than ever before, they still suffered from discrimination, prejudice and racism and little was done to improve their civil rights. The federal government developed a new role under Roosevelt, taking on more responsibility for the welfare of Americans and abandoning the policy of laissez-faire by ensuring the economic prosperity of the country. Yet for many this was a double-edged sword; the introduction of social security undoubtedly helped those in need but, some argued, it also took away their self-reliance. One letter to Eleanor Roosevelt complained in 1936, 'Personally, I have found that the more you give to the lower classes, the more they want.' The interference in people's lives and the affairs of the individual states was directly in contravention of the Constitution and many feared that the federal government and the role of the presidency were becoming too powerful, particularly when the independence of the Supreme Court was compromised. In his memoirs, Herbert Hoover wrote that under Roosevelt, 'We saw Congress reduced to a rubber stamp, and the Supreme Court subjugated' (*The Memoirs of Herbert Hoover*, 1953).

Perhaps Roosevelt's greatest achievement within the New Deal was to inspire hope and to raise the morale of the nation. His compassion for the American people was legendary and his 'fireside chats', although only numbering 27 in 12 years, gave the impression of 'a man talking to his friends,' as *The Washington Post* newspaper described them in 1933. The historian C. P. Hill agrees with this: 'It was not the least of Roosevelt's achievements that he gave new heart and new vigour to his fellow countrymen just in time to face the trial of the Second World War' (*The USA Since the First World War*, 1967).

The 1940 presidential election

In 1940 Roosevelt stood for an unprecedented third term in office. He had originally insisted that he was not prepared to break the George Washington precedent by actively seeking re-nomination for a third time, but his party had other ideas and re-nominated him as the Democratic presidential candidate with 946 votes to 72 for his rival James Farley. As conflict had already exploded in Europe and the forces of Nazism were conquering one European country after another, it was only natural that the campaign would revolve around the issue of war. Wendell Wilkie, the Republican candidate, raised fears that Roosevelt intended to take the USA into another European conflagration. Roosevelt reassured his audiences: 'Your boys are not going to be sent to fight in any foreign wars.' He was re-elected with 449 electoral college votes to Wilkie's 82 in November 1940. Just over a year later, the USA was once again at war.

08

the Second World War

This chapter will cover:
- Pearl Harbor and the USA's entry into the war
- the USA's role in the European and Pacific theatres of war
- the atomic bomb.

We must not be misguided by foreign propaganda to the effect that our frontiers lie in Europe. One need only glance at a map to see where our true frontiers lie. What more could we ask than the Atlantic Ocean on the East and the Pacific on the West?

Charles A. Lindbergh, famous aviator and a prominent isolationist, summed up the feeling of many Americans in 1939. A poll conducted at this time showed that less than 30 per cent of Americans wanted the USA to intervene in the war in Europe even if Britain and France faced defeat at the hands of Nazi Germany. If public opinion was so vehemently opposed to war, what eventually persuaded the USA to join the battle against the spread of Nazism in 1941?

Neutrality Acts

The 'Senate Investigation of the Munitions Industries', a report produced by the Nye Committee between 1934 and 1936, reported that greedy industrialists and munitions manufacturers had provoked the USA to enter the First World War by publishing gruesome tales of German atrocities in order to convince the USA to join the Allies and to invest heavily in war production. This report helped convince many Americans that they should ignore European 'propagandists' who publicized the atrocities of Germany, Italy and Japan during the 1930s.

Public opinion became increasingly vocal and anti-war and students on both sides of the Atlantic expressed the view that peace and negotiation was the way forward, not war. The major champion of isolationism was America First, a group of prominent businesspeople, celebrities and politicians, such as pilot Charles A. Lindbergh and automobile magnate Henry Ford, that spoke out against the war.

Between 1935 and 1937, Congress passed a series of Neutrality Acts hoping to avoid the kind of drift to war which had resulted in the USA joining the war in Europe in 1917. During 1935, Mussolini was busily extending his Italian empire into Abyssinia (Ethiopia), and the Neutrality Act passed in this year stated that, should the President proclaim that a state of war existed between two foreign states, the USA would stop all sales of arms to those involved in the war. It would also warn all American citizens of the dangers involved in travelling on vessels owned by those nations, in the hope that a situation such as the sinking of the *Lusitania*, and the loss of American lives, could be avoided. In 1935, Hitler reintroduced conscription in Germany in direct contravention of the Treaty of Versailles but few in Europe appreciated the implications of this since they were distracted by Mussolini's actions in Abyssinia (Ethiopia). In 1936, the fascist nations of Germany, Italy and Japan united in the Anti-Comintern Pact, and it was the inclusion of Japan that awoke some to the possibility of US interests being affected by the extension of fascist power, particularly their economic interests in the Pacific. Despite this, the Neutrality Act of 1936 extended the Act of 1935 for a further year and also stopped loans to countries at war. In 1937, the terms of the Act were again extended to include civil war since the Spanish Civil War had broken out that summer. The 1937 Neutrality Act passed in May of that year proved to be even firmer. Should the President declare that war existed anywhere in the world, the USA would forbid the sale of weapons and loans to those countries at war and would also forbid US citizens from travelling on ships owned by those countries. It is interesting to note that the Neutrality Acts did not differentiate between aggressive and peaceful nations, and many Americans were concerned that nations with 'just cause' for aid would be abandoned to their fate.

By 1938, Germany had been 'invited' by Austria to unite the two countries through an *Anschluss*, and by September of that year, it became apparent that Czechoslovakia was in danger of being incorporated into the ever expanding Germany. Neville Chamberlain, the British Prime Minister and his French counterpart, Daladier, attempted to appease Hitler in a series of meetings, the last of which was held in Munich in 1938. Here, an agreement was reached which gave Germany the Sudetan area of Czechoslovakia in return for a 'piece of paper' with Hitler's promise of 'peace in our time'. War seemed increasingly likely and Roosevelt was keen to prepare for what he saw as the inevitable conflagration beacuse he appreciated that the USA's security was bound up with that of Europe. In his State of the Union speech of 1939, Roosevelt warned of the storm clouds of war ahead but vowed to look again at the 'many methods short of war' that were open to the country. He was able to persuade Congress to permit a 20 per cent increase in the US navy and earmark over $300 million to build more aircraft for defence purposes, but at this point the US army, having been cut to the bone during the Depression years, numbered only 185,000. On 1 September 1939, Roosevelt was woken in the middle of the night to be informed that Hitler had invaded Poland; on the

3 September Britain declared war on Germany. In one of his fireside chats, Roosevelt promised that the USA would remain a neutral nation but he made no attempt to remain neutral in attitude. In 1939, a 'cash and carry' clause was introduced to the Neutrality Act. This insisted that belligerent countries pay cash for materials purchased in the USA and use their own ships to transport the materials.

The speed of Germany's progress through Europe stunned the American public; by June 1940 the Nazis controlled Norway, Denmark, Holland, Belgium and France in addition to Czechoslovakia and Poland. Only Britain and her Empire withstood the Nazi blitzkrieg, fighting the German Luftwaffe in the Battle of Britain throughout the summer and autumn of 1940.

It was increasingly obvious to Americans that a Nazi dominated Europe would be neither economically nor strategically to America's advantage. Defensive arrangements were hurriedly put into action: the Selective Service and Training Act introduced conscription for all men aged 21–36; the air force was increased; the National Defence Research Committee was established to develop new weapons of war, a programme which would result in the development of the atom bomb.

Britain continued to battle on alone, the Neutrality Acts preventing Roosevelt from providing aid, particularly with an election just around the corner and public opinion still vehemently anti-intervention. He succeeded in circumventing the Neutrality Acts by 'swapping' 50 old First World War destroyers for British naval bases in Newfoundland and the Caribbean, an act which raised both US and British protests; Americans believed he had once again undermined the constitution by evading congressional legislation while Britons believed Roosevelt had taken advantage of their dire straits to acquire bases which were extremely valuable. Sir Anthony Eden, a minister in the British government wrote in his memoirs:

> The destroyers were to be exchanged for a public assurance that the British fleet would sail to North American waters if Hitler gained control of the United Kingdom. The Prime Minister rightly protested that such an announcement would have a 'disastrous effect' on British morale. The West Indian bases alone were certainly worth more than fifty or sixty old destroyers.'

(Memoirs: The Reckoning,
Boston Houghton Mifflin Co., 1965)

The *New York Times* noted the importance of these ships for the British war effort: 'Were the control of the seas by Britain lost, the Atlantic would no longer be an obstacle – rather it would become a broad highway for the conqueror moving westwards'. Churchill, now the British Prime Minister, realized that without US aid Britain was in danger of being worn down by Hitler's forces and he began to put more and more pressure on Roosevelt to help Britain's cause.

The 1940 presidential election campaign

During the presidential election campaign, Roosevelt stated time and again his promise not to get the US involved in the war in Europe. He emphasized: 'I hate war now more than ever. I have one supreme determination: to do all that I can to keep war away from these shores for all time.'

On another occasion during his campaign, FDR said: 'I have said this before, but I shall say it again and again and again. Your boys are not going to be sent to any foreign war.'

His promises were believed by the majority of the American voters and he was returned for a third term as President. With his election victory in November 1940, Roosevelt was in a stronger position to give aid and to speak out against the dangers of isolationism. The President was well aware of the Johnson Act of 1934 which stated the USA could not make loans to governments that had failed to pay off their debts following the First World War; therefore he proposed an alternative way to aid Britain in her fight against Nazism.

The Lend Lease Act 1941

On 17 December 1940, Roosevelt made a radio broadcast to the nation about his intentions:

Now, what I am trying to do is to eliminate the dollar sign...let me give you an illustration: Suppose my neighbor's home catches fire, and I have a length of garden hose 400 or 500 feet away. If he can take my garden hose and connect it up with his hydrant, I may help him to put out his fire. Now, what do I do? I don't say to him before that operation, 'Neighbor my garden hose cost me $15; you have to pay me $15 for it.' What is the transaction that my garden hose cost goes on? I don't want $15 – I want my garden hose back after the fire is over. All right. If it goes through the fire all right, intact, without any damage to it, he gives it back to me and thanks me very much for the use of it. But suppose it gets smashed up – holes in it – during the fire; we don't have to have too much formality about it, but I say to him, 'I was glad to lend you that hose; I see I can't use it any more, it's all smashed up.' He says, 'How many feet of it were there?' I tell him, 'There were 150 feet of it.' He says, 'All right, I will replace it.' Now, if I get a nice garden hose back, I am in pretty good shape.

In imagery that was easily understood by all, Roosevelt both explained what the Lend Lease Act entailed and also hinted at the danger posed to the USA by Nazi control of Europe – after all, the fire in a neighbour's house could so easily spread to other properties. He was making it clear that he intended to loan Britain the supplies she needed to 'finish the job', as Churchill put it, rather than loaning money. Later that year Roosevelt clarified the role of the USA as the 'arsenal of democracy', not joining Britain in the war against Hitler but supplying the 'implements of war'. In January 1942, in his State of the Union speech, Roosevelt asked Congress to support all countries that were fighting for the 'four freedoms' – 'The first is freedom of speech and expression...The second is freedom of every person to worship God in his own way...the third is freedom from want...The fourth is freedom from fear.'

These were freedoms which he believed were central to the Allied cause and Roosevelt personally asked Congress to support his proposed Lend Lease Act in order to defend these freedoms. The isolationists were having none of this and warned again that the USA would be dragged into war, and accused Roosevelt of entering the war by stealth. The Lend-Lease Act that finally passed the Congress in March 1941 had been substantially altered from the original but it allowed the USA to lend or lease arms or other necessities to any country on whose safety the safety of the USA might depend. The final cost to Britain of this Act was almost $50 billion but in 1941 it ensured that Britain could continue her fight and marked a turning point in the war. When Hitler put into force Operation Barbarossa in June 1941 and invaded the Soviet Union, the Lend-Lease was extended to the Russians.

Since the British ships carrying the goods obtained from the USA were not accompanied by US convoys, the shipping lanes of the Atlantic were good hunting grounds for the German U-boats which were, by early 1941, sinking 500,000 tonnes of shipping per month. To ensure that supplies got through, Roosevelt secretly authorized actions that amounted to undeclared naval warfare with Germany; he extended the neutral zone to halfway across the Atlantic and gave instructions to US patrols to report any German submarine activity directly to the Royal Navy. This was later extended as far as Greenland and Iceland. When German U-boats were involved in a skirmish with the US destroyer *Greer*, Roosevelt engaged in some sabre-rattling warning that Axis vessels entered US waters at their peril. This was no avail as in October 1941 the US destroyer *Kearny* was attacked causing 11 fatalities and the *USS Reuben James* was sunk by a U-boat with the deaths of 115 crew. Following very narrow voting margins, Congress repealed the Neutrality Acts but not the clauses concerning loans to belligerent countries or the ban on Americans travelling on belligerent ships. The USA maintained neutrality but entry into the war continued to get nearer.

The Atlantic Charter

On 9 August 1941, President Franklin D. Roosevelt and Prime Minister Winston Churchill met in conference aboard *USS Augusta* at Placentia Bay, Newfoundland; after three days of talks they issued the Atlantic Charter. Originally designed to rally support for the war effort, it later became a blueprint for the post-war world.

The Charter announced that the signatories were not seeking more territory for their countries, and that they recognized the right of all peoples to choose their own form of government and to approve any territorial changes that might affect them. It also guaranteed all nations the right to trade and navigate anywhere in the world, and called for international co-operation to promote improved labour standards, economic advancement and social security. The ultimate purpose of the Charter was to ensure that, 'all the men in all the lands may live out their lives in freedom from fear and want'. Finally, Churchill and Roosevelt called for the disarmament of the Axis powers, pending the establishment of a 'permanent system of general security', a system later codified by the United Nations Charter.

Roosevelt had not committed the USA to declaring war, but before the end of that year the USA had joined Britain and the USSR in their fight against Germany, Italy and Japan.

Pearl Harbor

Very late on a cold, dark night in December, a British emissary was driven through the dreary streets of Washington. Inside his diplomatic pouch he carried a secret message marked Most Urgent Personal and Secret to the President. It was a triple priority message from the British Admiralty in London that the United States of America was going to be attacked at Pearl Harbor on December 7th. Lord Halifax was swiftly shown in to the White House and conferred with Franklin Roosevelt. Roosevelt's hopes soared; his long-laid plans were about to be fulfilled. It was December 5th, 1941.

(Mark Emerson Willey, *Pearl Harbor: Mother of all conspiracies*, Xlibris Corporation, 2001)

This description of the days before Pearl Harbor has been produced by an author who is convinced that President Roosevelt was aware that the Japanese were planning to attack Pearl Harbor days before the raid took place, which immediately begs the question 'Why didn't he do something about it?' In order to assess the accuracy of this theory it is necessary to review the known facts.

The 7 December 1941 was, in the words of Roosevelt, 'a day that will live in infamy'. Three hundred and fifty Japanese planes took off from six aircraft carriers and attacked the US naval base at Pearl Harbor in Hawaii. The surprise was complete. The attacking planes came in two waves: the first reaching its target at 7.53 a.m., the second at 8.55. By 9.55 a.m. it was all over and the carriers that had launched the planes were heading back to Japan. Behind them they left devastation: 2,403 dead, 188 planes destroyed as they stood in airfields, and a crippled Pacific fleet that included eight battleships, three cruisers and three destroyers which had been damaged or destroyed.

Because of the speed of the strike on Pearl Harbor it was assumed that the USA knew nothing of Japanese plans to attack US bases. However, it is now clear that as early as November 1941 the US government was aware that the Japanese were poised for attack, but it was presumed Pearl Harbor was too far from Japan to be a feasible target; far more likely to their thinking were bases in the Philippines or South-East Asia.

Word of the attack reached President Roosevelt in the Oval Room of the White House on Sunday afternoon. Later, when Winston Churchill called to tell the President of Japanese attacks on British colonies in South-East Asia and of Britain's decision to declare war the next day, Roosevelt responded that he too would be asking for a declaration of war against Japan when he went before Congress the following day. Churchill wrote: 'To have the United States at our side was to me the greatest joy. Now at this very moment I knew the United States was in the war...Hitler's fate was sealed. Mussolini's fate was sealed. As for the Japanese, they would be ground to powder.' On Monday, Roosevelt signed the declaration of war granted by Congress. One day later both Germany and Italy, as partners of Japan in the Tripartite Pact, declared war on the US.

The attack on Pearl Harbor has been surrounded in controversy with some historians going so far as to claim that there was a conspiracy on the part of several of the key players to use the attack as an excuse to bring the USA into the war in Europe. One rumour current at the time was that the Japanese in Hawaii had crept onto the bases in Hawaii early Sunday morning before the air attack and slit the throats of American servicemen. Another was that one of Roosevelt's New Deal colleagues, Harry Hopkins, had deliberately transferred planes away from Hawaii just before the attack. One story described how Roosevelt and Churchill plotted the raid with the Japanese, and it was even rumoured that British and Americans had piloted at least some of the attacking aircraft.

One more recent advocate of the conspiracy theory, Mark Emerson Willey, states:

> President Roosevelt (FDR) provoked the attack, knew about it in advance and covered up his failure to warn the Hawaiian commanders. FDR needed the attack to sucker Hitler to declare war, since the public and Congress were overwhelmingly against entering the war in Europe. It was his backdoor to war.
>
> (Mark Emerson Willey, *Pearl Harbor: Mother of all conspiracies*, Xlibris Corporation, 2001)

This argument had been hinted at by Doris Kearns Goodwin in her book *No Ordinary Time, Franklin and Eleanor Roosevelt: The Home Front in World War II* (1994). Roosevelt had warned the Cabinet about the likelihood of Japanese attack on 24 November 1941 and on the following day, in conversation with Stimson, the Secretary of War, had posed the question of how to manoeuvre the Japanese into firing the first shot without putting the US at too much risk. However, Doris Kearns Goodwin emphasizes that if Roosevelt had known about Pearl Harbor before the event he would have ensured that minimal damage be done to the Pacific fleet, after all, 'for the purposes of mobilizing the American people, one American ship torpedoed by the Japanese at Pearl Harbour would have sufficed,' and she finds it inconceivable that the President would have risked the lives of 3,500 US sailors and soldiers. The historian David M. Kennedy agrees with this, believing that to risk the entire Pacific fleet for an excuse to go to war constituted, 'too much danger to ourselves' especially since Roosevelt had not used previous naval incidents, such as the sinking of the *Kearney* and the *Reuben James*, as a pretext to declare war on Germany (*Freedom from Fear: The American People in Depression and War, 1929–1945*, 1999). It is likely that the US government expected the attack to be made on the Philippines, the Thai Peninsula or Borneo rather than Pearl Harbor, which was such a distance from Japan. Consequently, Pearl Harbor was left unprotected. General George C. Marshall had drafted a message to certain naval bases including Pearl Harbor to be on the alert following the request of Japan's Ambassador in Washington to meet the Secretary of State, but the message was sent by post rather than by radio and consequently arrived too late to warn the forces to be on their guard. John Toland suggests that there may have been a conspiracy to cover up mistakes made in Washington by blaming the commanders in Hawaii for the attack on Pearl Harbor:

> Roosevelt had been assured by Marshall that Oahu was the strongest fortress in the world and any enemy task force would be destroyed. The president, therefore, took a calculated risk and lost. This was understandable, but if he instigated a cover-up, as some evidence indicates, that was a serious offence. Perhaps the whole truth will never be known.

(John Toland, *Infamy*, Berkley Books, 1983)

Pearl Harbor remains a controversy which seems destined to continue. If the Japanese had intended the attack to deliver a mortal blow to the USA's Pacific fleet and defences, they would have been disappointed as it was fairly limited in its effect; the US Pacific fleet carriers were out of the port on manoeuvres and the Japanese attack failed to hit a vital fuel store whose destruction would have been a grave cause for concern.

On 8 December, Roosevelt announced to Congress that, 'our people, our territory and our interests are in grave danger'. In the vote on the declaration of war on Japan, which followed after the President's emotional speech, only one congressman voted against the motion; isolationism had been forgotten. On 11 December 1941, Germany and Italy declared war on the USA.

The New Deal at war

The mood of the country when war was declared in 1941 was one of grim determination unlike the one of jubilation that greeted the declaration of war in 1917. Few were under any illusion about the reality of war or the situation in Europe and most saw Adolf Hitler and the Japanese as real threats to the civilized world.

Roosevelt had already begun the process of preparing the country for war by increasing spending on defence, and the Selective Service Act (1940) had begun conscripting young men into the armed forces. The War Powers Act (1941) gave the President wide-ranging powers to mobilize the country and industry in preparation for 'total war'. Using similar tactics to those previously seen in the New Deal, Roosevelt set up a series of government agencies to organize mobilization: the Office of Price Administration (OPA) set prices in order to combat inflation; the National War Labor Board (NWLB) not only set wages but could also take over the running of industries should production be disrupted by strikes; the War Production Board (WPB) co-ordinated all the war-related industries.

The economic effect of war

In direct contrast to the New Deal policies of the 1930s, military spending was now given priority over social and economic reform and Congress rolled back much of the 1930's reform legislation during wartime. Many factories introduced longer working hours in order to increase industrial output. The federal government gave little attention to anti-trust legislation and, in order to overcome the shortage of labour, federal inspectors ignored laws which regulated the employment of children and women. The number of students leaving high school early increased significantly and the teenage workforce grew from 1 million to 3 million. For years, conservative politicians had fought against the New Deal agencies, but now that Roosevelt was concentrating on winning a war rather than reforming society, they succeeded in slashing funding for the CCC, WPA, and NYA. With the elimination of many New Deal programmes, poverty increased for many Americans in spite of the fact that wages were rising. One committee reported that 20 million Americans were on the border of subsistence and starvation. Twenty-five per cent of all employed Americans earned less than 64 cents an hour, while skilled workers often earned $7 or $8 an hour.

War changed the nature of the economy as a close relationship developed between big business and the military's expenditure on defence. Small companies disappeared as two-thirds of government contracts went to the 100 largest corporations. The transformation of the peacetime economy to one ready for war was remarkable, and within four years the USA had produced 300,000 war planes, 85,000 warships, 86,000 tanks and 50 million tonnes of ammunition – the USA had indeed become Roosevelt's 'arsenal of democracy' as these military supplies also helped Britain and the USSR. US industrial capacity increased as the average expenditure on military contracts increased to $250 million per day. The nation also became more urbanized – the six largest cities gained 2 million new inhabitants and 15 million Americans moved from rural areas to the cities. The theory of the British economist John Maynard Keynes that governments should intervene in the economy to reduce high unemployment was fulfilled in the US during the Second World War as nearly every worker with a useable skill was employed. The war was also responsible for the transformation of the USA into an invincible economic leviathan for the post-war world.

The internment of Japanese-Americans

In February 1942, Roosevelt issued Executive Order 9066 which forced the relocation of all Japanese-Americans from the West Coast, a region that Roosevelt and other US political and military leaders considered strategically vulnerable. The government established ten internment camps in Arkansas, Arizona, California, Colorado, Idaho, Utah, and Wyoming, which held a total of 100,000 persons of Japanese ancestry, many of whom were US citizens. The families lived in poorly built, overcrowded barracks with no running water, little heat and almost no privacy; they were surrounded by barbed wire and guarded by armed soldiers. The camps did provide some medical care and schools and, gradually, some young adults were released to do agricultural and defence work, to go to college, and even serve in the military.

Almost 50 years later, the US Congress passed, and President Ronald Reagan signed, the Civil Liberties Act of 1988 which formally apologized for its wartime imprisonment of these innocent people and awarded each of 80,000 survivors a $20,000 payment. The presidential Commission that recommended the 1988 apology explained the internment of Japanese-Americans as: '...race prejudice, war hysteria, and a failure of political leadership. Widespread ignorance of Japanese Americans contributed to a policy conceived in haste and executed in an atmosphere of fear and anger at Japan'. Although the Supreme Court at the time ruled that these camps were constitutional, they were closed in 1944 after Roosevelt had been re-elected for a fourth term.

The power and scope of the federal government and the presidency increased during the war years. The war increased the growth of the executive power so that the President and his advisers, more than Congress, seemed to direct both the nation's domestic and foreign agenda, a move which remained unchallenged by the Supreme Court. The number of civilian employees working for the federal government rose from 1 million to nearly 4 million and, at the same time, Washington's expenditure grew from $9 billion to $98.4 billion – twice the total that Washington had spent since the US was founded.

Domestic changes

Rationing of certain items was introduced. Within weeks of Pearl Harbor, rubber was rationed and was followed by items such as sugar, coffee and diesel; petrol stations were closed between the hours of 7 p.m. and 7 a.m. and the sale of new cars and trucks prohibited.

One of the most dramatic changes during the war was in the number of women who went out to work; more than 6 million women joined the workforce. As the armed forces took men to fill their ranks, industry filled the vacant jobs with women; since most of the machinery was automated, brute strength was no longer needed to operate it. In August 1943, *Newsweek* magazine reported: 'They [women] are in the shipyards, lumber mills, steel mills, foundries. They are welders, electricians, mechanics, and even boilermakers. They operate streetcars, buses, cranes, and tractors.'

Any job previously done by men who had been called up was now done by women and the song 'Rosie the Riveter' became the anthem for all women war workers. In 1939 only 36 women had been employed in shipbuilding; by 1942 there were 200,000 doing every conceivable job. Women not only went into industry to help the war effort; 3 million women served as Red Cross volunteers and in the nursing corps. Millions of women worked for the Civilian Defence as air raid wardens, fire watchers, messengers and drivers, and thousands found their way into military organizations such as the Women's Auxiliary Ferrying Squadron (WAFS) and the Women's Army Corps (WAC).

The war gave African Americans the perfect opportunity to press for an improvement in their civil rights. A. Philip Randolph planned a protest march through Washington in protest at the exclusion of African Americans from jobs in the defence industry. This alarmed the government to such an extent that Roosevelt agreed to ban discrimination against African Americans in industrial and government jobs and also to set up an agency, the Fair Employment Practice Committee (FEPC) to collect information on discrimination in private defence companies. In view of the fact that one of the reasons for the war against Hitler was his racist ideology of the Aryan race as *Ubermensch* or Supreme Race, the fact that African Americans had to fight in segregated units and could not fight at all in the Army Air Corps or the United States Marine Corps made little sense. It was not until January 1945 that the first formally integrated unit was introduced and not until 1948 that all jobs in the armed services were open to African Americans. The experiences of African Americans during the war would have a major effect on the civil rights movement in the 1940s and 1950s.

The war in Europe

The USA, Britain and the Soviet Union may have been allies, but there was a great deal of disagreement between them regarding the pursuit of the war, particularly the tactics to be employed. Churchill argued that the war should be concentrated in Europe and that the Axis powers should be attacked from the direction of the Mediterranean rather than France. Stalin was anxious for the Western powers to open a second front in order to take pressure off the Soviet army in the East; this request was put to one side by Roosevelt and Churchill in favour of an attack through Italy, the weakest of the Axis powers.

The first victory of the Allied powers came in October 1942 in North Africa. Britain's Field Marshall Montgomery defeated German forces at El Alamein and the next month General Dwight D. Eisenhower led Allied landings on the coast of North Africa. The Axis troops were trapped by British and US troops advancing from the West and the British 8th Army advancing from the East; in May 1943 250,000 Axis troops surrendered in Tunisia. The victory in North Africa gave the Allies two advantages: they now controlled the Suez Canal which afforded them easier access to oil supplies: and they won a perfect position from which to launch an attack on Italy. Sicily fell in July following an Allied attack by air and sea, and the Allies pushed their way up the Italian mainland. The Italian army surrendered in September 1943 but was replaced by the German army which slowed the progress of the Allied army with fierce fighting in the area of Monte Cassino; it was not until 1944 that Rome was taken.

In the Atlantic, the German 'wolf-packs', as the units of U-boats were called, had been extremely successful in sinking Allied shipping, but the development of technology such as radar and sonar, together with new weapons such as depth charges and the efficient replacement of ships when sunk, was gradually turning the tide against the Germans. Supply routes to Britain and the Soviet Union remained open and allowed the Allies to amass troops and supplies in preparation for the D-Day landings. While the Western Allies prepared for the invasion of Normandy, the bulk of the fighting in Europe fell to the Soviets who gradually began to push back the Germans from the East once the German 6th Army had surrendered at Stalingrad. The Allies continued to bomb German cities and industrial centres in an attempt to slow German war production – with limited success.

On 6 June 1944, the D-Day invasion was launched; in a space of two weeks over 1 million men landed on the Normandy beaches with some of the bloodiest fighting taking place on

Omaha beach. This landing has been immortalized in Spielberg's epic film *Saving Private Ryan* (1998). Although some of the film's historical details are a little suspect, the opening sequences give the viewer ample explanation of the origin of the name 'Bloody Omaha'.

By July, General Bradley's men had broken through the German lines at St Lô, and by August, Paris had been liberated, but then the Germans retaliated with the Battle of the Bulge in the Ardennes which pushed the US forces back, killing or wounding 55,000 men. By 1945, the Allies had regrouped and were advancing into Germany itself. President Roosevelt died on April 12 1945, less than a month before Germany's surrender; he did not live to see the victory to which he had contributed so much but left to his successor, Harry S. Truman, the problem of defeating the Japanese and making a lasting peace in Europe. Shortly before his death, Roosevelt had ordered that the presidential seal be changed so that the American eagle, which then faced the talon clasping the arrows of war, would instead face the olive branch – the symbol of peace.

The war in the Pacific

The attack on Pearl Harbor had given Japan a psychological advantage, especially when it was followed up by the conquest of the Philippines in 1942. However, the Doolittle Raid on mainland Japan and the Battle of the Coral Sea both raised American morale.

On 18 April 1942, Lieutenant Colonel James Doolittle of the US Army Air Corps led a force of 16 planes on a bombing raid to Japan; four cities, including the capital city of Tokyo, were bombed. Damage was very limited but the effect on the American people was exhilarating while the effect on the Japanese military leadership must have been rather more sobering. The raid had the effect of tying up Japanese planes and ships to defend the mainland, planes and ships which could have been used to counter US attacks as they began 'island hopping' their way closer to Japan.

The Battle of the Coral Sea, in early May 1942, was the first major aircraft carrier engagement of the Second World War and was also the first naval battle to take place at long distance: neither side's surface fleet sighted the other. The Americans lost the carrier *Lexington*, one destroyer, and one tanker while the

Japanese lost the carrier *Ryukyi*, four cruisers and two destroyers. Both sides withdrew from the Coral Sea at the same time, but even though it was a double retreat, the Americans were beginning to contain the Japanese expansion. The US navy learned a great deal from the Battle of the Coral Sea, such as better ways to contain aviation fuel and how to co-ordinate dive-bombers and torpedo-bombers to best effect; perhaps most importantly of all, it learned that there was a chance the Japanese could be beaten.

The Doolittle Raid on Japan had proved that Japan itself was not immune from air attack. In order to protect Japan more effectively it was decided to extend Japan's defensive perimeter eastward to create a more secure buffer zone. Midway, a tiny island 1,609 km (1,000 miles) from Hawaii became their target. The Japanese committed almost the entire Imperial fleet to the battle for Midway – six aircraft carriers, 11 battleships, 13 cruisers, 45 destroyers, submarines, transports and mine sweepers. However, this time the Americans had cracked the Japanese code, realized something was brewing and prepared a surprise reception committee consisting of three aircraft carriers, eight cruisers, 14 destroyers, and some aircraft stationed on Midway itself. The *Yorktown*, which had been badly damaged in the Battle of the Coral Sea, limped into battle following makeshift repairs at Pearl Harbor. Hardly an impressive force when compared to that of the Japanese, but one which was helped by the element of surprise.

On 4 June, the Americans discovered the Japanese fleet north-east of Midway. An air battle quickly developed which succeeded in setting fire to three Japanese carriers. *Hiryu*, the fourth Japanese carrier, fought back with an air attack which sank the *Yorktown* but later the *Hiryu* itself was badly damaged. The Japanese fleet retreated. The one-day battle of Midway reversed the tide of war in the Pacific; from that point on, Japan would be on the defensive.

The USA pursued a two-pronged attack across the Pacific Ocean 'hopping' from one island to the next: from the north came Admiral Chester Nimitz and from the south General Douglas MacArthur. The Japanese planned to take Australia by invading Guadalcanal and New Guinea, which were strategically well sited for a successful invasion. The Americans realized the intentions of the Japanese when it was discovered by a reconnaissance pilot on July 4 1942 that they were building an airfield on Guadalcanal; it was decided to invade the island in order to pre-empt the invasion. The Americans reached Guadalcanal in August 1942 and took six months to capture it completely because the US marines had little experience of jungle warfare; fighting conditions were hot and humid and the troops were constantly plagued by malaria-ridden mosquitoes. Japanese soldiers used animal cries to signal to their troops, but the Americans found it difficult to distinguish the sounds from genuine animal noises. Japanese snipers lay poised to attack both in the jungle underbrush and in the tree-tops above – small wonder that the US casualties were so high. The Battle of Guadalcanal officially ended during February 1943, and thus ended Japanese ambitions on Australia.

1943 saw the battles for other islands, including Tarawa and Saipan. Because of its position some 2,413 km (1,500 miles) from mainland Japan, Saipan was strategically important as a base for B-29 planes which were used to bomb the Japanese mainland. Further naval battles, including the Battle of Leyte Gulf, the largest battle in US history, were fought in 1944. This battle saw the appearance of one of the most feared Japanese weapons – the kamikaze pilot.

Kamikaze!

The word 'kamikaze' is usually translated as 'divine wind' in honour of a storm which saved the Japanese from a Mongol invasion in the thirteenth century. During the Second World War it came to mean Japanese suicide attack pilots, who deliberately flew their aircraft into Allied targets, usually ships; it is claimed that about 5,000 Allied personnel were killed by kamikazes at Okinawa alone. In the West it was difficult to comprehend what motivated these young men to fly their fatal missions. There are some clues in the manual they carried in their cockpits for inspiration. This advised them to, 'Transcend life and death. When you eliminate all thoughts about life and death, you will be able to totally disregard your earthly life. This will also enable you to concentrate your attention on eradicating the enemy.' Details in the manual included what emotions to expect as they dive towards their target and face death, 'Remember when diving into the enemy to shout at the top of your lungs: 'Hissatsu!' (Sink without fail!) At that moment, all the cherry blossoms at Yasukuni shrine in Tokyo will smile brightly at you.'

The atomic bomb

The type of fighting encountered by the Americans during the taking of Guadalcanal, Iwo Jima and Okinawa caused the US military many sleepless nights. There was no reason to suppose that the Japanese would not fight equally hard to protect mainland Japan thus dragging out the war for at least another 18 months, which would cost the USA dearly in both economic terms and in the loss of life that would accompany such a long, drawn-out campaign. In July 1945, President Truman warned the Japanese that if they did not surrender, the USA would use a new weapon against them, the like of which had never been seen before. This new weapon had been developed as part of the Manhattan project and had been tested at Alamogordo Air Force Base in the New Mexican Desert on 16 July 1945. After the explosion caused by this weapon, its creator, Robert Oppenheimer, observed: 'I am become as death, the destroyer of worlds.' The first atomic bomb was dropped on the Japanese city of Hiroshima on 6 August 1945. The bomb, nicknamed 'Little Boy', containing 64 kg (141 pounds) of uranium was dropped from the American plane *Enola Gay* and killed over 78,000 people, injured 80,000 and exposed 300,000 to radiation. Three days later another atomic device containing plutonium was dropped on Nagasaki killing 70,000. It was not until five days after the dropping of this second bomb that the Japanese surrendered unconditionally, the formal ceremony taking place on the *USS Missouri* on 14 September 1945.

The dropping of the bombs on Hiroshima and Nagasaki has been a subject of debate since 1945, with many claiming that the Japanese were already preparing to surrender and that the real reason behind the second bomb was to 'make Russia more manageable'. Others claim that the Manhattan project had cost $2 billion and that not to expect the Americans to use such a weapon was naïve – one particularly poignant cartoon shows two children in front of a mushroom cloud and a scene of devastation with the caption, 'Don't you see? They had to see if it worked.' The economic and human cost of taking the islands one by one to reach Japan certainly played a part in the decision to use the atomic bomb to end the war with as little loss of American life as possible – a decision few Americans involved in the Pacific war would have argued with.

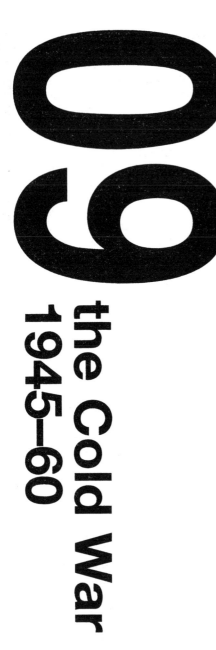

09

the Cold War
1945–60

This chapter will cover:
- the Cold War and why it began
- the Cold War in Europe
- the Cold War in Asia.

What was the Cold War?

At the end of the Second World War, relations between the Great Powers cooled and a tense rivalry which became known as the 'Cold War' developed between them. Although this conflict originated in Europe, it soon spread to the rest of the world. This 'Cold War' had all the features of a traditional war, such as two opposing sides each equipped with armies, navies and air forces and Allies, yet there was no direct, open fighting between the Great Powers. Instead, the emphasis of this war was on the flexing of muscles, the use of bluff and counter-bluff and the stockpiling of offensive and defensive weapons. Each side used spies and propaganda to extend their power or to persuade others to join them in their campaign against their enemies whom they believed were trying to destroy their political ideology and way of life. There was fear, hostility and suspicion, competition, threats and quarrels between the two sides, yet the existence of nuclear weapons meant that direct fighting was avoided.

Historians have long debated who was responsible for the beginning of the Cold War. During the 1940s and 1950s, the orthodox view believed that it was the USSR's expansionist nature and desire to spread communism to the rest of the world that had caused the Cold War. By the 1960s, many US historians revised the orthodox view and argued that it was the US that was responsible not only for the outbreak of 'hostilities' but also for their continuation and acceleration, simply because the US failed to appreciate Soviet defence issues. The post-revisionist view, which emerged in the 1970s and 1980s, took the middle line which avoided placing blame on one side or the other and instead saw the development of the Cold War in terms of mutual suspicion and overreaction to the other side's actions.

The difference in political, social and economic ideas between Communist Russia and the democratic West became apparent as early as the 1920s, but during the Second World War these contrasting ideologies had, out of necessity, united in an uneasy alliance against Hitler and Nazism – the Grand Alliance. On the surface they were Allies, but tensions were apparent, for example, in 1942 when Britain and the USA had refused to open up a second front against Hitler by invading Europe quickly and thus relieving the Soviet Union of some of the pressure upon her. These tensions increased following the defeat of Germany and her Allies, in 1945.

Yalta

In February 1945, the 'Big Three' leaders of the Allied forces – Franklin Roosevelt of the USA, Josef Stalin of the USSR and Winston Churchill of Britain – met in Yalta to discuss how Europe would be organized after the war. Mistrust was present on all sides, even Churchill and Roosevelt could not see eye to eye. It was decided that, once defeated, Germany should be disarmed and divided into four zones which would be occupied by the Big Three and France. Eastern European countries were to hold free elections and the USSR agreed to join the war against Japan a month after Germany had been defeated. All agreed that a United Nations (UN) organization would be established.

Disagreements arose about how Poland would be governed, Britain favouring the exiled Polish government while the Soviets wanted the pro-Soviet government of Lublin. It was clear that Stalin was eager to move the Soviet frontier with Poland westwards in line with the USSR's need for security. There were also differences regarding reparations (money to repair the damage done during the war) from Germany, Stalin wanting a far higher level of reparations than the USA and Britain. The meeting at Yalta exposed the cracks in the Grand Alliance; once the unifying ambition to defeat Hitler had been removed, only the trust between the three leaders could hold the Alliance together.

On 25 April 1945, the US and Soviet troops met on the banks of the Elbe near Strehla, and within weeks the Germans had surrendered. Roosevelt had died on the 12 April so it was President Harry S. Truman who celebrated the Allied victory. When the Allies met in Potsdam to discuss Germany's future, there had been another change in the leaders representing the Allied powers; Churchill had been defeated in a general election and was replaced by Clement Attlee.

Potsdam conference

Some decisions were made at Potsdam; details regarding the zones of occupation were finalized; the Nazi Party was to be banned and Nazi leaders were to be put on trial as war criminals; each power was to collect industrial equipment from their zone as reparations and Poland's western border was to be along a line defined by the Oder and Neisse rivers. Although the

Conference ended amicably enough, there had been areas of disagreement, possibly because a change of attitude had developed along with the change of leading players. Although Truman had played an important role in the USA's war effort, his knowledge of foreign affairs, and in particular the European situation, was superficial. However, unlike Roosevelt, he was unwilling to compromise with 'Uncle Joe' Stalin, whom he believed was little more than a bully. Truman was determined not to appear 'soft' on communism especially since public opinion at home had become distinctly more anti-communist. Increasingly the West was concerned about Stalin's intentions in eastern europe, and Truman became convinced that Stalin was planning world conquest which only force could prevent. The USA's 'trump card', the atomic bomb, became a vital factor.

On 16 July 1945, as mentioned in Chapter 8, the first atomic bomb had been tested at Almagordo in the New Mexico desert. Churchill noted that the USA's new power had transformed Truman's mood. Stalin was informed of this new weapon on 24 July, but it is likely that Stalin already knew of the bomb's existence thanks to his spies. On 10 August, after the US atomic bombings on Japan, the Emperor of Japan announced his decision to surrender and terms were agreed on 14 August. The Second World War was over.

Stalin's speech to the Supreme Soviet in February 1946, where he insisted that the very existence of capitalism made war inevitable, alarmed Washington, and the US Embassy in Moscow was asked to explain Stalin's foreign policy. The 8,000 word-long reply from George Kennan, a diplomat in Moscow, which came to be known as the 'Long Telegram', predicted nothing less than a fight to the death between communism and democracy. Amidst fears of communist influence infiltrating Iran, Turkey, Greece and Italy, Winston Churchill made an inflamatory speech in Fulton, Missouri on March 5th 1946: 'From Stettin in the Baltic to Trieste in the Adriatic, an iron curtain has descended across the continent.' This speech warned of the spreading influence of the Soviets and of the need to stop this expansion westwards. It declared that Soviet policy divided Europe into two separate halves – the West comprising of free democratic states, and, behind an iron curtain, the East where the countries were ruled by communist parties directly controlled by the Soviet Union. The American public was horrified and, although Truman denied all prior knowledge of the content of the speech, in reality it was just what the President and his advisers wanted to hear.

The Truman Doctrine

Stalin was keen to establish a cordon sanitaire in eastern Europe – a buffer zone of countries controlled by the Soviets which could protect mother Russia's western frontier from the threat of invasion. To this end, as the Soviet Red Army freed Poland, Czechoslovakia, Bulgaria and Hungary, Romania and Eastern Germany from German occupation, they established Communist governments that were closely controlled from Moscow. The Soviets also took direct control of the Baltic States – Latvia, Estonia and Lithuania – and seemed to be taking too keen an interest in Iran and Greece. Britain had been helping the monarchist forces in Greece in the civil war against the communists but, following the devastating effects of the severe winter of 1946–7, the British government decided to end economic aid to Greece and to withdraw British troops as the country was financially unable to cope with foreign commitments. Greece would be open to a communist takeover unless the USA could be persuaded to take up the cause. The US Secretary of State, General George C. Marshall, soon realized the gravity of the situation but appreciated that the solidly Republican Congress would oppose giving aid to Greece. Dean Acheson (the Under-Secretary of State) came to the rescue with a compelling report. He painted a picture of a barrel of apples being infected by one rotten one – if Greece fell to communism so too would other countries in the eastern Mediterranean. The analogy struck home and the congressional leaders pledged their support for President Truman when he asked Congress for $400 million to aid Greece and Turkey.

On the 12 March 1947, Truman made a speech which spelled out the realities of the world in the aftermath of the Second World War and, although it was prompted by the Greek crisis, he clearly intended it to have wider implications. Truman explained that he believed the USA should help any country threatened by communism and asked for $400 million to aid Greece and Turkey and for US civilian and military personnel to help reconstruct both countries. In effect, Truman was setting a precedent – the USA was promising to help any country withstand communism whether this be from an external attack or from internal revolution. His deliberate exaggeration of the communist threat worked: Congress approved the money to aid the anti-communist forces in Greece. The communists were defeated and the spread of communism in the Mediterranean contained. The speech became known as the 'Truman Doctrine' and meant that the USA was ready to take a major part in world affairs by sending money, weapons and advisers to any country in the world that felt threatened by communism. The USA was prepared to draw a line and say to the Soviets 'no further' – this was the policy of containment.

Marshall aid

Truman planned to attack the roots of communism. He believed that misery, poverty and want were fertile soil in which communism could grow, and two years after the end of the war, governments in Europe were still struggling to overcome the effects of that war. Churchill had described Europe as: 'a rubble heap, a charnel house, a breeding ground of pestilence and hate'. Truman believed that if the USA used its wealth to help Europe recover from this economic misery and regain prosperity, fewer countries would be tempted by communism. In addition, the USA's own economy would benefit by encouraging the revival of trade. Superficially his objective was economic – the reconstruction of countries devastated by the war, yet beneath the surface was a political motive, to deprive communism of the conditions needed to flourish.

On 5 June 1947, General George C. Marshall announced a programme of aid to help war-torn Europe – the Marshall Plan. Marshall insisted that the policy should bring order to the chaos caused by poverty and hunger and that the offer of aid was open to all countries: 'Our policy is directed not against any country or doctrine, but against hunger, poverty, desperation and chaos. Its purpose should be the revival of a working economy in the world: so as to permit the emergence of political and social conditions in which free institutions can exist.'

Over the next five years, $13.5 billion was paid out to 16 countries through the Organisation of European Economic Co-operation (OEEC). This aid took the form of cash, equipment, food and technical assistance to countries willing to co-operate to create economic recovery. These countries would then agree to buy US goods and allow US companies to invest in their industries. This move would stimulate the US economy and consolidate American influence in western Europe. The Marshall Plan helped the economic recovery of Europe and it initiated a period of prosperity in Europe which lasted into the 1970s. Churchill called it the 'most unselfish act by any great power in history', but it also protected US interests and enabled the USA to dominate Europe economically. Often the aid was given in the form of goods – grain or industrial machinery – and this enabled the USA to control its end use rather more easily; the OEEC requested 67,000 tractors but received only half of that number since most US farmers feared competition from European farmers.

National Security Council Resolution 68

In January 1946, Truman had ordered a major review of security policy. The report which emerged advocated a major build-up of arms immediately in order to ensure that the policy of containment was no empty threat. The report was submitted to the President in April 1946 and approved in September of that year. Thus prepared with National Security Council Resolution 68 (NSCR 68), US policy makers could now defend the 'Free World' against the spread of communism. The communist takeover in China in October 1949, the testing of the nuclear bomb by the Soviets in September 1949 and the invasion of South Korea by Communist North Korea in June 1950 all contributed to a feeling that NSCR 68 was justified and contributed to the decision to expand the US nuclear programme.

The German question

After the war, Germany had been divided into four zones each controlled by the victorious Allies, the USA, Britain, France and the Soviet Union. Berlin, the capital city, had been divided in the same way. It was hoped that the country would eventually be reunited as a democratic country sometime in the near future. Unfortunately, disagreements between the Allies about the political future of Germany became so heated that it soon became clear that a unified Germany was impossible.

The Allies put 22 surviving Nazi leaders on trial in Nuremberg in November 1945. The setting for the trials was symbolic as it was here that the major Nazi rallies had taken place before the war. Of the 22 accused, 12 were sentenced to death, seven to varying terms of imprisonment and three were acquitted. The trials were controversial. Some said they were show trials or acts of revenge of dubious legality but they did rid Germany of the

Nazi political leadership, and the publicity and detailed documentation and evidence did much to publicize the Nazi atrocities to the German people.

It had been agreed at Potsdam that the Soviet Union could take a portion of the reparations from the Soviet zone of Germany as it was unclear how long it would be before reparations could be paid. It was also agreed that a quarter of the industrial goods made in the Western sectors would be given to the Soviet Union in exchange for food and coal from the Soviet zone. By May 1946, the agreements made at Potsdam were faltering; the Soviets had not delivered the food and coal they had agreed to supply from their zone and they were busy stripping Germany's industry to be shipped back to mother Russia. Britain and the USA brought their deliveries of industrial goods to the Soviet zone to an end and concentrated instead on improving the economy of their own zones. They demanded that Germany be treated as a single economic unit. This naturally alarmed the Soviets as they feared that the USA would dominate a revived German capitalist economy and this would be a direct economic and political threat to them. The unification of the US and British zones to form Bizonia in 1947 began the process of economic reconstruction and handing back to the Germans the responsibility for their own affairs. By 1948, the British, French and US zones had been merged into one, a development which Stalin regarded with distrust.

The Berlin blockade and airlift

Berlin was 160 km (100 miles) inside the Soviet zone of Germany but it had been divided into four zones, one for each of the Allied powers. Britain, the USA and France relied on free access through the Soviet zone for road, rail and canal links with the city. On the 23 June 1948, a message from the Soviet News Agency was sent to the main newspaper in Berlin: 'The Soviet administration is compelled to halt all traffic to and from Berlin tomorrow at 0600 hours because of technical difficulties.'

These technical difficulties closed the roads, canals and railways from Western Germany to Berlin. The city had only enough food and fuel to last six weeks and it was clearly the aim of the Soviets to force the West to withdraw from Western Berlin by reducing the population to starvation. General Clay was convinced that if Berlin fell to the Soviets, Western Germany would be the next to fall and communism would triumph. However, the air corridors remained open and the British and

Americans organized a round the clock airlift into the city. At the peak of the airlift, 13,000 tonnes of goods a day were provided and aircraft were landing in Berlin every three minutes, day and night. US B-29 aircraft capable of carrying atomic bombs were stationed in Britain within easy reach of Berlin to warn the Soviets what would happen should they try to stop the airlift by shooting down Western planes. In the West, the blockade was presented as a plan to probe the weak spots in the Western Alliance. However, in the USSR, it was presented as a Western plot to drag the USSR into war; because the Soviet Union was so moderate, this plot failed and the West was forced to abandon the blockade.

North Atlantic Treaty Organization

On 4 April 1949, the North Atlantic Treaty was signed in Washington. In its determination to halt the expansion of communism, the USA had committed itself to close military collaboration. The treaty was based on article 51 of the United Nations Charter, but it was clearly a military rather than defensive alliance as the members agreed to regard an attack on any one of them in Europe or North America as an attack against them all. If such an event took place the members agreed to assist each other, 'by taking such action as it deems necessary…to restore and maintain the security of the North Atlantic area'. The necessary action included the use of armed force.

The 12 original members comprised Britain, France, Belgium, Holland, Luxembourg, Portugal, Denmark, Ireland, Italy, Norway, Canada and the USA. All agreed to place their defence forces under a joint North Atlantic Treaty Organization (NATO) command, which would co-ordinate the defence of the West. At one level, NATO was a sign that the USA was determined to make European defence a priority. At another level, it marked a significant militarization of Cold War conflict. In May 1955, West Germany became a member of NATO and this reawakened Soviet fear of German rearmament and the emergence of a militarist Germany hell bent on reunification. In response to this perceived threat, the Soviet government organized the Warsaw Defence Treaty (1955) with her seven European satellites. It was a military alliance in which the communist countries of eastern Europe all agreed to help each other and the Soviet Union in the event of armed attack from the West. It indicated the division of Europe into two armed camps.

Eisenhower and Dulles: Cold War warriors

In 1952, former General Eisenhower became President of the USA following an election campaign which had accused Truman of being 'soft on communism'. It seemed likely that this campaign would set the agenda for the USA's relations with the Soviets, especially considering the domestic preoccupation with the anti-communist utterances of Senator McCarthy which were gripping American people with a real fear of 'Reds under the beds'. Instead of responding to the more moderate Soviet leader, Khrushchev, in a positive way, Eisenhower and his Secretary of State, John Foster Dulles, used deliberately provocative language such as 'roll back' (their intention to aid any eastern European countries wishing to rise up against their Communist government) and 'massive retaliation' (their intention to use nuclear weapons to counter any attempts made by the Soviets to attack the USA). However, their 'roll back' intentions were proved to be empty threats during the Hungarian uprising in 1956.

Hungary 1956

Khrushchev's de-Stalinization speech to the Twentieth Congress of the Soviet Communist Party in February 1956 had hinted at peaceful coexistence with other countries and different roads to socialism within eastern Europe. The Hungarian people took this to mean that the repressive communist regime in their country would be reformed and, in an attempt to speed things up, there was open criticism of the government from the intellectuals and students and mass demonstrations in Budapest. The Hungarian government panicked and called on Moscow for help. On the 25 October 1956, 30,000 Soviet troops sealed off Budapest and declared martial law. Following street fighting it became apparent that the Soviet troops were not strong enough to overcome the protestors, and so they withdrew. Throughout Hungary there was an atmosphere of expectation: industrial workers formed revolutionary councils; open elections were held in villages and towns across the country; and a coalition government was formed between some of the parties which had existed before the communist takeover. It seemed at first that the Soviets would accept this multi-party government, but the Suez Canal crisis broke out in Egypt. This distracted Washington's attention from eastern Europe and offered the Soviets a perfect opportunity to clamp down on Hungary's dissidents. On the 3 November 1956, Soviet troops and tanks encircled Budapest and entered the city using maximum firepower against the citizens of Budapest. The tactics were extreme and even non-combatants were targeted as queues of housewives outside shops were machine gunned. There was no mercy shown to the 'freedom fighters': as the last 30 defenders of the Kilan Hungarian Army Barracks surrendered, they were shot as they emerged. The Hungarians made desperate radio appeals: 'Civilized people of the world! Our ship is sinking. Light is fading. The shadows grow darker over the soil of Hungary. Extend us your aid.' But no aid came. Eisenhower was distracted by the Suez crisis and the final stages of the American presidential election. He only condemned the action in the final speeches of his campaign and formally protested to the Kremlin. Dulles' promises of liberation and 'roll back' had proved to be empty words. The USA settled for containment; however deep Eisenhower's hatred of communism, his fear of war was deeper.

The Cold War in Asia

Following the surrender of Japan in August 1945, the country was occupied by US forces under the command of General Douglas MacArthur who was given wide powers to transform Japan from a feudal, militaristic state into a democratic, constitutional one. The Japanese army was disarmed and demobilized; Emperor Hirohito was demoted from a divine being to a constitutional monarch; and a constitution which excluded the influence of the army and provided for a democratically elected government was drawn up. Communists were banned from government posts, trade unions were legalized but discouraged, and votes for women were introduced. The Soviets had little say in the post-war treatment of Japan as they had entered the war against Japan at such a late stage, instead the USSR was given a role to play in the occupation of Korea.

The communist takeover in China and the invasion of South Korea led to a re-evaluation of Japan's role in the area on the part of the USA, and a change in the relationship between the two countries. Japan was now seen to be strategically important as a counter-balance to the rise of 'red' China and a far more acceptable trading partner than the emerging Communist State. Japan needed to be economically prosperous to withstand the temptations of communism, therefore the US began to rebuild

Japanese industry and encouraged the USA's allies in the Far East to trade with Japan. In 1951, a Peace Treaty which formally ended the war between Japan and the USA was signed and, in September, a Mutual Security Treaty was signed which allowed the USA to maintain military bases on Japanese territory and allowed Japan to develop a defensive army of 110,000 troops.

The change in the US attitude towards Japan caused the Soviets some concern, and several countries that had been invaded by Japan expressed their unease. In Japan itself there were several demonstrations against the US bases and anti-American riots in 1954 led to a cancellation of Eisenhower's visit to Japan. In spite of these concerns, Japan's economy prospered and proved to be strong enough by the 1960s to compete with the USA.

China

During the Second World War China had fought on the side of the Allies against Japan, but when the war ended, fighting between the ntionalists and communists began again. The USA poured hundreds of millions of dollars of aid into Chiang Kai-shek's nationalist campaign, and almost all of his equipment had been provided by the US government. This was not enough against the enmity of the Chinese masses. Chiang Kai-shek's Kuomintang Party had made little attempt to tackle China's problems: inflation was high and US aid often went into the pockets of Chiang and his family; the Kuomintang had been unwilling to reduce the powers of the landlords thus alienating the millions of peasants in the country – a force which Mao Zedong and his Chinese Communist Party successfully harnessed.

Mao naturally looked to the Soviets for aid, but while Stalin believed the Chinese Revolution should be based on support from the industrial workers (as had the 1917 Revolution in Russia), Mao was only too aware of China's primitive industrial development and instead gathered his support from the millions of peasants in rural China.

During the Second World War China had fought on the side of the Allies against Japan, but in 1945 civil war between nationalists (or Kuomintang) led by Chiang Kai-Shek and communists led by Mao Zedong had recommenced. The communists had emerged from the war far stronger than the nationalists, controlling 482,700 sq. km (300,000 sq. miles) and

95 million people. In December 1945, General Marshall had negotiated a truce between the Kuomintang and the communists, but this collapsed within a matter of months. By the end of 1948, the communists had taken Manchuria and won decisive battles in the North of China since in the areas controlled by the Kuomintang there were food shortages, corruption and hyper-inflation which turned the people against Chiang Kai-shek. From the beginning of 1949, the major cities fell one by one to the communists and on 1 October 1949 Mao announced the establishment of the People's Republic of China. Chiang Kai-shek fled to Formosa (Taiwan) where he complained loudly about the lack of US support for his government. Some in the USA were also critical of Truman for not applying the Truman Doctrine to China, but in reality the $3 billion of aid given by the USA to Chiang Kai-shek since 1945 had little effect and Truman's attentions were firmly on the growing crisis in Berlin. Dean Acheson wrote in 1949: 'nothing this country did or could have done...would have changed the result'. The US refused to recognize the Communist government of the People's Republic of China and vetoed the Soviet-backed claim to have communist China installed in the Chinese seat in the UN, a seat which was still occupied by the nationalists.

Fear of communist expansion

In the USA, events in China revived the fear of worldwide communist expansion. John Foster Dulles called the loss of China 'the worst defeat the United States has suffered in its history', which was perhaps rather an exaggeration, but 'containment' once designed to prevent the expansion of communism in Europe now seemed necessary on a worldwide scale. In 1950, all trade and travel links with China were banned in the USA and for the next 20 years the USA tried its utmost to exclude Communist China from world affairs. The USA tended to overestimate the influence of the USSR in China. The Soviet Union had welcomed Mao in Moscow, had praised China's success, signed a Treaty of Friendship to last for 30 years and promised loans, military aid and technical expertise to develop China's industrial strength. However, it was clear that Stalin saw Mao as a 'junior partner' and failed to appreciate China's potential power. A new Red Star was rising in the East and a 'bamboo curtain' was about to fall.

The Korean War

Japan had ruled Korea since 1910, but following the Second World War it was decided by the Allies that Korea would receive independence. Japan surrendered to Russian forces in the North of Korea and to US forces in the South of the country, and the dividing line between the two was drawn on the thirty-eigth parallel of latitude. This division was to be a temporary measure until free elections could be held and Korea reunited, but when the Americans applied to the UN to hold elections in 1947, the USSR refused to co-operate. Elections were held in the South in 1948, and both the US and the USSR withdrew their troops leaving a divided Korea with a democratic South and a communist North. The Communist government was led by Kim Il Sung while South Korea was led by Syngman Rhee. Each government claimed to rule the whole of Korea.

With two friendly communist countries in its borders, North Korea increased in confidence in its dealings with the South. Attacks between the armed forces of North and South intensified along the thirty-eighth parallel but it still came as a surprise when, on 25 June 1950, North Korean forces invaded South Korea. Within three days these forces, armed with Soviet weapons, had taken Seoul, the capital of South Korea and had overrun much of the country. It seems likely that the war started because neither Syngman Rhee nor Kim Il Sung was prepared to accept a divided Korea any longer and baited each other until one side launched an all-out attack on the other. If this was the case, the Korean War had its origins in a civil war. In the USA, Truman viewed the situation differently. To Truman it seemed obvious that the war had been initiated by Stalin for a variety of reasons: Stalin had lost the initiative in Europe and saw another possible sphere of interest in Asia; Stalin could directly threaten US control of Japan if he controlled Korea and this would in turn threaten the USA's position in the Pacific. Truman had domestic concerns also. His standing in the opinion polls had diminished and he had been heavily criticized by McCarthy and the Republican Party for losing China; he could not afford to stand by and watch Korea fall to communism. Truman promptly sent the US 7th Fleet to Formosa (Taiwan), where he feared China might attack, and made use of diplomatic pressure on the UN which passed a motion demanding that the North Koreans should withdraw from South Korea. A second motion to help South Korea to resist and repel the armed attack and restore the balance of power was passed in the United Nations

Security Council. The USA was given unlimited authority to direct the military operation in Korea. Had the USSR been present in the Security Council, the US motion would have been vetoed but the Soviet government had been boycotting the Security Council in protest at the USA's refusal to recognize Communist China. US policy in Asia had changed completely and the Truman Doctrine had been extended to the whole of Asia.

The USA called on her NATO Allies to provide military assistance in Korea, but US troops formed the greater part of the UN forces (50 per cent of land forces, 93 per cent of air forces and 86 per cent of naval forces) with General MacArthur as the overall Commander in Chief. MacArthur had been given a virtual carte blanche by the President, reporting to and taking orders only from him, a situation which led to problems in the long run.

The first US troops landed in Korea in July 1950 but faced a number of initial setbacks, including an entire US regiment being ambushed and wiped out, and Major General William Dean being captured and paraded in a Korean propaganda film. On 15 September, these troops were supported by UN troops under the command of General MacArthur, landing at Inchon behind North Korean lines. The invasion fleet of 269 ships that landed at Inchon was the largest since D-Day. Following a massive bombardment which flattened Inchon, huge numbers of US soldiers streamed ashore. The military tide began to turn in favour of the UN–US forces and intense fighting forced the North Koreans back behind the thirty-eighth parallel by 8 October. The objectives of the UN resolution had been achieved, and the US had achieved containment. Instead of being satisfied with containing the spread of communism in Korea, the USA saw this as a chance to reunite Korea and expel communism from North Korea. The US-led forces pushed northwards and, by October, had succeeded in capturing Pyongyang, the capital of North Korea. The Chinese became increasingly nervous since North Korea could be used as a base from which to bomb industrial areas in China or to attack the Chinese border. An official warning was issued: if the Americans crossed the thirty-eighth parallel into North Korea, China would intervene. Truman called their bluff. Having captured Pyongyang, the US–UN force advanced towards the Chinese border in a clear attempt to destroy the North Korean Communist government. On 19 October, 250,000 Chinese 'volunteers' poured over the border, overwhelmed the US–UN troops who were pushed back, permitting the Chinese to occupy Seoul in the South. Following weeks of fierce fighting, the Chinese were pushed back to the thirty-eighth parallel and the war became one of attrition – neither side willing to extend the fighting into an all-out conflagration but neither willing to back down. MacArthur's ultimate aim was to extend war into China itself and defeat Mao Zedong using nuclear weapons if needs be, something which was not in the brief issued by the UN. Following a series of confidential meetings in the White House, MacArthur was removed from his command on 10 April 1951, a decision which was fully supported by the Chiefs of Staff. MacArthur and many Americans were furious at his treatment, and on his return to the USA he was greeted by enthusiastic crowds, which did nothing for Truman's failing popularity.

At the suggestion of the Soviets, peace talks began at a tea house in Panmanjom in June 1951 while the war continued. The peace talks were complex and frequently broke down and, in spite of pressure on the Chinese from General Dwight Eisenhower who had become President in November 1952, the fighting continued. It was after Stalin died in 1953 that the situation changed. Following Stalin's death. the new Soviet leadership decided that the war must be ended; China, no longer sure of receiving Soviet arms and supplies, had reached the same conclusion. Eisenhower bombed dams in North Korea, which caused extensive flooding, and threatened to use nuclear weapons against Beijing in an attempt to bring the communists to the peace talks. Only Syngman Rhee remained against peace, so the talks continued without him and an armistice was agreed on 27 July 1953. There followed a complicated exchange of prisoners. Of over 12,000 UN prisoners, only 21 Americans and one Scot decided to stay on in Communist China; 50,000 Communist Prisoners of War (POW) were released, of which two-thirds wanted to go to Taiwan. Of the prisoners returning to the North, some cast off their US-made POW uniforms in an act of defiance and crossed the border naked, carrying flags they had made out of rags dyed red with their own blood. No peace treaty could be agreed upon, and peace talks continued for over 40 years.

The forgotten war

The Korean War was called the 'forgotten war' because it came soon after the Second World War and was overshadowed by the

Vietnam War. Perhaps because the war only lasted three years (1950–3), it is not thought of as significant, and it is often not even mentioned in history books. However, if one compares the fatalities of the Korean War (54,246) to those of Vietnam (58,226) which lasted over 16 years, by ratio the Korean War was far bloodier than Vietnam. In 1995, the memorial to the Korean War was dedicated by President Clinton. It consists of 19 larger-than-life US ground troopers equipped for battle moving towards an American flag. Etched into the granite wall which runs alongside these figures are photographs of hundreds of faces taken from photographs of the Korean campaign kept in the military archives. The 19 figures are reflected in the granite wall and together add up to 38 – to recall the thirty-eighth parallel along which the country still remains divided.

10

1950s' consumerism and communism

This chapter will cover:
- the age of affluence –
  keeping up with the Joneses
- the suburbs and their effect
  on US society
- Macarthyism – 'Reds under
  the beds' fear of
  communism.

I drive my car to supermarket / The way I take is superhigh / A superlot is where I park it / And Super Suds are what I buy. / Supersalesmen sell me tonic / Super-Tone O, for relief. / The planes I ride are supersonic. / In trains I like the Super Chief. / Supercilious men and women / Call me superficial, me! / Who so superbly learned to swim in / Supercolossality. / Superphosphate-fed foods feed me / Superservice keeps me new. / Who would dare to supercede me / Super-super-superwho?

This is how John Updike described American materialism in 1954. Films and magazines carried the message of US success to all corners of the world. Supermarkets, motorways, rock and roll music, television shows and huge cars shining with chrome fittings and sporting dramatic tailfins were being pushed as symbols of a successful economy. One member of Eisenhower's cabinet commented, 'What's good for General Motors is good for the whole country.' A housing boom, increasing numbers of consumer goods, low unemployment, generous public funding and technological advances created tremendous economic growth. Writers like Updike, social critics, and artists lamented the rise of consumer culture and the reign of the product but for most Americans the 1950s were a period of peace, prosperity and plenty.

The standard of living

The US standard of living soared in the 1950s with Americans setting the pace as the best fed, best dressed, most comfortable people in the world. Unlike the prosperity of the 1920s, the 1950s' affluence had a broader base and reached most groups in US society. The advent of the Cold War and the Marshall Plan of the 1940s all contributed to higher living standards in the USA as American factories churned out goods for war-devastated Europe and weapons for defence against the Red Menace sweeping the world. US workers once again felt secure in their employment, and this security gave them spending power unequalled by the rest of the world for several decades.

Between 1945 and 1960, because of the Baby Boom which took place after the war, the population of the USA soared to 179,323,175, a rise of 30 per cent. During the same period the Gross National Product (GNP), that is, the total worth of all the goods and services that were produced in a year, almost doubled from $284.6 billion to $502.6 billion. During the 1950s, the USA was producing half of the world's goods. The standard of living, as well as the GNP, rose rapidly during the 1950s. The gap between the rich and the poor actually increased during the post-war years, but in many ways the country seemed to be overflowing with abundance.

Rise of the suburbs

The 1950s are closely associated with the rise of suburban living. As people became more wealthy, many moved out of the city centres into the suburbs which were designed in such a way as to make trips into the city, even for shopping, unnecessary. The most famous suburban housing estate in Levittown, NY, opened its office in March 1949 and enjoyed immediate success providing 17,000 homes for 82,000 people. Abraham Levitt adopted assembly-line techniques to build houses; they arrived flat-packed on the back of a lorry and were bolted together on site. Many commentators derided the 'little boxes' of 'Levittowns', but they were never short of buyers particularly young, white, lower-middle income families. By making every home identical and employing assembly-line construction techniques, Levitt homes sold at $7,900, or $65 a month with no deposit, and the house came complete with major appliances.

Several factors encouraged a move to the suburbs in the USA. Owning a house was a goal for many families, especially those with young children, and suburban housing offered a way for young couples without a lot of extra income to get a head start on the American Dream. The increase in car ownership and the 1956 Interstate Highways Act ensured that there were 65,970 km (41,000 miles) of new roads, designed to aid commuting, running into the city centres via giant 'spaghetti junctions'. The existence of long-term low-interest mortgages, a benefit of the New Deal, enabled people with quite modest incomes to become home-owners. There was an element of 'white flight' in the popularity of the suburbs, with white couples moving away from the more ethnically diverse urban areas to more homogeneous environments in the suburbs. Increasingly, work and living spaces were separate, particularly with the rise of white-collar employment.

Life in the suburbs was family-centred. Fathers went out to work (and yelled out 'Honey, I'm home' on their return); mothers went shopping and looked after the children. The rest of their life was defined by school, church and the television set.

People began to regard refrigerators, televisions, washing machines and other consumer goods as necessities rather than as luxuries, and items such as Hi-Fi record players and cars were regarded as status symbols; after all this was the era which coined the phrase 'Keep up with the Joneses'. Each family purchase depended on what the next door neighbours had bought recently and what had been advertised on television. The invention of the transistor radio was a revolutionary step forward in the world of television and radio since it made obsolete the old-fashioned expensive valves on which these items had previously depended. The result was that televisions and radios became commonplace in homes all over the USA.

Television

The numbers of homes that had a television increased dramatically during the post-war period:

- 1946: 7,000 TV sets existed in the USA
- 1948: 148,000 sets
- 1950: 4.4 million sets
- 1950: 50 million sets.

By 1960, 90 per cent of homes had televisions and this certainly had an effect on American life. The 1950s was, for many, the golden age of television, a period when society embraced television and made it an integral part of their lives. The USA still watches TV programmess from the 1950s, and frequently episodes of *I Love Lucy* are shown on late-night TV. TV situation comedies from the 1950s upheld the traditional values and mores that were being challenged in real life. Domestic comedies were popular and emphasized the nuclear suburban white family in neighbourhoods seemingly untouched by ethnic conflicts, and where mothers never needed or wanted to work outside the home; *I love Lucy* was a prime example of this. Westerns were also extremely popular, not only did they hark back to a simpler time in history but also the notion of frontier living, where right and wrong were totally apparent, appealed to many during the rapidly changing times.

Television changed domestic architecture and the interior layout of houses altered when large sitting rooms became necessary for watching TV. It even changed how Americans ate their meals since watching TV needed snacks and finger foods, and because speed was of the essence, convenient TV dinners appeared on TV trays. Americans used their free time in a completely different way to the pre-war years. Television ushered in the information age, providing the public with almost instantly accessible information about what was going on in the country and even the world, and about what to buy, what to wear and how to behave. It was blamed for all manner of social problems from juvenile crime to the demise of the traditional family.

By 1959, the quiz shows had pushed aside almost everything else, that is until scandals about rigged results shamed the television companies and brought about tighter federal regulation. Airtime was dominated by three national 'networks'. The usual diet of game shows, sitcoms and soap operas eventually drove away more thoughtful viewers and teenagers. Television certainly exerted power; in 1954 it undermined Senator McCarthy when his rantings were televised and subsequently lost him a great deal of support. Conversely in 1960 television put Kennedy in the White House by showing him at his best while Nixon appeared unshaven and ill at ease. Nearly all television stations depended on advertising for their revenue and at least 20 per cent of transmission time was given over to adverts for a variety of products. The power of the commercial sponsors increased to such an extent that many stations became obsessed with the number of viewers who watched the 'ads'. The 1950s saw the birth of marketing research and consumer surveys. These adverts encouraged consumer spending, and if consumers didn't have the necessary cash, there was always hire purchase; between 1945 and 1957 hire purchase (consumer credit) rose by a massive 800 per cent. 'Spend, Spend, Spend!' could have been the motto of US society at this time as Americans saved only 5 per cent of their income on average. Shopping became a popular leisure activity, especially amongst teenagers who appeared as a distinctive group within society during this period. In fact, teenagers were soon targeted by advertisers and manufacturing companies who began manufacturing goods specifically to appeal to them. For the first time teenage fashion made a healthy profit, and goods such as transistor radios, magazines, rock and roll records and films drew young people to spend their money. A survey in 1959 found that the average American teenager had $555 spending money that year at a time when a school teacher in Mississippi could expect to earn $3,000 a year.

Teen culture

It was in the 1950s that 'teenagers' emerged as their own cultural and social category. Although adolescence had been recognized as a distinct developmental stage in life, it was not until the 1940s that this rite of passage was given a specific name and teenagers were given recognition as a group apart. The prosperity of the 1950s gave young people spending money that their parents had never had, and in the 1950s this group began to assert themselves in ways that sometimes worried their parents. There was a new concern in general with youth. In the 1940s, the images of the teenager were taken from movies such as the *Andy Hardy* movies which were made between 1937 and 1945 and starred Mickey Rooney as Andy, and Judy Garland, Lana Turner and Ann Rutherford as his female co-stars. Andy Hardy may have been a bit wild but he was no threat to suburban USA nor were the 'bobbysoxers' who appeared in the late 1940s. These played their Frank Sinatra records loudly, screamed and fainted at concerts, but were, in reality, suburbanites at heart in training for mainstream American adult life. The new teenager of the 1950s was very different and could be seen in J. D. Salinger's *The Catcher in the Rye* (1951). Holden Caulfield, the novel's 'hero', was disparaging about the society he lived in and the 'phoney' values of the adults he saw about him. Along with many others the sugar-coated, goody-goody message transmitted by US culture at this time disgusted many American youths who turned away from such wholesome heroes as Curly in the film *Oklahoma* (1955) to embrace the more exciting Marlon Brando in *The Wild One* (1953) and James Dean in *Rebel without a Cause* (1955). The role models that these film characters provided teenagers summed up the general frustration and lack of direction that many felt in the 1950s. They wanted to rebel against everything, but especially against what their parents believed. Juvenile delinquency was seen to be something of a national crisis, although it was not statistically more prominent than in other eras. Teenagers flouting authority, even if it was as harmless as wearing a vivid combination of pink and black, was regarded by many adults as deeply disturbing in an era when everything seemed to be changing so fast. There was bewilderment too; why was this rebellion going on during a period of such prosperity? The historian Neil DeMarco believes that teenagers were acting out the ideas of William Motley, a novelist, whose novel *We Fished all Night* (1951) and whose idea of 'live fast, die young, and have a good-looking corpse' struck a note with a generation looking for excitement and growing up under the threat of nuclear war; if one push of a button could end the world tomorrow, why not enjoy it today? Conversely, their parents looked for stability in the years following the Second World War.

Rebel without a Cause (1955) was one of the major teenage movies of the decade and starred James Dean as a juvenile delinquent from a middle-class family who gets drunk, clashes with his father and the police, and plays 'chicken run' with a local gang leader who is killed. Dean's death in a high speed crash at the age of 24, just a few weeks after the release of the film, ensured that both the movie and his image would achieve cult status and reinforced the desire of teenagers to 'live fast and die young'.

Rock and roll

Rock and roll belonged to teenagers. It marked a fundamental break from the kind of music popular among their parents – the crooners such as Perry Como and Bing Crosby with their safe, romantic and rather sickly lyrics held little appeal for the teenagers. Rock and roll also marked the first significant form of desegregated popular culture since early rock music was very much associated with black US culture. It was a blend of white 'country and western' and black 'rhythm and blues' music, the latter being a type of folk music originating among Black Americans at the beginning of the twentieth century. A disc jockey from Cleveland, Alan Freed, claims the credit for coining the term 'rock and roll'. His popular radio show, which featured black artists and rhythm and blues songs, ensured that black recording artists were heard by thousands of teens all over the USA between 1954 and 1955. Many white parents were horrified not only by the fact that 'black' music was having an influence on their children but also because the contents of many of the songs contained, in their opinion, too many references to immoral behaviour in the rather suggestive lyrics!

Rock and roll music was characterized by a steady, pulsing beat and prominent guitar work, and soon white rock musicians began to appear. Bill Haley and the Comets had what has been considered the first rock hit with 'Rock Around the Clock', featured in the 1955 film *The Blackboard Jungle*. This film played on fears about the youth of the 1950s, depicting teens running amok, fired up by the pounding beat of rock music and indulging in anti-social behaviour. John Lennon recorded his disappointment with the film when he eventually saw it in England – he had expected the audience to go wild and be dancing in the aisles; they did not – clearly the British teenagers were more reserved than their American counterparts! Soon rock and roll hits topped the charts: Fats Domino's 'Ain't It a

Shame' (1955); Chuck Berry's 'Maybelline' (1955), Little Richard's 'Tutti Frutti' (1955); and Elvis' first hit 'That's All Right' (1954). Elvis Presley was the real 'danger' in the development of rock 'n' roll. His blatantly sexualized persona with his thrusting hips and tight trousers caused many parents unease, so much so that some television companies would only film him from the waist up! Jack Gould in the *New York Times* fuelled the concerns of parents: 'these gyrations have to concern parents unless we're the kind of parents who approve of kids going around and stealing hubcaps, indulging in promiscuity and generally behaving like delinquents'.

Elvis represented a white lower class that had been forgotten by suburban America, the 'flipside of the conventional male image. His fish-white complexion, so different from the 'healthy tan' of the beach boys; his brooding Latin eyes, heavily shaded in mascara', as his biographer Albert Goldman wrote (*Elvis Presley*, 1981). Clearly Elvis opened the door to a world that middle-class suburban Americans preferred to ignore, but Little Richard was even worse in their eyes. Not only was Little Richard black but his shows attracted a truly integrated crowd of black and white teenagers; he shocked the parents and delighted the teenagers with his flamboyance, wearing make-up and sporting outrageous hairstyles, jumping and screaming on stage, and flaunting his ambivalent sexuality.

Literature

One aspect of popular culture that seemed to provide an alternative to the dull predictability of 1950s' culture was a loosely affiliated group of writers, poets, and critics known as the 'Beat Generation'. These people rebelled against the humdrum self-satisfied suburban lifestyle that seemed to be taking over the country. The most famous figures of the Beat Generation were Allen Ginsberg and Jack Kerouac. Ginsberg's poem 'Howl' (1955) was a scathing attack on the 'robot apartments' and 'invisible suburbs' of mainstream USA and became a manifesto for the next generation of the 1960s. Kerouac's book *On the Road* (1957) denounced modern life, espoused a life of cultural rebellion and nonconformity, and experimented with genres, lifestyles, and sexualities.

Another major trend in 1950s' literature saw the world in quite a different way to that of the Beat Generation. In 1956, Mickey Spillane's pulp fiction accounted for seven out of the ten

American best-sellers. Spillane was influenced by the Cold War. Detective Mike Hammer, Spillane's 'hero', was the epitome of machismo, busy gunning down 'commies' and 'bedding babes', an antidote to post-war paranoia about gender roles and delinquent behaviour.

The car culture

The car industry centred in Detroit was, and still is, central to the US economy. During the 1950s, the city supplied the majority of the cars driven on US roads. To match the confident, almost boastful atmosphere of society, cars were designed to look extravagant and every car manufacturer was churning out huge, gas-guzzling (a term coined in the 1960s), multi-toned, shiny chromed beasts which were a hallmark of the period. The shape of car tailfins changed every year, but by the 1960s this style detail had disappeared – the number of lawsuits pursued by people who had injured themselves on these accoutrements had increased dramatically as the tailfins themselves grew even more outrageous! Ever aware of the overproduction of the 1920s, the automobile industry, and other consumer industries, introduced the concept of 'planned obsolescence', ensuring that all consumer products needed to be replaced. Spares for old models became difficult to obtain; new designs made earlier designs look old-fashioned. The car industry aimed to sell each family a second car, a better car or a different car year after year. The consumer cycle was described as 'Borrow, Spend, Buy, Waste, Want (the next purchase)'. Car names were designed to appeal to a sense of adventure – Comet, Fury, Thunderbird – and came complete with features which promised a heady mix of elegance, comfort and fingertip control such as comfort-aire ventilation, speed-trigger transmission, robotop convertible roofs. Not all of these lived up to expectations. The Ford company produced a car called the Edsel which not only failed to start when it made its public debut on national television, but was so riddled with faults that the company pulled the plug on the car only two months after going into production.

By the mid 1950s, 67.4 million cars were privately owned and driven in the USA. Men drove back and forth from work and their home in the suburbs, rather than using public transport. Housewives frequently had to drive, rather than walk or take public transportation, to suburban shopping centres since there was little option but to do so; frequently the shopping malls were so far 'out of town'. In 1956, as part of a plan for mass evacuations in case of nuclear attack, Congress passed the National Defense Highway Act, which earmarked $41 billion for the construction of 64,360 km (40,000 miles) of high speed, limited access roads: these ran directly into city centres and demonstrated the government's acceptance of the car as a way of life for the majority of Americans. As the country began to be connected by highways, the 'road trip' increased in popularity and families took more and more vacations and weekend trips. The entrepreneurs responded by opening hotel or motel chains to provide accommodation. In 1952, the first Holiday Inn opened, the forerunner of many other chain hotels which can be found across the USA and which provide a uniform standard of service.

The automobile even influenced the way Americans ate. In 1937, the McDonald brothers opened their first drive-in restaurant near Pasadena but did not, at this point, sell hamburgers. In 1948, they evolved a completely new concept; the menu was cut to just seven items – hamburgers, cheeseburgers, pie, crisps, coffee, milk and pop. The hamburgers came with ketchup, mustard, onions and pickle already applied and, although they were small in size, the burgers cost only 15 cents. Initially this idea was a disaster, however, when they added French fries and milkshakes a whole new clientele developed – the family. Young suburbanites realized that a whole family could be fed for a few dollars and that there was no time wasted waiting for food to be prepared – the food was already waiting, enabling the customers to place an order and immediately collect it.

Prosperity in the 1950s

Certainly during the post-war period the USA did experience an economic boom, and it is tempting to regard this period as one in which all Americans enjoyed wealth and prosperity. The standard of living did rise for the vast majority; when one looks at the figures for three common consumer items – cars, televisions and refrigerators – during the 1950s it is clear that more and more families owned these items and were experiencing a rise in their living standards. Looking at the employment statistics for the 1950s, the percentage of the adult population unemployed never went higher than 6.8 per cent while during the Great Depression the percentage stood at 25 per cent. Yet if one examines the figures, it is clear that

39.5 million Americans lived below the poverty line, that is, had barely enough to survive. Of those, 11 million were African Americans which means that 56 per cent of the black population in the USA lived in extreme poverty.

Politics in the 1950s

In 1945, Vice-President Harry S. Truman succeeded Franklin D. Roosevelt as President of the USA and immediately faced both problems and opportunities as the country passed from a wartime to a peacetime economy. War had seen the economy flourishing and there were fears that once wartime spending came to an end there would be a massive increase in unemployment; this was not the case. As we have seen above, unparalleled consumer spending replaced government spending and ensured that there were plenty of job opportunities for the GIs (abbreviation of government or general issue) returning to the workforce. Before his death, Roosevelt had signed the Servicemen's Readjustment Act (1944) known as the 'GI Bill of Rights'. These laws included an Employment Act to ensure that servicemen and women who had been in employment before the war were given the chance to get their jobs back, and they were also given offers of cheap loans and free training at a college or university; between 1945 and 1955 $20 billion was given out to help 7.8 million veterans. Truman had presented a 21-point programme to Congress following the end of the war in 1945 proposing to build on the New Deal and defend the most vulnerable in society; in order to do this he called for a $4 billion tax increase, which Congress rejected. The first few years of the Truman administration were not economically successful with inflation rising to 25 per cent in 1945–6 but by the end of the 1940s the Baby Boom, the Marshall Plan and the Korean War had all contributed to a rise in the demand for US goods. When he was re-elected in 1948, Truman used his State of the Union speech to call for a Fair Deal for America which included a rise in the minimum wage from 40 cents to 75 cents per hour; a repeal of the Taft-Hartley Act (which called for a 60 day cooling-off period before any strike could take place); the expansion of Social Security; the setting up of public work schemes; and a health care programme. All this was to be paid for out of taxation.

Social Security was extended to 1 million more Americans and the minimum wage did increase; the National Housing Act built subsidized low-income housing and contained measures for slum clearance and urban renewal. Yet Truman found it difficult to work with Congress on many major issues, particularly federal health care and education as both conservative Democrats and Republicans worked against him. Increasingly, Congress was losing interest in New Deal-type politics and was becoming more concerned with issues such as communist subversion and the war in Korea, and Truman was forced to abandon his Fair Deal in order to concentrate on these areas.

McCarthyism

Fear of 'Reds under the beds' or communist infiltration and subversion was rampant in 1950s America. The historian William Chafe believes that the USA suffers from a 'seasonal allergy', a traditional intolerance which surfaces from time to time, and that the period of anti-communism seen in the late 1940s and early 1950s was an example of this (William Chafe, *The Unfinished Journey*, 1991). Some historians suggest that the foreign policy of 'containment' spread to domestic policy, while other historians emphasize the coming of the Cold War and the fear of communist expansion making the leap across the Atlantic to conquer the USA; just as the USA had to prevent communism from sneaking over international borders, so families had to protect themselves from undesirable elements sneaking into their neighbourhoods. Still other historians believe that US society was changing so fast in the 1950s that some people could not come to terms with the psychological impact these changes had and consequently looked for scapegoats on which to blame their unease; this unease evolved into a mass hysteria and a panic fed by unscrupulous politicians.

In 1947, Congress formed The House Un-American Activities Committee (HUAC), best known for a series of hearings it held during an investigation into communism in the film industry. The HUAC interviewed 41 people who were working in Hollywood. These people attended the interviews voluntarily and became known as 'friendly witnesses'. They named 19 people during their interviews whom they accused of holding left-wing views. Of these, ten refused to give evidence. Known as the 'Hollywood Ten', they claimed that the first amendment of the American Constitution (the right to freedom of speech and free assembly) gave them the right to do this. The HUAC disagreed and they all were found guilty of contempt of

Congress and each was sentenced to between six and 12 months in prison. (In 1948 the Supreme Court ruled that first amendment rights could be withheld by Congress if national security was at risk; some then went on to plead the fifth amendment but this was taken as proof of their guilt since the fifth amendment gives a person the right to silence so as not to implicate themselves in a crime).

The HUAC pressured actors, writers, and producers to 'name names', that is, to point the finger at other actors supposedly engaged in communist activities. Larry Parks was the only actor in the original 19 people named. He agreed to give evidence to the HUAC and admitted that he had joined the Communist Party in 1941 but left it four years later. However, when asked for the names of fellow members, Parks at first refused but later in a private hearing named other actors who had joined the party. One of them was Lee J. Cobb who described his experiences:

> When the facilities of the government of the United States are drawn on an individual it can be terrifying. The blacklist is just the opening gambit – being deprived of work. Your passport is confiscated. That's minor. But not being able to move without being tailed is something else. After a certain point it grows to implied as well as articulated threats, and people succumb. My wife did, and she was institutionalized.

> (*Naming Names*, by Victor Navaskypub. The Viking Press, 1980)

He later 'did a deal' with the HUAC in order to be removed from the blacklist and be able to earn money to keep his family together. If people refused to name names when called up to appear before the HUAC, they were added to a blacklist that had been drawn up by the Hollywood film studios. Over 320 people were placed on this list which stopped them from working in the entertainment industry and included names such as Charlie Chaplin, Larry Adler, Paul Robeson, Orson Welles, Aaron Copeland and Arthur Miller. The latter was questioned about meetings of communist writers he had attended but refused to name others present. He was prosecuted for contempt of court and given a suspended gaol sentence and fined $500. His play *The Crucible* about the witch-hunts in Salem, Massachusetts during the seventeenth century was based on his experiences during this period.

In 1948, the State Department accused Alger Hiss, a State Department official and former aide to Dean Acheson, of passing department secrets to a communist agent in the late 1930s. Hiss maintained his innocence throughout but he was charged with lying at the HUAC hearing and he eventually served a five-year jail sentence in 1950. Within a month of this sentence being passed, the British arrested Klaus Fuchs, a physicist who had worked on the Los Alamos nuclear project, for spying. Out of his arrest came the arrest of Ethel and Julius Rosenberg who were convicted of passing secrets to the Soviets, and were executed in 1953. These events proved two things to Americans in the 1950s: communism could be found at the highest levels of government and those who dared to undermine the US government would be caught and punished. Although Hiss and the Rosenbergs all proclaimed their innocence, recent decoding by the Verona Project has discovered that they were indeed spying for the Soviets.

On 9 February 1950, Senator Joseph McCarthy made a speech at the Ohio County Women's Republican Club in West Virginia. This little-known Republican Senator from Wisconsin then dropped a bombshell:

> While I cannot take the time to name all of the men in the State Department who have been named as members of the Communist Party and members of a spy ring, I have here in my hand a list of 205 – a list of names that were made known to the Secretary of State and who are nevertheless still working and shaping the policy of the State Department.

Although he never produced a list of these names, the media flocked to McCarthy's press conferences and some historians have argued that the media should be held partially responsible for McCarthy's rise to power, by encouraging the publicity-hungry Senator to go a little further each time. McCarthy provided the Republican Party with the perfect issue with which to attack the Democrats. In order to counter their charges of being soft on communism, the Democrats had to denounce the ideology forcefully and act decisively against any hints of communist activity in the USA. It was the time of the Korean War and the public felt that the USA was not doing as well as it should have been in attempting to contain the spread of communism; scapegoats were sought and seemed to have been found in subversive communists within the very heart of the US government. The Tydings Committee investigated McCarthy's accusations but found no evidence of truth in them and went so far as to call them 'a fraud and a hoax', yet the HUAC investigations continued and spread their net wider.

McCarthy was made Chairman of the Government Committee on Operations of the Senate, and this gave him the opportunity to investigate the possibility of communist subversion. He began receiving information from his friend, J. Edgar Hoover, head of the FBI, and William Sullivan, one of Hoover's agents, later admitted that: 'We were the ones who made the McCarthy hearings possible. We fed McCarthy all the material he was using.

For two years, McCarthy's Committee investigated numerous government departments and questioned many about their political past. Some admitted they had been members of the Communist Party and lost their jobs as a result. Politicians became afraid to challenge McCarthy for fear that they would be accused of being communists. One exception was Senator William Benton from Connecticut. McCarthy and his supporters began smearing Benton, claiming that while Assistant Secretary of State Benton had protected known communists; not only that but he was guilty of purchasing and displaying 'lewd art works'. Benton was defeated in the 1952 elections. McCarthy portrayed Truman as a dangerous liberal soft on communism and his anti-communist crusade helped the Republican candidate, Dwight Eisenhower, win the presidential election in 1952. McCarthy too was re-elected in 1952 and again drew headlines by stripping Robert Oppenheimer, the inventor of the atomic bomb, of his security clearance. By publicly questioning the ethical implications of the atomic bomb, Oppenheimer was suspected by many of subversion.

While many feared being accused of communism, others decided to fight fire with fire. Hank Greenspun, a journalist, published an article in the *Las Vegas Sun* in October 1952 in which he accused McCarthy of homosexual activities. It is interesting to note that McCarthy did not take Greenspun to court for libel as he would have had to answer questions about his sexuality; instead McCarthy decided on a damage limitation exercise – he married his secretary and they adopted a child from an orphanage in New York.

By the mid 1950s, McCarthy had become an embarrassment, with his friends, Cohn and Schine, touring US Embassies searching for leftist books. In 1954, McCarthy overreached himself. He accused the US army of harbouring communists at its top levels, and the Senate finally condemned McCarthy's actions. Perhaps even more importantly, the McCarthy-Army hearings were televised and many Americans were shocked and disgusted by McCarthy's public hysterics. He was exposed as a bully and a liar. When McCarthy was censured by the Senate by a vote of 67 to 22, his career was at an end.

The damage done to the USA by the McCarthy witch-hunts was extensive. Americans became social conformists for fear of getting into trouble by taking part in political activities. Controversy in education was avoided by teachers and pupils alike. The congressional hearings and blacklists affected the lives of the men and women caught up in them, but exactly how many others lost their jobs is difficult to tell; statistics suggest around 10,000 people.

McCarthyism may have prevented much-needed reforms in social policy as the government abandoned the New Deal and the nation swung to the right after the war. Measures such as national health insurance were simply abandoned. In foreign policy matters, opposition to the Cold War had been identified with communism to such an extent that it was no longer possible to challenge the basic assumptions of US foreign policy.

The cultural and intellectual life of the nation was affected: TV offered a bland combination of quiz shows and Westerns during the late 1950s for fear of appearing too controversial or challenging the status quo; the film industry avoided social or political issues which might challenge the traditional 'American Way'. Even intellectuals avoided controversy. It was not until the civil rights movement and the Vietnam War brought reality to the fore that intellectuals challenged US mores.

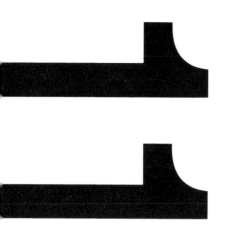

11

race relations and civil rights

This chapter will cover:
- the effect of the World Wars on civil rights
- the rise of the NAACP and its attempts to amend the Jim Crow laws
- Martin Luther King and his role in the civil rights campaign
- radical solutions: Malcolm X, the Black Panthers and the Nation of Islam.

The situation in 1900

After the American Civil War in 1865, slavery was abolished but African Americans did not gain equality with whites. Approximately 90 per cent of the USA's 12 million African Americans lived in the south where they remained second-class citizens. The powers given to the states by the constitution enabled most southern states to pass laws between 1881 and 1915 which discriminated against African Americans, and enforced African Americans and whites to have separate transport, theatres, churches, parks, schools, restaurants and public toilets. The Supreme Court in the Plessy v. Ferguson ruling (1896) approved these 'Jim Crow' segregation laws by stating that separate but equal facilities were not against the fourteenth amendment which gave equality before the law to all. Yet separate facilities did not mean equal. Most African Americans remained second-class citizens with unskilled, poorly paid jobs and many former slaves were sharecroppers who rented land at a high rent from white landlords. Their schools were under-funded, oversubscribed and in a shabby state – even their textbooks could not be kept in the same place as white textbooks, and less than 1 per cent of African-American children went to high school. The South also ignored the fifteenth amendment which said the right to vote, 'shall not be denied…on account of race, color or previous condition of servitude'. In order to vote one needs to register, but the South prevented African Americans from registering in a variety of ways. All those who registered to vote had to pay a poll tax, which prevented African Americans from registering as they were too poor to pay the tax; literacy tests, which were often rigged, prevented other African Americans from voting; if all else failed African Americans might lose their jobs or credit, be beaten or even killed to prevent them registering to vote. Only 5 per cent of African Americans eligible to vote actually did so in the South. Violence against the African-American population was endemic, and unlawful lynchings by white supremacist groups such as the Ku Klux Klan were commonplace: in 1919 alone, 70 African American people were lynched.

African Americans in the industrialized North fared a little better, having legal and political equality with whites. Yet here too they suffered discrimination in a number of ways; they were the last to be hired and the first to be fired should the economic situation deteriorate. The whites in the North resented black competition for jobs, and before long some restaurants, hotels and theatres refused to admit African-American customers. Increasingly, African Americans found themselves confined to black ghettos such as Harlem in New York where rents were higher than in the white neighbourhoods.

Booker T. Washington and accommodationism

At the beginning of the twentieth century, a variety of ways of improving relations between African American and white Americans were suggested, not always with the full support of either side. One of the first to attempt to change the lives of African Americans was the son of a white man and slave, himself a former slave, Booker T. Washington. He succeeded in educating himself to such a standard that he became a successful teacher and head of an institute of higher education for African Americans in Tuskegee, Alabama. The fact that a black ex-slave should occupy the position of principal of an educational establishment for African Americans in the heart of the South might seem unlikely, but Washington's leadership of the school was so conservative that it was acceptable to the white administration that controlled Macon County. Washington had many ideas which today seem alien to one who was trying to improve the situation of African Americans in the southern states. Washington did not believe that African Americans should campaign for the vote, and urged African Americans to prove their loyalty to the USA by stoically working hard before being granted their political rights. These ideas were supported by many white southerners as they were regarded as a means of social control, encouraging African Americans to accept their inferior economic and social status, and white businesspeople such as Andrew Carnegie and Collis Huntington donated large sums of money to the school. Washington's reputation grew as he lectured to conferences on aspects of both African-American and Native-American education, was awarded an honorary degree from Harvard, met and became friendly with several Presidents, took tea with Queen Victoria, and dined at the White House. However, Washington's influence was not as great as these achievements might at first suggest. President Theodore Roosevelt paid lip-service to the advancement of African Americans, but was also responsible for limiting the number of African-American political appointments, of dismissing all African-American soldiers in Fort Brown Texas after a fracas, and justified the lynching of African Americans because they had apparently raped white women, a far greater crime in his opinion. The advent of President Wilson to the presidency in 1912 saw attempts by this southerner to introduce segregation in the civil service, and praise for the Ku Klux Klan for saving the South from black rule. Increasingly African-American militants regarded Booker T. Washington as an 'Uncle Tom', a black man who was too deferential to the whites – because of his views that it was the role of African Americans to serve whites, and that those black leaders who demanded social equality were political extremists. Yet Washington did achieve many things for African Americans of the early twentieth century. Through Tuskagee he ensured that generations of African Americans obtained a vocational education and, through this, economic opportunities. It was also a major achievement to gain acceptance in the South for black education. In 1900 Washington helped establish the National Negro Business League, ensuring that the organization concentrated on commercial issues rather than civil rights; in his opinion the ability to earn a living and own property was more important than the right to vote. To many he was a role model; to others his ideas perpetuated racial inequality. Even his former friend, W. E. B. Du Bois, clashed several times with Washington and his ideas, in particular quarrelling over the establishment of the National Association for the Advancement of Coloured People (NAACP) in 1909.

Booker T. Washington died in November 1915; to some he was the 'great accommodator', yet although he gave the impression that he was trying his utmost to appease and reassure whites his private papers show that he was discreetly using the law courts to campaign against segregation on trains, discrimination and disenfranchisement. As Vivienne Saunders notes, 'Given the degree, extent and longevity of white hostility to African Americans, 'accommodationism' probably stood more chance of consolidating black gains in America than confrontation – in his lifetime at least' (*Race Relations in the USA since 1900*, Hodder & Stoughton, 2003).

W. E. B. Du Bois and the NAACP

William Du Bois was born a free man in Great Barrington, Massachusetts on 23 February 1868. He was educated at Fisk University in Nashville, and after he graduated he spent two years at the University of Berlin before returning to the USA and going to Harvard to complete his dissertation, *The Suppression of the African Slave Trade*. He became the first African American to receive a Ph.D. from Harvard in 1895. Du Bois' methods differed from those of Booker T. Washington; while the latter emphasized the importance of economic equality and separate but equal status for African Americans, Du Bois aimed at legal and political equality and racial integration. Although the two had worked together on attacking the segregation on trains, their aims gradually forced them apart and they became rivals. In 1905, Du Bois formed the Niagara Movement which aimed to end inequality. The group drew up a plan for aggressive action and demanded manhood suffrage, equal economic and educational opportunities, an end to segregation and full civil rights, and it pointedly excluded Washington from their proceedings. The Niagara Movement had little impact on influencing those in power and, in February 1909, Du Bois joined with other campaigners for African-American civil rights to form the pressure group, NAACP. The Association began publishing its own magazine, *Crisis*, in November 1910, and soon built up a large readership amongst black people and white sympathizers, selling 100,000 copies a month by 1919. In the magazine, Du Bois campaigned against lynching and the Jim Crow laws, and in favour of female emancipation. As a pressure group, NAACP used a variety of tactics to draw the public's attention to the poor treatment of African Americans, in particular the rise in incidences of lynching and the racial tensions which resulted from the success of the film *Birth of a Nation* (1915) which glorified the actions of the Ku Klux Klan. The campaign against lynching did help decrease the number of lynchings and Du Bois' writing was inspirational, helping to raise African-American self-confidence and pride and contributing to the Harlem Renaissance during the 1920s.

At first Du Bois was supportive of black nationalism, but after the First World War (which he supported) he became highly critical of Marcus Garvey and the Universal Negro Improvement Association (UNIA), describing Garvey as 'a lunatic or traitor' and being called a 'white man's nigger' by Garvey in return.

During the 1950s, Du Bois became a victim of McCarthyism and was accused of being a Soviet agent in 1951. He was acquitted of the charge but the State Department refused to issue him a passport until 1958. Du Bois did join the

Communist Party in 1961, and at the age of 91 moved to Ghana where he died on 27 August, 1963.

Marcus Garvey and Black Pride

The First World War had seen some African-American soldiers fighting in France, although most were used for labouring duties in all-black units. The African Americans experienced little racism on the part of the French, and the Germans tried to persuade black American soldiers not to fight for a country that treated them so badly, dropping pamphlets on the trenches where black soldiers were stationed asking, 'Do you enjoy the same rights as the white people do in America, the land of Freedom and Democracy, or are you treated over there as second-class citizens?' Following demobilization, many US towns and cities saw race riots develop as blacks and whites competed for jobs and housing. Some of the worst rioting took place in Chicago, where the riots lasted a fortnight following an incident where a 15-year-old African American was stoned for crossing onto the 'white' part of a beach on Lake Michigan. Following a report ordered by the Governor of Illinois, it was found that the white police had treated African Americans unfairly. Not only did the report call for desegregation but it was also critical of living conditions in the ghetto and remarked on the growing black consciousness.

This increasing black consciousness was fanned by the work of Marcus Garvey, a Jamaican who moved to the USA in 1916. Garvey had founded the UNIA in 1914, which aimed to raise African-American awareness of their culture and to make them proud of their colour. As he said, 'Black is beautiful', and in his newspaper, *Negro World*, he refused to include advertisements for products which claimed to bleach the skin and make the user look white; for him the blacker a person's skin, the better.

Garvey campaigned against lynching, Jim Crow laws, racial discrimination and the denial of voting rights in much the same way as other civil rights groups, but UNIA proposed a radically different solution to these problems. As Garvey did not believe that white Americans would ever treat African Americans as equals he argued for segregation rather than integration. He suggested that African Americans should go and live in Africa and called for 'Africa for the Africans at home and abroad', that is, that Africa should become the defender of blacks all over the world.

Garvey began to recruit African Americans who were willing to travel to Africa and 'clear out the white invaders'. He appealed to the new militant feelings of African Americans that had emerged at the end of the First World War by forming an army, equipping them with uniforms and weapons, and asking those African Americans who had fought in Europe to join his army to fight for equal rights. By 1919, Garvey had formed the Black Cross Navigation and Trading Company. He purchased two steamships with $10 million which had been invested in his venture by his supporters; these would be used to take African Americans to Africa. He even had talks with the Ku Klux Klan about his plans to repatriate African Americans! However, after making a couple of journeys to Africa, the Company ran out of money. Several people in his company had been involved in corruption, and Garvey was arrested, charged with fraud and sentenced to five years' imprisonment. Halfway through his sentence he was deported to Jamaica.

The end of the 1920s

By the end of the 1920s, the work of individuals such as Washington, Du Bois and Garvey had helped raise black consciousness, and some political progress had been made by the NAACP. The association's anti-lynching campaign had led to a decrease in the numbers being lynched, and there had been several court victories such as the one which abolished the 'grandfather clause'; this clause said that a black person was not eligible to vote unless he could prove his grandfather had voted which, considering slavery had only been abolished in 1865, would rule out the vast majority of African Americans in the South. Yet in the South, the main problems of poverty, lack of education, segregation and intimidation continued, and even in the North most African Americans were preoccupied with earning a living rather than becoming politically active. It was not until the Great Depression of the 1930s and the efforts of the federal government to overcome its effects through the policies of the New Deal that change began to gather pace.

Roosevelt and the New Deal

The Wall Street crash in 1929 triggered an economic depression which affected all Americans but African Americans in particular. Clifford Burke commented: 'The Negro was born in depression. It didn't mean much to him…It only became official when it hit the white man' (Studs Terkel, *Hard Times*, The New Press, 1970). In other words, the government only started to pay attention to poverty and unemployment when it happened to the white Americans. In agriculture, African-American farmers left the land for the cities as the price of produce tumbled, but they found little improvement in their economic circumstances. Black unemployment rose, fluctuating from 30 per cent to 60 per cent during the 1930s, as whites, desperate for jobs, competed with African Americans for their traditional unskilled work as servants, porters, street cleaners and rubbish collectors. African Americans were the last to be hired and the first to be fired, and even had to contend with white vigilante groups that tried to prevent African Americans being employed at all. In the presidential election of 1932, few southern African Americans voted, prevented by the cost of the $2 poll tax. In the North, Roosevelt's Democratic Party, associated as it was with the South, consequently won 50 per cent of the white vote but only 23 per cent of the black vote.

Once elected, Roosevelt's New Deal saw government intervention attempting to prevent the USA sliding into anarchy by getting people back to work and by promising 'Relief, Recovery and Reform'. Yet African-American leaders were disappointed to find that many of the early New Deal projects discriminated against the African Americans and, in 1935, the NAACP's newspaper, *Crisis*, informed it's readers that they should realize that, '…the powers that be in Roosevelt's administration have nothing for them'. By the 1936 election, the black vote had swung dramatically in favour of Roosevelt mainly because of the relief cheques African Americans received from the New Deal which they felt had enabled them to survive. New Deal programmes helped to provide jobs, housing, relief and training for thousands of African Americans; the Farm Settlement Act enabled many African-American sharecroppers to become independent farmers; in the field of black culture, the New Deal enabled African Americans to record their experiences for posterity as the Federal Writers' Project recorded African Americans' experience of slavery, their songs and history. Mary MacLeod Bethune became the highest ranking African American appointee in the Roosevelt administration as the head of the NYA. However, the New Deal did not always reach the people who needed help the most. It did little for unskilled workers who formed the greater part of the African-American population. In the South, racism and segregation continued in the New Deal as African Americans were segregated in the CCC camps. In the Tennessee Valley the new town of Norris excluded African Americans from living there. Lynchings increased during the Depression years, but Roosevelt refused to support a proposed law against lynching for fear he lose the support of southern Democrats. Eleanor Roosevelt, however, supported groups opposed to racism and publicly denounced segregation; her actions at a segregated conference in Birmingham, Alabama in 1938 made her opposition clear – not even Eugene 'Bull' O'Connor, the city's racist police chief could prevent her from making her point.

The New Deal, by attracting so many African-American voters to the Democratic Party, placed civil rights firmly on the political agenda.

The Second World War and civil rights

The Second World War had a galvanizing effect on African-American communities and provided American Americans with the ideal opportunity to press for civil rights. In 1941, the government was so alarmed by a 100,000-strong protest against the exclusion of African Americans from jobs in the defence industry proposed by A. Phillip Randolph, that they came to an agreement; if Randolph agreed to call off the march, Roosevelt agreed to ban discrimination in the defence industry and establish the Fair Employment Practice Committee (FEPC) to investigate discrimination in private firms. Randolph agreed and the FECP found widespread discrimination and attempted to rectify the situation by refusing to award government contracts to firms that discriminated – with some success. The armed forces were quite a different matter. African-American soldiers who experienced racism within the armed services found the ill-treatment they received in attempting to serve their country deeply disturbing. The army initially refused to train African-American officers, the air force would not train them as pilots and the navy used them exclusively in the kitchens. African-American blood could not be used to treat white servicemen and all African-American soldiers fought in segregated units. African-American publications during the war published many letters of outrage and complaint written by African-American military personnel noting that African Americans were good enough to fight against racist Germany but were expected to suffer discrimination and humiliation in a segregated US army.

In contrast to the treatment they received at the hands of their own countrymen, African-American soldiers were surprised to find the British attitude towards them very different. Shops served African-American GIs without comment, churches and chapels welcomed them into their services and in the South Wales valleys, who had already adopted Paul Robeson as one of their own, the African-American soldiers found kindred spirits who shared a common experience. Some African Americans were inspired by Mahatma Gandhi's peaceful confrontation with the British during his struggle for independence for India, and one, James Farmer, believed that such tactics could be usefully employed during wartime in order to win concessions from the government. To this end, he founded the Congress for Racial Equality (CORE) and called for a campaign of 'non-cooperation, economic boycott and civil disobedience'. CORE organized sit-ins in Chicago restaurants that were segregated and also demanded desegregation on inter-state transport. However, during the war most African Americans remained inactive, not wanting to be accused of being unpatriotic, and many were also fearful of a repetition of the race riots which took place in 1943 in places such as Detroit and Harlem.

When the troops were demobilized at the end of the war, a disproportionate number of African Americans lost their wartime jobs. It seemed that having been instrumental in defeating one of the most racist regimes in history, African Americans could not hope for an end to racism in their own country.

Truman and civil rights

In his youth Harry Truman had paid $10 to become a member of the Ku Klux Klan, his ancestors had been slave owners and he made no bones about his belief that: 'Negroes ought to be in Africa, yellow men in Asia and white men in Europe and America' – hardly a promising start. Yet, by 1940, Truman was making speeches which argued for greater rights for African Americans. In Missouri in 1940 he said to his audience: 'The majority of our Negro people find but cold comfort in shanties and tenements. Surely as free men they are entitled to something better than this?' As President, Truman set up a civil rights committee to investigate the increasing violence towards African Americans in post-war USA. The report which the committee presented to him the following year advised the federal government to eliminate segregation, pass legislation against lynching, to abolish the poll tax, to end discrimination in the armed forces and to establish a United States Commission on Civil Rights. Using his presidential (executive) power, Truman issued orders to end discrimination in the armed forces, established a fair employment Board in 1948, appointed an African-American judge to a federal court and tried to use federal purchasing power to encourage other employers not to discriminate on grounds of race when hiring employees. Although his attempts were often hampered by conservatives, Truman had raised the USA's awareness of civil rights issues through his actions and his speeches, which emphasized the need for the USA to 'guarantee freedom and equality to all our citizens'.

Civil rights in the 1950s and 1960s

The civil rights movement came directly into the spotlight during the 1950s in spite of the fact that President Eisenhower was less inclined to champion racial equality than his predecessor. In his State of the Union speech in 1953, Eisenhower re-emphasized the federal government's commitment to desegregate the armed forces and to work against discrimination in federal employment and facilities, but without any real conviction. Nevertheless, because of his liberal appointments to the Supreme Court, Eisenhower inadvertently took a significant step towards racial equality.

The Supreme Court 1954: Brown v. Topeka Board of Education

In 1953, President Eisenhower appointed Earl Warren as Chief Justice of the United States Supreme Court, thinking that Warren would support his moderate stance on social issues. Earl Warren was liberal but not a radical, but he could not agree with Eisenhower on the issue of racial segregation in public schools, and was shocked when the President defended the southerners, who wanted to keep segregation in schools, by saying: 'These are not bad people. All they are concerned about is to see that sweet little girls are not required to sit in schools alongside some big black bucks.' Warren could not agree.

The particular issue at stake in the case of *Brown v. Topeka Board of Education* was whether an African-American girl,

Linda Brown, could attend a local all-white school rather than having to walk more than 20 blocks to get to the shabby, under-funded black school she was supposed to attend. With the help of the NAACP, her father Oliver Brown appealed against a ruling by the Topeka Board of Education that his daughter could only attend the black school. On 19 May 1954, Chief Justice Warren announced the Court's decision that the Constitution was 'color-blind' and ordered the Topeka Board of Education to end segregation in its schools. The Court, by ruling in favour of Brown, had overturned the *Plessy v. Ferguson* decision of 1896 (the 'separate but equal' ruling). Education continued to blaze a trail in the field of civil rights and to drag a reluctant President Eisenhower behind it.

Little Rock, 1957

In 1957, the school board in Little Rock, Arkansas bowed to the Supreme Court decision made three years earlier and voted to desegregate a white high school. Nine African-American students of outstanding academic ability were chosen or volunteered to begin attending the white high school in the working-class neighbourhood of Little Rock. Orval Faubus, the state's Governor, had been regarded as a fairly moderate politician. Yet, with an eye on being re-elected the next year, Faubus called out National Guard troops to prevent the students from entering the school. Eisenhower may not have grasped all the ethical issues at stake in Little Rock, but he did understand a personal challenge and sent in troops from the 101st Airborne and federalized the Arkansas National Guard. The students were able to enter the school, but when the 101st pulled out a few weeks later, the African-American students faced systematic harassment and abuse. Elizabeth Eckford, one of the nine African-American students who tried to enrol in Little Rock, recalled her experience: 'I tried to see a friendly face somewhere in the mob – someone maybe who would help. I looked into the face of an old woman and it seemed a kind face. But when I looked at her again, she spat at me' (Ron Claybourne ANC news, Little Rock, 23 September, 1997). Will Counts took a famous photo of Elizabeth Eckford being followed by the hostile crowd; in the background the face of Hazel Bryant can be seen, contorted in what appears to be hatred. Bryant recalled: 'I was behind her and the crowd was jeering saying; "go home nigger ...go back to Africa" and things like that' (Ron Claybourne ANC news, Little Rock, 23 September, 1997). Thirty-five years later the two women met again and Hazel Bryant was able to apologize to the girl she had prevented from going to school on that day in 1957; to date, she is the only white person in Little Rock to publicly apologize. Her message to whites who still harbour a grudge against the Little Rock nine is: 'If you had been born black, if that had been you, you'd feel the same way wouldn't you?'

Although Eisenhower had apparently taken the initiative in Little Rock, two years earlier he had failed to provide moral leadership in the case of Emmett Till, a 14-year-old African-American boy from Chicago who, while on holiday in Mississippi, had been beaten to death for whistling at a white woman. An all-white jury found his murderers not guilty after his defence team had argued that Till was still alive in Chicago and that the whole incident was a NAACP plot. Eisenhower made no comment on the trial.

Eisenhower did, however, pass two Civil Rights Acts. In 1957, in an attempt to win the African-American vote, he introduced a bill which aimed to ensure all citizens could exercise their right to vote but the Democratic senators used a variety of tactics to weaken the bill including a 24-hour filibuster by Strom Thurmond. The result was that the Act that was eventually passed did little to help African Americans exercise their right to vote since any public official accused of hindering them would be tried by an all-white jury. A further bill in 1960 was again diluted in its effectiveness by the southern democrats, and although it established penalties for obstructing African Americans from voting, the two Acts together only added 3 per cent more African-American voters to the electoral roll. It was clear that African Americans could not rely on Eisenhower and the federal government for substantial support in their struggle to gain their civil rights and that they must 'do it themselves'.

The Montgomery bus boycott

According to many history books, a tired old lady refused to give up her seat to a white man and thus sparked the year-long Montgomery bus boycott. This account is inaccurate in several ways. Rosa Parks was only 42 and the secretary of the Montgomery branch of the NAACP. After discussions with her husband and mother, Rosa Parks decided to deliberately challenge the law which kept buses segregated and on 1 December 1955, Rosa, after a day working as a tailor's assistant, refused to give up her seat to a white man. Contrary to many historical accounts, the year long bus boycott by the black community was not a spontaneous response to the arrest of Rosa Parks but part of a long running protest against the discriminatory practices of the Montgomery transport system. Women's organizations had been sending letters and petitions and meeting with top city officials for months before the boycott actually began. The Parks incident simply provided the activists with the final outrage needed to challenge the law. The boycott required tremendous organization to be effective and to avoid public disorder, therefore, the NAACP turned to the churches for help. One 26-year-old African-American Baptist minister proved to be the ideal leader for the bus boycott – Martin Luther King Jr. The demands of the campaign were simple: the bus companies should use the 'first come first served' system of seating; drivers should be polite to African-American customers; and African-American drivers should be employed. African Americans, who accounted for 75 per cent of the bus company's business, refused to use buses. They walked or shared cars instead. Martin Luther King preached non-violence in spite of trumped-up speed charges being filed against him and in spite of a firebomb attack on his house. The Supreme Court declared that the segregated buses were unconstitutional and the boycott was called off when desegregated buses began to run. Although this victory was quite limited, as the rest of the city of Montgomery remained segregated, it had wide implications: it had demonstrated how powerful the black community could be if organized and united; it demonstrated that non-violence could be effective; it emphasized the growing importance of the churches and the continued importance of the NAACP in the civil rights struggle; and it brought Martin Luther King to national prominence.

Martin Luther King and direct non-violent action in the South

The choice of Martin Luther King to 'front' the bus boycott proved to be an inspired one. King was a great admirer of Mahatma Gandhi and his use of *satyagraha* (non-violent protest) as a political weapon. King's position as a Baptist minister allowed him to preach eruditely about the use of such tactics as an effective means to fight discrimination and segregation and to unite the disparate black groups in Montgomery. In 1957 a group of clergy from the South, including King, formed the Southern Christian Leadership

Conference (SCLC) to fight against racial discrimination and to provide a focused direction for the various civil rights groups and organizations.

One of the most effective methods used to bring about change in the segregation laws was the sit-in protest. This had been used by a group of four African-American students who sat down at the all-white lunch counter in Woolworth's Greensboro, North Carolina in 1960. Although denied service, they continued to sit in the cafeteria as part of their protest; as one set of students left their seats, another set would take them, and this went on for days. Within a couple of days, a group of African-American and white students had staged another sit-in and so on; over 70,000 people took part in similar sit-ins in opposition to segregated services over the next 18 months, drawing the attention of the world to the inequity of the situation as television crews filmed whites attacking the peaceful protesters. The sit-ins did have some success, and Atlanta's schools and department stores were soon desegregated and the action of the students inspired others to follow.

The freedom rides

In 1946 the Supreme Court had ruled against segregation on inter-state transport (*Morgan v. Virginia*), and in 1960 against segregation on inter-state bus facilities (*Boynton v. Virginia*), but in 1961 an integrated group travelled to the South to test these judgements. The group were members of CORE, which had tried using the same tactics in the 1940s to little effect. This time they believed that the publicity, which was bound to ensue once 'southern bigots' reacted to this passive assault on segregation,would bring results.

On 4 May 1961, four white and four African-American students boarded inter-state buses from Virginia to Mississippi to test the law. The buses and their African-American passengers were attacked by racists; one bus was firebombed, but the press coverage of these incidents did bring results. The Attorney General, Robert Kennedy, sent John Seigenthaler to accompany the 'freedom riders' on their trip. However, in Birmingham the passengers were greeted by members of the Ku Klux Klan and further acts of violence which the Ku Klux Klan hoped would dissuade other people from taking part in freedom rides. Birmingham's police chief had ensured that the riders had received no police protection from the mob by giving his police officers the day off to celebrate Mother's Day.

Over 1,000 people took part in freedom rides during the next six months, and with the local authorities unwilling to protect them, President John F. Kennedy sent Byron White and 500 federal marshals from the North to accompany them. In Montgomery, they too were attacked and this sparked off a race riot. Finally, Robert Kennedy persuaded the Interstate Commerce Commission (ICC) to draft regulations to end racial segregation in bus and rail terminals and at airports. These took effect on 1 November 1961. Martin Luther King had contacted the riders but had not personally taken part in the rides himself, for which he was criticized by the students of the Student Non-Violence Co-ordinating Committee (SNCC). However, King had succeeded in getting the CORE, the SNCC and the SCLC to work together and this, together with worldwide publicity, had brought results. These three organizations decided to work together with the NACCP on their next project – to increase African-American voter registration.

Birmingham, Alabama

In 1963, Martin Luther King and other African-American leaders organized a campaign against segregation in Birmingham, Alabama where relations between the races were amongst the worst in the South. King was aware that Birmingham's hot-headed, racist police chief, Eugene 'Bull' O'Connor would react violently. In April 1963, 'freedom marches' began in Birmingham although in the beginning the local populace was unwilling. As King had expected, O'Connor soon attracted media attention by turning police dogs on the peaceful demonstrators. King was arrested and denied access to his lawyer, and it was only his wife Coretta, who phoned Robert Kennedy, who succeeded in getting him released, having been kept in solitary confinement for a week. As press interest was waning, the local branch of the SCLC enlisted the help of school children, some as young as six years old to march through the streets of Birmingham. Soon, 500 of these young marchers were in prison but the *pièce de résistance* came when O'Connor ordered his men to turn water on a crowd of young protesters and the force of the water knocked them down and tore the clothes off their backs. The police dogs were attacked by the crowd and O'Connor was filmed urging his men to use the dogs: 'I want to see the dogs work. Look at those niggers run!' The deliberate use of the media was vital to the success of the Birmingham campaign, as an SCLC officer noted: 'There never was any more skilful manipulation of the news media than there was in Birmingham.' The situation spun out of control with the Klu Klux Klan holding a big rally with flaming crosses and inflammatory racist speeches, but the marches continued and the violence grew. Birmingham's jails were full to overflowing and there were fears in Washington that the violence could spread to other parts of the USA. Robert Kennedy urged his brother to take action. The President demanded the Birmingham council end segregation and the council complied; this was the biggest victory yet for the civil rights campaign.

The march on Washington, August 1963

In February 1963, President Kennedy introduced a Civil Rights Bill to Congress which proposed giving African Americans equality in public housing and education and ending discrimination in any government-funded schemes. As usual, southern Democrats objected to the Bill which made slow progress through Congress. King proposed a march on Washington DC to help the Bill on its way. Kennedy was unsure about the wisdom of this, fearing that it might give the Congress sufficient excuse to reject the Bill rather than vote for it 'at the point of a gun'. King ignored the President's fears, believing that if the march was called off it could lead to the use of violence by more militant African-American leaders. The march went ahead and over a quarter of a million people heard Martin Luther King give one of the most memorable speeches of the twentieth century in front of the Lincoln memorial on 28 August 1963:

> I have a dream that my four little children will one day live in a nation where they will not be judged by the colour of their skin but by the content of their character. I have a dream today!...Let freedom ring...when we allow freedom to ring, when we let it ring from every village and hamlet, from every state and every city, we will be able to speed up that day when all of God's children...will be able to join hands and sing in the words of the old Negro spiritual. 'Free at last, free at last; thank God almighty, we are free at last!

This was King at his very best which, coupled with the emotional impact of the Washington march probably helped the civil rights legislation to pass through Congress.

Martin Luther King in the northern cities

Having concentrated for so long on the South, King now turned to the living conditions of African Americans in the northern ghettos. It was his experience in Watts, Los Angeles that led King to call for a better distribution of wealth in America. In 1966, King and his family moved into a ghetto apartment in Chicago, which was promptly renovated by the landlord when he realized just who had rented it! Although King's stay in Chicago did attract publicity, little was achieved by it and his book, *Where Do We Go from Here?* (1967), posed a question which he himself could not answer. Before his death, King had spoken out against the war in Vietnam and was planning a Poor People's Campaign, a multi-racial movement against poverty, but he felt that people were not responding to the campaign in the same way they had to his civil rights campaign. In 1968, African-American sanitation workers on strike in Memphis Tennessee were dispersed violently by the police and, during a battle between Black Power demonstrators (see p. 166) and the police, a boy was killed. King was asked to speak in support of the strikers, but on a protest march part of the crowd became violent and broke shop windows. King retreated to his motel in despair, wondering if the time for violence had arrived and the time for non-violent protest had passed. That evening on 4 April, King was standing on the balcony of his motel in Memphis when he was shot dead by a sniper. As news of his death spread across the country, there were riots in the black areas of many cities with thousands of injuries and up to 30 deaths.

Martin Luther King: saint or sinner?

King's assassination at the hands of a lone gunman, James Earl Ray, ensured his status as a martyr of the civil rights movement, and his birthday is now celebrated as a national holiday in the USA. King was a winner of the Nobel Peace Prize and was posthumously awarded the Presidential Medal of Freedom. His funeral was attended by world leaders and the funeral oration emphasized that: 'His activities contributed mightily to the passage of the civil rights legislation of 1964 and 1965.' King's speeches are quoted and misquoted to this day, and his message of non-violent protest has been heard all over the world. King inspired others to take part in the civil rights movement, united civil rights groups under one umbrella, learned how to manipulate the media and reached out directly to the White House from 1960 to his death in 1968.

However, some have argued that it was not King that made the civil rights movement, rather it was the movement that made him. Sometimes his actions and tactics were less than successful and frequently they were open to criticism. For instance, not every one agreed with King's tactics in Birmingham. Malcolm X commented: 'Real men don't put their children on the firing line.'

King's area of influence was the Old South as his lack of impact on the North shows in the later 1960s, and in his later years he was losing ground to black nationalism and the writings of Malcolm X. King's sternest critics were usually 'Black Power' extremists who were impatient with King's tactics of non-violence and patience; African-American Muslims advocated physical violence as the only way to defeat racism but King realized that with the strength of the US army behind them, the US government would always be able to meet violence with greater violence. Martin Luther King has been accused of being a self-publicist, a seeker of self-glory giving the impression that the whole movement depended on him alone. In his personal life King was no saint – his public career affected his family life and his raunchy extra-marital sex life could have been used to discredit him. Yet when all is said and done, King was a moderate leader who contributed a great deal to the black cause and who has come to symbolize the civil rights struggle of 1955–68.

King's death, like that of President Kennedy's, has been surrounded by conspiracy theories fuelled by a reported statement from King's son in 1997 that the family believed Ray to have been an innocent party in the assassination and that the real assassins were still at large.

Black radicalism 1965–8

Although Martin Luther King had acted as the spokesperson for the civil rights movement for a period during the late 1950s and early 1960s, more radical voices and points of view began to emerge from the mid-60s onwards. Violence such as the killing of four young African-American girls in a Baptist Sunday school in Birmingham, Alabama on 6 September 1963 led many African Americans to view violence as the only way to fight white racism because the civil law had patently failed to protect the African-American population from such outrages. This led to the growth of the Black Power movement led by Malcolm X.

Born Malcolm Little, he had dropped his surname since he argued it was a mark of slavery as slaves were given their owner's surname. Malcolm X preferred to see African Americans using a simple letter or number instead. By 1963, Malcolm X had become a member of the Nation of Islam led by Elijah Muhammad; the African-American Muslims believed that the white man was evil and that African Americans should live apart from whites, and were in favour of black nationalism and social revolution. As all African Americans were good and all white people were evil, integration was not an option; hence Malcolm X's disdain for the work done by Martin Luther King, whom he accused of being an Uncle Tom. Malcolm X disliked Christians equating the religion with white supremacists, and felt that the Christian teachings such as 'turning the other cheek' encouraged white violence against submissive African Americans. Malcolm X's followers were poor African Americans from the northern ghettos and, because of his preaching, membership of the Nation of Islam rose to 40,000 by 1964. However, in 1964 Malcolm X quarrelled with Elijah Muhammad, who tended to ignore the strict moral code of Islam when it suited him. Muhammad tried to prevent Malcolm X from making political speeches and was jealous of his popularity, fame and influence. They had disagreed about the methods to be used to improve the lives of African Americans, as Malcolm X moved gradually towards the civil rights activists seeing political participation as the best way to achieve his aims. Following a visit to Mecca in 1964, Malcolm X saw black and white Muslims co-operating and he became increasingly tolerant of whites provided they aimed to help American blacks. These ideas became increasingly distasteful to the Nation of Islam and, in 1965, Malcolm X was assassinated in all probability by one of their members.

Black Power and the Black Panthers

The term 'Black Power' was first heard around 1966, during a march organized by James Meredith, the University of Mississippi's first African-American student, but it came to prominence as part of the Black Panther movement of the late 1960s. It is not an easy term to define as it was, indeed is, constantly evolving and meant different things to different people. To Elijah Muhammad it meant black people would rule the world; to Richard Nixon it meant black capitalism; to Floyd McKissack it meant political and economic power and a new self-image. There was certainly an emphasis on black pride and culture, with Afro hairstyles and African clothing being very fashionable. In ideological terms, Malcolm X's ideas had a great influence on other black radicals such as Stokely Carmichael and Floyd McKissick, who both wanted to adopt a far more radical approach to civil rights than their chairmanships of SNCC and CORE respectively allowed them. The slow progress African Americans were making towards equality in the USA was frustrating to both men, and gradually they moved away from the non-violence preached by Martin Luther King towards Black Power which hinted at the use of violence, and which King believed would make white people feel threatened.

In *Black Power: The Politics of Liberation* (1967), Carmichael suggested that African Americans ally themselves with other nations in the developing world who were at that time also trying to rid themselves of white rule. Amongst their demands were that African Americans be compensated for the wrongs done to them since the time of slavery, and that they be exempt from military service. By 1968 the SNCC had merged with the Black Panther movement.

The leaders of the Black Panthers were influenced by the ideas expressed by Malcolm X towards the end of his life. Their calls for working-class unity on an international scale and joint action with white revolutionary groups led naturally to their evolution into a Marxist revolutionary group. In their characteristic black berets, leather jackets and gloves, they looked every bit the part of a black revolutionary movement. Small wonder that J. Edgar Hoover of the FBI described the Panthers as 'the greatest threat to the internal security of the country' and authorized tough measures to be taken against them. Although the Panthers were a small group consisting of at the most 5,000 members, they achieved a great deal of publicity. For example, in the Mexico Olympics in 1968, during the Olympic 400 m award ceremony, Tommy Smith and John Carlos stood on the winners' podium to accept their medals wearing black gloves, and gave the Black Power salute. The US establishment was outraged, and neither man represented his country again.

The Black Panther Party had been formed in October 1966 by Bobby Seale and Huey Newton, initially to protect the local African-American community in Oakland, California from police brutality and racism; the group also did humanitarian work running medical clinics and providing school children with free food. The movement was continually harassed by the police, and some of its members were involved in shoot-outs.

During one of these incidents, Huey Newton was wounded and later charged with killing a police officer.

By 1968, there was a chapter of the Black Panther Party in Chicago. Its founder, Fred Hampton also established a community service programme which provided free breakfasts for school children and a free medical clinic. Perhaps his greatest achievement was to persuade Chicago's most powerful street gangs to stop fighting against each other.

Following Hoover's orders to take action against the Panthers, several incidents occurred during the late 1960s which deprived the Panthers of several of their leaders. One such incident occurred early on 4 December 1969 when the Panther headquarters in Chicago was raided by the police. The police later claimed that the Panthers opened fire first and a shoot-out developed during which Fred Hampton was killed. This was a different story to the one told by eye witnesses who claimed that Hampton had been wounded in the shoulder and then executed by a single shot to the head. The surviving Panthers were arrested and charged with attempting to murder the police. Further ballistic evidence revealed that only one bullet had been fired by the Panthers while the police had fired nearly 100 shots. By the end of 1969, a total of 27 Panthers had been shot by police and 750 arrested.

Black Power raised the morale of African Americans and increased pride in black culture. This led to the establishment of many academic courses on black history, and the work done by the Black Panthers in inner cities gave practical aid to many poor African Americans. However, it could be argued that the movement contributed to the decline of the civil rights movement because the first generation of leaders lost support to the new radical ideas which failed to come to fruition. Dr Clayborne Carson, a participant in and observer of African-American political movements noted: '...the black power movement...promised more than the civil rights movement but delivered less' (*The Autobiography of MLK junior*, Warner Books, 1998). The movement has been criticized for its overtly macho image which resulted in many African-American women being limited in their role within Black Power because of their gender, just at a time when the feminist movement in the USA was beginning to come to prominence. By the 1970s it was clear that tackling economic inequality was next on the agenda, as King had noted in his book *Where do we go from here?*, but this was to prove a difficult problem for both civil rights and Black Power.

The conservatism of the 1970s and 1980s

The attempt on the part of Richard Nixon to appoint two southern Conservatives to the Supreme Court, when he became President in 1968, did not bode well for the civil rights movement. However, although more conservative in nature, the Supreme Court during this period continued to expand desegregation in education with the *Swann v. Charlotte Mecklenburg Board of Education* judgement in 1971. This ordered bussing of school children to ensure racially mixed schools; by 1972 only 8 per cent of African-American children in the South attended segregated schools. Progress was also made in the fields of employment discrimination with the passing of the Equal Employment Opportunity Act (1972). Federal anti-poverty action such as raising social security and welfare payments helped to raise living standards amongst the African-American community.

President Carter faced increasing economic and foreign policy problems during his one-term presidency, and hence had little time for the plight of black America. Even so, he appointed more African Americans and Hispanics to the judiciary, the cabinet and to diplomatic posts than any President before him.

Ronald Reagan's years as President saw an unprecedented attack on the welfare state which had been evolving since the 1930s. Reagan's economic programme, 'Reaganomics,' cut taxes, but in order to fund these tax cuts federal spending on welfare was also cut. Reagan's Family Support Act (1988) insisted that people who received social welfare payments either took part in community service or undertook government training schemes. It was these changes in the welfare payment system which hit many poor African Americans as 43 per cent of African Americans received payments under the Aid to Families with Dependent Children scheme. Thirty-five per cent received food stamps and 34 per cent lived in subsidized housing. It was interesting to note that Reagan had a great deal of support from middle-class African Americans.

The George Bush (senior) election campaign saw much emphasis placed on law and order, but one particular advert also stirred up racial fears. It featured the convicted black murderer Willie Horton who raped and murdered a white woman while on a furlough from prison, and it helped Bush score points against his liberal Democrat opponent Michael

Dukakis. In 1992, race riots took place in Los Angeles following a judgement in the Rodney King case. In 1991 a black driver, Rodney King, had been stopped by four white police officers for a trivial motoring offence. He was pulled from his car and beaten up by the police officers using batons as he lay on the ground. King sustained 12 broken bones during the attack. The whole incident was filmed on video by a passer-by. In 1992, a jury (ten of whom were white), found the four officers 'not guilty' of assault, and the worst riots in US history erupted. President Bush was forced to send in federal troops to restore order. During the riots there had been what the media called a 'looting free-for-all' as crowds broke into shops and loaded up their cars with goods. Rioters started over 5,000 separate fires, 55 people were killed and 2,500 people seriously injured. The Rodney King affair had shown that African Americans still did not have the same civil rights as white Americans since the legal system was still regarded as biased against African Americans. The Los Angeles riots also emphasized the economic divisions in US society; the fact that violence had been directed against Korean shopkeepers accused of exploiting poor African Americans showed that little had changed since the 1960s when Jewish shopkeepers had been similarly reviled.

During the Reagan and Bush years, the Supreme Court had become gradually more conservative as the appointment of Clarence Thomas proved. Although Thomas himself had profited from affirmative action, which had enabled him to go to Yale Law School, he was personally against this policy and preferred black self-help. He supported Supreme Court judgements such as *Freeman v. Pitts* (1992) and, during Bill Clinton's presidency, *Missouri v. Jenkins* (1995), which attacked school desegregation and also opposed the proposal to widen voting rights; it seemed that many of the civil rights gained since the 1950s were under attack.

President Bill Clinton

In 1994, Republicans took control of both houses of Congress, and this made the Democratic President Bill Clinton's task of getting legislation through the Congress almost impossible. In addition to rejecting health care legislation and limiting affirmative action programmes, Congress made severe cuts in welfare spending, all of which affected African-American citizens. On 16 October 1995, the Million Man March took place in Washington to demonstrate black male's concern about social issues. It was organized by Louis Farrakhan, the leader of Nation of Islam, and called for a separate black nation while speaking out strongly against white people and the Jews. President Clinton objected strongly to this separatism: 'Whether we like it or not we are one nation. White Americans must acknowledge the roots of black pain. To our black citizens we must say your house too must be cleansed of racism.' In the same year, the black US football star, O. J. Simpson, went on trial accused of stabbing to death his ex-wife Nicole and her friend Ronald Coleman. The trial was televised throughout the world with more than 180 million watching the jury find Simpson not guilty. This trial divided the USA; while most white people believed Simpson was guilty, most African-American people were convinced he was innocent, something Johnnie Cochran, Simpson's defence lawyer realized and emphasized when he said: 'Race plays a part in everything in America and we need to understand that.'

The situation at the end of the twentieth century

In 1988, Jesse Jackson ran for president, something that would have been unthinkable at the beginning of the century. However, ten years later in 1998 there was still not one African-American Senator. It was estimated that approximately one-third of African Americans were middle class, yet black poverty remained a major problem intensified by the conservative policies of the Republican Party. The problems of crime, unemployment and poverty remained in black ghettos in spite of the efforts of African-American mayors such as Tom Bradley in Los Angeles. The Supreme Court welcomed Clarence Thomas, son of a sharecropper, into its ranks, yet proceeded to erode civil rights and affirmative action programmes designed to give aid to the poorest in society. It seems that although progress has been made in legal and political rights, and the fields of culture and sport, the USA remains, in certain aspects such as housing and schooling, a segregated society.

Kennedy and the 1960s

This chapter will cover:

- Kennedy – the hope of a new generation
- Kennedy's policies at home and abroad
- Kennedy's assassination and the many theories surrounding it.

The torch has passed to a new generation of Americans. We must bear the burden of a struggle against the common enemies of man: tyranny, poverty, disease and war itself...And so my fellow Americans: ask not what your country can do for you – ask instead what you can do for your country.

This is an extract from the inaugural speech of John Fitzgerald Kennedy on 20 January 1961, thirty-fifth President of the United States of America, the youngest person to be elected President, and the first to be a Roman Catholic.

Kennedy's election did indeed seem to mark a break with the generation who had led the country during the 1950s: his youthful good looks, charm, wit, attractive wife and young family appeared to offer the promise of a new beginning. Youth, style, glamour and culture seemed to epitomize the administration as Kennedy attracted the 'brightest and best' to positions in his government. Kennedy displayed a vigorous reforming energy as his 'New Frontier' increased social security, established training schemes for the unemployed, and initiated housing programmes; he was committed to the cause of racial equality and sent an innovative Civil Rights bill to Congress; he took the USA towards a completely new frontier when he began the Apollo Moon Project; and in foreign affairs he personally prevented a third world war breaking out during the Cuban crisis. Kennedy did all this during his 1,000 days in office – no wonder the White House was nicknamed the court of 'Camelot'. Yet all this promise was tragically cut short on 22 November 1963 when an assassin shot and killed John Fitzgerald Kennedy as he drove through the streets of Dallas, Texas. This event stunned the world and created a myth which remains a subject of controversy to this day. Every aspect of Kennedy's life has been subjected to intense scrutiny, but what had John Fitzgerald Kennedy done for his country?

Kennedy during the war

Politics was not Kennedy's first choice as a career – on leaving college he had considered both law and business but in 1941 joined the navy. In December 1941, he underwent torpedo boat training, was commissioned as an ensign and shipped out to the South Pacific within a year.

In the early hours of 2 August 1943, Kennedy, now a lieutenant, was in command of the torpedo boat PT-109 on patrol near the Solomon Islands when a Japanese destroyer cut Kennedy's boat in half. Kennedy, in spite of being injured himself, collected his men together on the remains of the boat before ordering them to make for an island about 5 km (3 miles) away. Kennedy took charge of a member of the crew who had been badly burned, towing him to the island while holding the straps of the man's life vest between his teeth. Once they had reached the island, Kennedy and another officer scouted around and found two natives in a canoe who carried a message to a US naval base that Kennedy had scratched on a coconut. Kennedy and his men were rescued five days later. For his courage and leadership, Kennedy won the Navy and Marine Corps Medal.

Politics and marriage

On his discharge from the navy, Kennedy tried journalism and covered such stories as the British elections and the Potsdam Conference. He finally found his way into politics in 1946 when he gained the Democratic nomination as a representative for a Boston district. In 1952, he won election to the US Senate and, two years later, he married the beautiful Jacqueline Bouvier with whom he had three children, one of the children died shortly after birth. During his eight years in the Senate, Kennedy's voting record was difficult to pigeonhole: he supported raising the minimum wage and increasing welfare benefits, but also advocated reform of the unions; and he avoided censuring Senator McCarthy because he was in hospital recovering from a reoccurrence of his old back injury.

In 1960 Kennedy decided to run for President. Many people thought that his Catholicism and his age would handicap him, but Kennedy declared his support for the separation of church and state, and he attracted many Democrats to his side by winning every state primary he entered. Once he gained his party's nomination, Kennedy chose Lyndon B. Johnson as his vice-presidential running mate even though he had originally opposed him for the nomination. The choice of Johnson as his running mate ensured Kennedy's southern votes. Kennedy's youth, confidence and personality contrasted with Nixon's image which seemed to belong to a different era, even though there was only four years difference in their ages. During a televised debate in September 1960, the difference in their images counted. To those who had heard the debate on the radio, Nixon had won easily, but to those who had watched the debate on television, Kennedy's image was one of youthful exuberance in comparison with Nixon's grey, tired, elderly appearance. In fact, Nixon was ill with the flu and newly out of hospital following a knee operation, but television made no allowances for this. Kennedy not only used his image to win the election, he was also able to profit from the Republicans' poor record in foreign and domestic affairs; just before the election the U-2 spy plane incident had shown Eisenhower's dishonesty, and the economic recession with inflation at 3.5 per cent and unemployment at 6.5 per cent, suggested that the government had not done all it might to ensure prosperity.

Johnson's popularity in the South, Kennedy's support for civil rights (he phoned Coretta King to offer his support when her husband had been imprisoned), the monetary support Kennedy received from his influential father Joseph Kennedy (the former bootlegger and diplomat), and Kennedy's catchy reference in the campaign to the 'New Frontier' ensured that Kennedy won the election by a fine margin of 0.1 per cent of the popular vote. There was evidence of electoral malpractice in Illinois and Texas, but Nixon chose to accept the result rather than undermine the democratic credentials of the USA. Kennedy now had to put his fine words into action.

Poverty

Kennedy was regarded as a liberal so it was with some anticipation of reform that he began his period of office. In the midst of prosperity there was 'The Other America' with 40 million citizens living in poverty. An official Senate report in 1960 found 8 million people living on incomes that were lower than $1,000 a year: poverty was officially defined as a family of four that lived on an income of less than $3,000 per annum. Over 8 million of the poor were over the age of 65. Poverty was not confined to certain regions nor to certain racial or social groups, and the causes of poverty were many and varied. With such a complex problem, Kennedy's task was not an easy one. He hoped his economic improvements would eventually trickle down to the poor, but he was also aware that direct action was needed instantly. Increases in social security and the minimum wage, and their extension to the retail trade helped many, especially women: over $400 million was provided for training in schools and jobs; $500 million of grants and loans were provided for depressed areas. In December 1962, the President gave his approval for an anti-poverty package which was to be introduced after the 1964 election since Congress was, at that time, log-jammed with legislation. Kennedy's assassination prevented this.

Kennedy proposed a health care funded from a tax on pay-rolls; it was rejected. He proposed giving money to states, especially the poorest states, for scholarships and buildings; this bill also failed. It seems likely that Kennedy would have tackled social problems more energetically once re-elected; this was not to be, but he certainly laid the foundations for what followed – Johnson's 'Great Society'.

After Kennedy's assassination, Lyndon B. Johnson, who was enthusiastic about the contents of the package, gave it his immediate go-ahead; he also had far more success with health care and education. Johnson's vision of the 'Great Society' was one in which the federal government would act to eliminate poverty, extend civil rights, ensure that education was open to all, work towards full employment, and one in which no one was denied basic health care because of a lack of money. It was President Johnson who succeeded where Kennedy had failed, persuading Congress to pass a series of bills providing federal aid for health care for the poor and the elderly, improvements in education, and both urban and rural regeneration.

The economy

Getting the USA 'moving again' was Kennedy's priority in domestic affairs because a strong economy would not only be of benefit domestically, it would also strengthen the USA's standing in the world. Although anxious to cut taxes, Kennedy was aware that this was unlikely to be popular with the southern Democrats and so he postponed proposing his $10 billion tax cut, leaving it to be passed by Johnson in 1963. Kennedy did however reduce business taxes and cut tariffs to stimulate trade. His spending on defence and the space programme did much to stimulate the economy and, through encouraging the states to spend federal grants on schools highways and housing, unemployment was reduced to 5.3 per cent in 1964.

In an attempt to keep inflation and unemployment down, Kennedy had asked employers to keep wage and price rises within certain limits. US Steel challenged this by putting up their prices. Kennedy was able to call their bluff by putting pressure on US steel's competitors not to raise prices and by threatening the company that it would not receive any further government contracts. This double whammy of being undercut by their competitors and threatened by the government 'persuaded' US Steel to get back in line.

Civil rights

Kennedy is remembered as a campaigner for civil rights, but when he first became President he was unwilling to take a strong stand on the issue for fear he alienate the southern congressmen and thus put his New Frontier measures in jeopardy. During his presidential election campaign, it was reported that Kennedy asked his adviser on civil rights, Harris Wofford, to 'Tell me the ten things I have to know about this goddamn civil rights mess.' Kennedy was personally not prejudiced against blacks in any way but his interests lay mainly in foreign affairs and the New Frontier reforms. It was Robert Kennedy, the President's brother and Attorney General, who proved to be the most active member of the Kennedy administration with regard to civil rights; his actions ensured that lunch counters, inter-state bussing and universities in Mississippi and Alabama were desegregated. Indeed, President Kennedy has been openly criticized for giving his approval for the FBI's tap on Martin Luther King's phone and for the appointment of several openly pro-segregation judges in the South. He did, however, demonstrate his support by appointing African-Americans to high office within his administration, and he did send troops to support the registration of James Meredith, an African American student, in the university of Mississippi following the refusal of Governor Ross Barnett to desegregate the university 'whatever the federal courts say'. The events in Birmingham, Alabama in spring 1963 did much to persuade the President of the need for a Civil Rights Bill. Within a month of seeing scenes on television, which he admitted made him feel physically sick, Kennedy had made a public statement which was televised from the Oval office. In it he listed the actions he would be asking Congress to take including the right for all Americans to be served in public facilities, the end to segregation in public education, and a greater protection for the right to vote. The Civil Rights Bill introduced by Kennedy into Congress in 1963 had little chance of success with some politicians, such as George Wallace, promising they would fight it every inch of the way. Kennedy's assassination later that year changed the situation; on a wave of emotion President Johnson succeeded in getting through Congress the Civil Rights Act (1964) and the Voting Rights Act (1965).

Kennedy and Congress

At first glance it appears that Kennedy would have no problem in dealing with Congress since both houses were controlled by the Democrats. However, closer inspection reveals that there was a large group of southern Democrats who were so opposed to Kennedy's 'liberal' ideas that they were happy to vote with the Republican Party to prevent many of Kennedy's bills becoming law. Because of this, many of the key features of Kennedy's New Frontier programme such as Medicare, urban reform and aid to education were blocked. The historian Maldwyn Jones noted that, 'in most cases the margin of defeat was narrow and it may be that a President less preoccupied with foreign and defence matters and more skilled in handling Congress could have achieved more' (M. A. Jones, *The Limits of Liberty: American History 1607–1992*, OUP, 1995).

Support of space programmes

During the 1960 presidential campaign, Kennedy made it clear that he was eager for the USA to lead the way in the race to send man into outer space. He emphasized that not only had a 'missile gap' developed between the USA and the USSR but also that the Soviet Union was ahead of the USA in its exploration of space – a situation that Kennedy was determined to remedy. He said, 'No nation which expects to be the leader of other nations can expect to stay behind in this race for space,' and asked Congress to approve more than $22 billion for the Apollo Project, which aimed to land an American man on the moon before the end of the decade. Kennedy's speech at Rice University, Texas in 1962 stressed the importance of the space programme to the USA: 'We choose to go to the Moon and to do the other things, not because they are easy, but because they are hard, because that goal will serve to organize and measure the best of our energies and skill.' This goal was finally realized six years after Kennedy's death.

Kennedy and foreign affairs

In the opinion of the historian James N. Giglio, 'President John F. Kennedy always gave his greatest attention to foreign affairs' (*The Presidency of JFK*, Kansas University Press, 1991). Kennedy is certainly remembered for his handling of several international crises: the Berlin Wall crisis, the Cuban crisis, and the situation in Laos and Vietnam, with varying degrees of success.

Berlin

After the Second World War, the city of Berlin found itself isolated; an island within the communist sector of East Germany. The city had been divided between the victorious powers and had gradually polarized itself into East and West Berlin; the East under communist control and the West controlled by the democratic powers. The two parts of the city developed at different rates, with the citizens of West Berlin enjoying a higher standard of living than those living in the East. The prosperity of the Western part of the city was a constant thorn in the flesh of the communist authorities, particularly since so many of their citizens used Berlin as a gateway to Western Europe. East Germany was losing the skilled citizens that were needed to rebuild the country as they moved to the West in search of a better standard of living than that available in the East. The communist authorities were keen to stop this haemorrhage of skilled labour but were unsure how far the USA and NATO would be willing to go to defend West Berlin.

The USA had three basic principles with regard to Berlin: the citizens of Berlin should be free to choose the form of government they wanted to rule over them; US, British and French troops should remain in West Berlin for as long as the citizens of Berlin wanted them there; and there should be free access to West Berlin through East Germany via roads, canals and flight paths. By supporting West Berlin, the USA showed its strong opposition to the expansion of communism, and the USSR remained uncertain as to how far the USA was prepared to go and whether it was prepared to use nuclear weapons to defend its sector of the city.

When Kennedy was elected President, his youth and relative inexperience convinced Khrushchev, the Soviet leader, that pressure could be put upon him regarding Berlin. When the two met in Vienna (1961), Khrushchev insisted that the USA withdraw from Berlin by the end of the year and, when Kennedy refused, Khrushchev lost his temper, banged on the table and exploded, 'I want peace but if you want war that is your problem.' Kennedy emphasized his standpoint when he addressed the nation on 25 July: 'We cannot and will not permit the Communists to drive us out of Berlin.' Khrushchev could not allow the floods of skilled refugees to continue to leave the East and so, on 13 August 1961, barriers were built to stop free movement between the Western sectors of Berlin and the Soviet sector. On the 17 August, the barbed wire began to be replaced with stone – the construction of the Berlin Wall had begun. Recently-released documents reveal that Kennedy contemplated the use of nuclear weapons and one of his advisers, Carl Kaysen, even produced a report proposing a limited first strike which would deter the Soviets from attacking the USA. Kennedy sent General Lucius Clay to Berlin as his special representative, but Clay was under the impression that he was being sent to Berlin to take on the Soviets and even built a replica 'Berlin Wall' so that his soldiers might practise knocking it down! In October, a US diplomat and his wife were refused admission to a function in East Berlin because they refused to show their passports. Clay sent armed troops to accompany the diplomat into East Berlin, and US tanks were parked near to Checkpoint Charlie, the main crossing point from East to West Berlin. On 27 October, ten Soviet tanks drove to Checkpoint Charlie where they lined up to face the US tanks. The atmosphere grew tense and the US garrison in Berlin, NATO and Strategic Air Command were all placed on alert; Khrushchev issued orders that should the Americans start to fire the Soviet Commander should reply in kind. Kennedy contacted Khrushchev directly and assured him that if the Soviet tanks withdrew, the US tanks would also withdraw. The end of the crisis came when a Soviet tank started its engine and pulled back five yards; minutes later a US tank did the same, pulling back just 4.5 m (5 yards), gradually the tanks withdrew, one by one. The crisis was over. The Wall remained – 'not a very nice solution, but a wall is a hell of a lot better than a war,' said Kennedy. The President visited Berlin on 26 June 1963 to inspect the Wall and look over into East Berlin. He addressed a huge crowd of Berliners in Rudolph Wilde Platz and ended his speech, 'All free men, wherever they may live, are citizens of Berlin, and therefore as a free man, I can take pride in the words *Ich bin ein Berliner*.' The crowd cheered. Some historians have wondered if the President was aware that 'ein Berliner' was also the term for a doughnut, however, German linguists assure us that Kennedy's grammar was correct.

The Cuban Missile crisis

In April 1961, President Kennedy called his press secretary, Pierre Salinger, into the Oval office and declared that he needed around 1,000 cigars and asked Salinger to collect as many as he could by the next day. The following morning Salinger was again summoned to the Oval office. Kennedy asked how he had fared, to which Salinger announced that he had succeeded in collecting 1,100. On hearing this, Kennedy produced a decree banning all Cuban products from entry into the USA. 'Good,' he declared. 'Now...I can sign this!'

What had caused Kennedy to prohibit Cuban cigars and other produce from being imported into the USA? Approximately 150 km (240 miles) off Key West, on the coast of Florida, lies the Caribbean island of Cuba. Since early 1933, Cuba had been ruled by a pro-American dictator, Fulgencio Batista y Zaldivar. The USA not only helped keep him in power but also dominated Cuba's trade and bought most of Cuba's main crop, sugar cane. The USA owned most of the land and the larger industries, and Cuba became well known as a holiday destination for rich Americans. Tourism in this Caribbean playground was dominated by the Mafia, and the island gave many Americans a weekend taste of the tropics and access to prostitution, drugs and gambling. The gulf between the rich and poor in the country was tremendous; living conditions in the rural areas were almost medieval. Batista's government was harsh and corrupt and very unpopular with many of the Cuban people.

In 1959, Batista was overthrown by Fidel Castro who began a series of reforms designed to end corruption and terror in Cuban politics and to improve Cuban prosperity, particularly that of the peasants who worked on the land and in US-owned sugar mills. At first, Castro appeared not to have had any political affiliation other than vaguely socialist ideas, but following a visit to the USA where he was snubbed by President Eisenhower, Castro began distributing land he had confiscated to the landless peasants who had been exploited by both Batista and by US companies. When the US oil companies in Cuba refused to refine oil bought from countries other than the USA, Castro nationalized the refineries and, although compensation was offered, the USA refused to come to terms. In February 1960, Castro signed a trade agreement with the Soviet Union and nationalized US interests in Cuba worth over $1 billion, and the USA retaliated by refusing to buy sugar, the country's main export. The Soviet Union stepped in to buy the crop and also to ship petrol to Cuba when Eisenhower refused to sell petroleum products to Cuba – as a result Cuba moved closer towards the Soviets. An associate of Khrushchev's claimed that Castro was not communist, but had been pushed to become so by the USA as US policies became increasingly anti-Castro.

During this period, the Central Intelligence Agency (CIA) became involved in a series of covert operations against Cuba, and also trained a force of Cuban exiles in Guatemala with the intention of leading an uprising against Castro and his government. Kennedy had been briefed by Eisenhower on the CIA plan to help the anti-Castro guerrillas prior to his inauguration in 1961. Kennedy had not objected to the proposed plan because while campaigning for the presidency the Democrats had frequently been accused by the Republicans of being soft on Cuba, and Kennedy had promised action if elected. However, he did insist that US involvement be kept secret and he refused to consider any US military involvement.

The invasion of the Bay of Pigs, where a group of approximately 1,400 poorly armed Cuban exiles landed on Cuba to face 20,000 Cuban troops in an attempt to provoke an armed uprising against Castro, was a disaster. The people did not rise up to support the rebels, and many previously non-political Cubans hurried to defend their country from the invaders. Following three days of fighting, the survivors of the invading exile brigade surrendered; 100 men had been killed, 1,200 were taken prisoner, and 14 were rescued by the US navy. The CIA had not only overestimated the Cuban support for the invasion but had wrongly assumed that Kennedy would support the invasion with direct action should it run into difficulties. However, Kennedy was too aware of world opinion and anxious to avoid any political repercussions. When Kennedy met Khrushchev in June, the Soviet leader beamed with confidence and rubbed salt in the wound by insisting that communism would eventually win the day.

In July 1962, 65 Soviet ships, some carrying military equipment, set sail for Cuba. By September, construction of missile sites in San Cristobal in western Cuba had begun. From here, nuclear missiles could be launched at the USA.

On 14 October 1962, these sites were photographed by a U-2 spy plane. The photographs were analysed by the photo intelligence branch of the CIA and the President was informed of their existence on 16 October. Immediately, Kennedy created the Executive Committee of the National Security Council

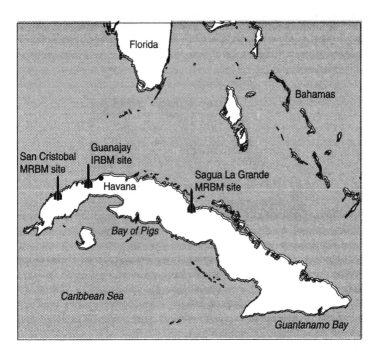

figure 6 Cuban missile sites

(ExComm) to deal with the crisis. This was a group of senior advisers which met almost continuously for the next two weeks in an attempt to calculate the implications of every move made by both sides during the crisis. ExComm divided into two groups – the hawks and the doves. The hawks, mainly military men, wanted to invade Cuba and eliminate communism; the doves wanted to avoid anything which may lead to open warfare, they preferred a more diplomatic approach.

Kennedy was faced with several choices: do nothing other than protest to Cuba and the USSR – not really an option since this would be dangerous to the USA and would appear as though the USSR had scored a major victory; attack Cuban military bases and the missile bases by air, which could easily escalate into a war with Cuba and possibly the USSR, with many civilian and military casualties; invade Cuba with the US armed forces, which could result in an estimated 25,000 US casualties and might escalate into war with the USSR; attack Cuba and the USSR with nuclear weapons, which could lead to a full-scale nuclear war and the end of humanity; blockade Cuba with the US navy and prevent Soviet ships from accessing Cuba. Kennedy chose the latter.

figure 7 Kennedy and Khrushchev realize the dangers of nuclear war following the events in Cuba.

(Source: "Lets get a lock for this thing", *Herblock: A Cartoonist's life*, Times Books, 1998. Image courtesy of the Prints & Photographs Division, Library of Congress.)

The blockade began on 24 October when Cuba was encircled by 100 US warships. Kennedy addressed the nation from the White House, setting out the evidence of Soviet missiles on Cuba and outlining the US policy of quarantine – the word blockade had been dropped as it was considered too aggressive. While he was speaking, all US military forces around the world went on Defcon 3 – a heightened state of nuclear alert. The Secretary General of the UN, U Thant, sent identical letters to both Kennedy and Khrushchev pleading with both governments to suspend the blockade and the shipments for a couple of weeks in order to reduce the risk of war.

At 10.25 a.m. on 24 October, reports came that some of the Soviet ships had stopped dead in the water. In the immortal words of Dean Rusk, the Secretary of State, 'We're eyeball to eyeball, and I think the other fellow just blinked' (*The Cold War*, C. B. Jones, Hodder Arnold, 2004).

On 26 October, Khrushchev sent a long personal letter to Kennedy which said, 'We and you ought not to pull on the end of the rope in which we have tied the knot of war, because the more we pull the tighter the knot will be tied.' Krushchev offered a political solution – the Soviets might withdraw the missiles if the USA agreed not invade Cuba in the future nor to support other forces who might invade. In the early hours of 27 October, Robert Kennedy met Anatoly Dobrynin, the Soviet Ambassador, who raised the question of US missiles in Turkey and the threat they posed to the security of the Soviet Union. Robert Kennedy consulted his brother by phone and replied that the President was willing to examine the question of Turkey favourably. This news was immediately relayed to Moscow. On 27 October, a second letter from Khrushchev to Kennedy had been broadcast on Radio Moscow. At this time no direct link existed between the Kremlin and the White House, and a broadcast from Moscow Radio was an effective way of reaching the White House. This second letter was far more formal than the previous one. It stated that the Soviet missiles on Cuba would be removed in return for the removal of US missiles in Turkey. The hawks in ExComm were furious as there had been no mention of Turkey in the previous letter – they were unaware that Khrushchev was responding to the proposals made between Robert Kennedy and Dobrynin. Although Kennedy believed that world opinion would accept the deal over Turkey in order to avoid nuclear war, he became increasingly aware that should he push the USSR further he might possibly spark a nuclear conflagration, while should he retreat it might look like surrender. Kennedy decided to gamble; he ignored Khrushchev's second letter and replied instead to his first. Consequently at 8 p.m., President Kennedy signed a letter which guaranteed an end to the blockade and to not invade Cuba if the Soviet Union withdrew its missiles. The world held its breath for the USSR's reply. The Kremlin was aware that time was running out, as they had been given 24 hours to reply to Kennedy's letter, and after some deliberation it was agreed to accept Kennedy's proposal. The acceptance was broadcast on Moscow Radio at 9 a.m. Sunday 28 October. Within hours, Kennedy had broadcast a statement of acknowledgement and the world breathed a collective sigh of relief.

In the USA the result was hailed as an American victory. In Moscow, Khrushchev also claimed a victory and hailed the conclusion as a triumph for common sense. Kennedy emerged as the young hero who kept his cool and taught the Soviets a lesson. His failure in the Bay of Pigs forgotten, Kennedy had become a world statesman and peacemaker, and the Democratic Party won their biggest majority in the Senate in 20 years only ten days after the crisis.

The USA and the Soviet Union had realized that the policy of brinkmanship – of pushing each other to the very brink of war – was too deadly a game, and with the existence of nuclear weapons it could result in worldwide catastrophe. It was decided to set up a 'Hot-line' teleprinter link between Moscow and Washington in order not to repeat the difficulties the two leaders had faced as they attempted to communicate directly during the crisis. The Cuban crisis had exposed the dangers of nuclear weapons and a series of nuclear arms control talks began, culminating in 1963 with a nuclear test ban treaty signed between the USA, Britain and the Soviet Union.

South-East Asia

In South-East Asia, particularly in Laos and South Vietnam, the perceived threat of Chinese communism against the pro-American governments in this area forced President Kennedy to strengthen the defence of that region. In Laos, where communist guerrilla warfare seemed to be gaining ground, he refused to involve US troops preferring instead to come to an agreement with the Soviet Union in Vienna in June 1961 whereby both the USA and the USSR agreed to support a neutral government in Laos.

In Vietnam, Kennedy was determined to act. Although small numbers of US military advisers had been present in South Vietnam for anti-guerrilla operations since 1954, they increased in numbers under the Kennedy administration from about 700 to more than 15,000. These military advisers were accompanied by an increase in the supply of equipment to the South Vietnamese army, although Kennedy stopped short of sending in US troops disguised as flood relief workers as advocated by General Maxwell Taylor and Walt Rostow. The latter was one of Kennedy's advisers who had reconnoitred the situation in South Vietnam. In addition to this, a 'strategic hamlet' programme was introduced whereby Vietnamese villagers were moved into defensive stockades in an attempt to deprive the Vietcong guerrillas of aid. This programme was bitterly resented by the Vietnamese villagers and proved to be a costly failure (see

Chapter 13). In spite of Kennedy's belief in the domino effect (that is, that should one country fall to communism others would follow suit) and his belief that 'Vietnam represents the cornerstone of the Free World in Southeast Asia', he showed no inclination to send in US troops. Notwithstanding this reticence to commit troops, Kennedy was prepared to withdraw US support for the South Vietnamese regime led by Ngo Dinh Diem and acquiesce to a coup to remove the leader, though the murders of both Diem and his brother Nhu during the coup deeply affected Kennedy.

Historians have debated whether Kennedy, had he not been assassinated, would have withdrawn the USA from involvement in Vietnam. Some point to the fact that he refused to become militarily involved, and cite Kennedy's television interview with Walter Cronkite on 3 September 1963 (where he emphasized that the war was one that the South Vietnamese had to win or lose themselves) as evidence that Kennedy had decided to withdraw from Vietnam. Others believe that Kennedy was merely continuing Eisenhower's policy, trying to put off the day when he would be forced to come to a difficult decision regarding the USA's future in Vietnam. Dean Rusk denied that Kennedy considered withdrawal from South-East Asia, and the speech Kennedy had prepared to give at Dallas Trade Mart on the fateful day of 22 November 1963 gave no indication of a change in policy: 'Our assistance to...nations can be painful, risky and costly, as is true in Southeast Asia today. But we dare not weary of the task.'

Assassination

John F. Kennedy was once asked how, if given the choice, he would prefer to die. 'You never know what's hit you,' he replied. 'A gunshot is the perfect way.'

In November 1963, while campaigning for the 1964 presidential election, Kennedy visited Florida and Texas, two of the most populated southern states. He had been warned that Texas might be hostile. Indeed, only a month earlier, Adlai Stevenson, US ambassador to the UN, had been spat upon and assaulted during a visit to Dallas. However, in San Antonio, Houston, and Fort Worth the crowds were friendly, and clearly delighted with Jacqueline Kennedy who accompanied her husband together with Vice-President Johnson and Mrs Johnson.

On arrival in Dallas it was decided that Kennedy and his party would travel in a motorcade of open-topped cars through the business district of Dallas, with one car and several motorcycles riding ahead of the presidential limousine which was, in turn, followed by a car carrying eight Secret Service agents and a car containing Lyndon Johnson and Ralph Yarborough. A large and enthusiastic crowd greeted the presidential party, and all along the route crowds of people stood applauding.

As the car passed the Texas School Book Depository, Governor Connally's wife said: 'Mr. President, you can't say that Dallas doesn't love you.' 'That's obvious,' replied Kennedy – his last words before he was shot.

At 12.30 p.m., shortly after the presidential limousine entered Elm Street, a shot was fired. Secret Service agent Roy Kellerman urged the driver, William Greer, 'Let's get out of here,' but Greer braked instead of accelerating away. Further bullets were fired and President Kennedy was hit by bullets in the head and the left shoulder, while another bullet hit Governor Connally in the back. The car rushed the President and Governor Connally to Parkland Memorial Hospital where the men were carried into separate emergency rooms. Connally had wounds to his back, chest, wrist and thigh; Kennedy's injuries were far more serious. He had a massive wound to the head and at 1 p.m. he was declared dead. Within two hours, Vice-President Johnson took the oath as President.

Meanwhile, back in Dealy Plaza, police investigations into the assassination were underway. Witnesses claimed they had seen shots being fired from two locations; from behind a wooden fence on the Grassy Knoll and from the Texas School Book Depository. During a search of the Texas School Book Depository, the police discovered three empty cartridge cases on the floor by one of the sixth-floor windows and a Mannlicher-Carcano rifle hidden beneath some boxes.

At 1.16 p.m., a Dallas police officer, J. D. Tippit, was shot by a man he had stopped to question on East 10th Street. Later, a manager of a shoe shop called the police after seeing a man acting suspiciously and hiding from passing police cars. The man had entered a cinema where he was later captured and arrested by police officers following a brief struggle. The man arrested was Lee Harvey Oswald, a 24-year-old ex-Marine, who worked at the Texas School Book Depository, and his palm print was later found on the rifle that had been found in the

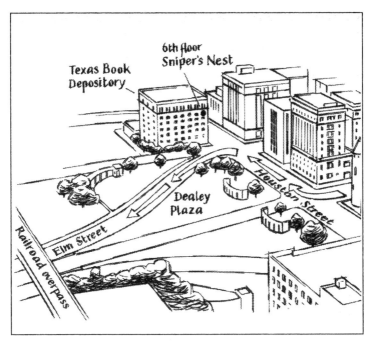

figure 8 map of Dealy Plaza

Depository. Several witnesses testified that they had seen Oswald at the sixth-floor window that day, but during his interrogation by the police Oswald denied he had been involved in the killing of Kennedy and claimed that he had been 'set up'. On 24 November 1963, the Dallas police decided to transfer Oswald to the county jail, but as he was led through the basement of police headquarters, a local nightclub owner, Jack Ruby, rushed forward and shot him fatally in the stomach.

On that same day, the President's body lay in state in the rotunda of the US Capitol prior to a state funeral attended by the leaders of 92 nations. A million people lined the route from the Capitol to St Matthew's Cathedral as a horse-drawn caisson carried the body to requiem Mass. Who can forget the haunting photo of Jacqueline Kennedy's dignified figure as she bade her husband farewell, holding the hand of her young daughter Caroline and watching her three-year-old son, John F. Kennedy Junior, saluting his father's casket?

President John Fitzgerald Kennedy was buried on a slope in Arlington National Cemetery where his grave is marked by an eternal flame. The assassination was a shattering event in the lives of most contemporary Americans. 'Where were you when Kennedy was shot?' was a frequent question asked in the years that followed, and was still asked for decades afterwards.

The Warren Commission

On November 29, President Johnson appointed a seven-member commission, headed by Chief Justice Earl Warren, to conduct a thorough investigation of the assassination of President Kennedy, and report to the nation. The commission's report, made public on 27 September 1964, concluded that the three shots which killed President Kennedy and wounded Governor Connally were fired from the sixth-floor window at the south-east corner of the Texas School Book Depository by Lee Harvey Oswald, who acted alone. The report also stated that the same bullet that penetrated the President's throat also caused Governor Connally's wounds. The Commission found no evidence that either Lee Harvey Oswald or Jack Ruby was part of any conspiracy, domestic or foreign, to assassinate President Kennedy, nor was there evidence of conspiracy, subversion, or disloyalty to the U.S. government by any federal, state, or local official.

In 1979, however, the House Select Committee on Assassinations concluded that, 'scientific acoustical evidence establishes a high probability that two gunmen fired at President John F. Kennedy,' and that, 'on the basis of the evidence available to it', President John F. Kennedy was probably assassinated as a result of a conspiracy of which Oswald probably was a part, and may also have included members of organized crime and/or anti-Castro Cubans.

The Committee was critical of both the Warren Commission, that had:

> ...failed to investigate adequately the possibility of a conspiracy to assassinate the President.

and of the Secret Service which was:

> ...deficient in the performance of its duties. The Secret Service possessed information that was not properly analyzed, investigated or used by the Secret Service in connection with the President's trip to Dallas; moreover, Secret Service agents in the motorcade were inadequately prepared to protect the President from a sniper.

The House Select Committee on Assassinations refused to publish all the documents obtained during the investigation but it is expected that they will be published in 2017.

In 1998, a congressional records review board discounted the 1979 finding and confirmed that Oswald acted alone.

Conspiracy theories

It seems incredible that so many theories have come to light regarding who assassinated John F. Kennedy. Perhaps the most likely reason for this is the explanation put forward by William Manchester:

> ...if you put the murdered President of the United States on one side of a scale and that wretched waif Oswald on the other side, it doesn't balance. You want to add something weightier to Oswald. It would invest the President's death with meaning, endowing him with martyrdom. He would have died for something...A conspiracy would, of course, do the job nicely.

(William Manchester, *The Death of a President*,
Galahad Books, 1967)

The conspiracy theories are many and varied, and some are given more credence than others.

The Warren Commission came to the conclusion that Kennedy was assassinated by a lone gunman, Lee Harvey Oswald, a theory that has been supported by several other investigators. Yet this theory has its weaknesses: according to the Commission, Oswald had accurately fired a cheap rifle with distorted sight at a moving target using old ammunition, and succeeded in making two hits with three shots in 5.6 seconds. It was clear at the time that Oswald could not fire his bolt-action rifle fast enough to wound both the President and Governor Connally with separate shots, therefore the commission developed the so-called 'magic bullet' theory which argued that a single bullet hit Kennedy in the back of the neck and exited from the throat just below the Adam's apple. The same bullet then entered Connally's back, exited from his chest, went completely through his right wrist, and lodged in his left thigh.

Anthony Summers, the author of *The Kennedy Conspiracy* (1980), believes that Kennedy was killed by a group of anti-Castro activists, funded by Mafia mobsters who had been thrown out of Cuba following Castro's revolution, and that some members of the CIA took part in this conspiracy. The House Select Committee on Assassinations also discovered evidence to suggest that anti-Castro Cubans were involved in the assassination.

Several theories have been put forward by Jack Anderson and Michael Kurtz to suggest that Fidel Castro ordered the assassination of Kennedy. This is a natural enough theory considering the Bay of Pigs debacle, the CIA's plots against the Cuban leader's life and the many US military plans for the invasion of Cuba. Yet on hearing of Kennedy's death, Castro reacted grimly saying, 'This is bad news.' Castro was convinced that the forces that conspired against Kennedy were also out to get Cuba, and he prepared his troops for a US invasion. In a two-hour speech broadcast on Cuban radio and television on November 23, Castro warned the Cuban people that Kennedy's death, 'may have very negative repercussions with regard to the interests of our country.'

The hand of the Mafia has been seen behind the assassination of the President. The Mafia had lost their gambling interests in Havana when Castro seized power, and had been disappointed when the Kennedy administration failed to reverse the situation. Furthermore, President Kennedy appointed his brother, Robert, as Attorney General, and proceeded to conduct an all-out war against the Mafia and organized crime, with great success. The instinct of the Mafia was to kill Robert Kennedy, but they knew that this would only cause the President to pursue his policies more vigorously. According to Edward Reid's book, *The Grim Reapers* (1969), one Mafia boss, Carlos Marcello, was determined to assassinate the President first; if the President was removed, the Attorney General would be replaced by the President's successor, since the appointment was one of patronage.

Matthew Smith, in his book, *JFK: The Second Plot* (Trafalgar Square, 1992), claims that the oil industry was involved in the assassination:

> The oil industry in Texas had enjoyed huge tax concessions since 1926, when Congress had provided them as an incentive to increase much needed prospecting…John Kennedy had declared an intention to review the oil industry revenues. There was nothing in the world which would have inflamed the oil barons more than the President interfering.

Even the CIA has been implicated in the assassination of John F. Kennedy. Daniel Marvin had volunteered for counter insurgency and guerrilla warfare training while in the US army, and in 1964 became a student at the Special Warfare Centre in Fort Bragg, North Carolina. There he remembers attending lectures from CIA 'advisers' on the events in Dallas in 1963. He recalls feeling:

> …that our CIA instructors had first-hand knowledge of what happened in Dallas. During a coffee break one day, an instructor casually remarked on the 'success of the conspiracy in Dallas,' tending to confirm my suspicions that the President's murder was conceived, executed and covered up by high-level echelons within our government.

Kennedy's life and the subsequent conspiracy theories surrounding his death have been the inspiration for many films. These include Nigel Turner's 1988 mini-series, *The Men Who Killed Kennedy*, Oliver Stone's 1991 blockbuster, *JFK*, and 1993's *JFK: Reckless Youth*, which looked at Kennedy's early years.

The President's health

In November 2002, long-secret medical records were made public, revealing that Kennedy's physical ailments were more severe than previously thought. He was in constant pain from fractured vertebrae, despite multiple medications, and in addition suffered from severe digestive problems and Addison's disease. Under observation by an army of doctors for most of his life, three physicians treated him during his presidency: his official doctor, who was a navy officer; Dr Janet Travell, who injected novocain into Kennedy's back muscles to deaden pain for two hours at a time, sometimes several times a day; and Dr Max Jacobson, who gave Kennedy amphetamines so he could be bright-eyed and bushy-tailed when meeting his public.

Moreover, Kennedy took Demerol, a controlled pain killer that Jackie got from a Secret Service guard. Alistair Cooke, in one of his *Letter from America* broadcasts for the BBC, recalls how, when watching missiles being tested from the safety of a US warship, he noticed a rocking chair being carried to the bridge from the presidential helicopter. On enquiring about this incongruous object he was told that it belonged to the President who frequently used the rocking motion of the chair to alleviate the constant pain he suffered.

The President's love life

Kennedy is well known for his many affairs with a succession of women; during his time as a congressman in Georgetown, women were frequently seen around his residence. There were reports that he would take one girl out for dinner, and a different girl would come down to breakfast the next morning. As President, he had two girls in the typing pool that he could always fall back on. He famously told Harold MacMillan that if he didn't have a woman every two or three days, he got terrible headaches! His personal secretary, Evelyn Lincoln, recalls that Kennedy even asked her to help sneak women into the White House: 'You know women chased him. Let's face it. There were young women. There were older women. They all did. I spent half of my time talking to women' (CNN Interview, 18 March, 1998). In Seymour Hersh's book, *Dark Side of Camelot*, (1998), there are many details about Kennedy's extra-marital affairs and it is widely believed that the President had affairs with no less than Marilyn Monroe and also the girlfriend of a notorious Mafia boss. It is interesting to note that the media during Kennedy's presidency did not report any of his shenanigans – it is difficult to imagine them turning a blind eye today!

Vietnam

This chapter will cover:
- the reasons that the USA became involved in South-East Asia
- the tactics used by US troops and why they were ineffective
- the effect the war had on US society
- the role played by the media in bringing about the end of the war.

The words of Country Joe McDonald and the Fish's song 'I-Feel-Like-I'm-Fixin'-To-Die-Rag' (1965) made some very perceptive observations about the causes of the war that developed in South-East Asia. Anti-communist feeling was clearly high on the singer's list of causes, but he also referred to the amount of money that could be made by the armaments industry by going to war, and a general gung-ho attitude on the part of the American public. Perhaps his most memorable verse brings home the reality of war:

Come on mothers throughout the land:
Pack your boys off to Vietnam.
Come on fathers don't hesitate,
Send your sons off before it's too late.
You can be the first one on your block
To have your boy come home in a box.

Between 1961 and 1975, 56,869 US troops were killed and another 153,329 were seriously wounded. The long-term psychological damage to the 3 million soldiers who fought in Vietnam, and the resulting social problems are still being counted. How did the USA become embroiled in such a war so far from home?

Before the Second World War, Vietnam, known then as Indo-China, was part of the French empire. During the war the Japanese had conquered Indo-China and were resisted by the Viet Nam Doc Lap Dong Minh Hoi (Vietminh) – the league for the independence of Vietnam – led by Ho Chi Minh who organized a guerrilla resistance to the occupying power. The Vietminh accepted members of many different political opinions, united by the desire to fight for freedom from both the Japanese and the French, and had the support of the USA during the war. The Vietminh were led by General Vo Nguyen Giap, a former history teacher, who trained elite groups of guerrillas, both male and female, in the art of jungle fighting. At the end of the Second World War, France resumed the running of the area. Ho Chi Minh and his supporters had hoped to create a country free from external influence, and a bitter war resulted. The USA criticized France's policy in Indo-China, but it soon became clear that the USA believed the Vietminh were receiving aid from the USSR. Taken in conjunction with the establishment of a Communist government in China, the USA reassessed their policy of supporting independence for all colonial people and supported France's efforts to re-establish her empire in the area in an attempt to stop the spread of communism. In spite of this support and initial military successes, the war went badly for France and 8,000 troops were killed in Dien Bien Phu in 1954. With a total of 90,000 French troops killed, wounded or missing, the French surrendered. Despite the huge amount of financial aid provided by USA, the French blamed their defeat on the Americans for refusing to send in US aircraft manned by military crews. As it was, the defeat at Dien Bien Phu was too much for the French, who agreed to most of the Vietminh demands at peace talks held in Geneva. The Geneva Agreement that resulted from this meeting between the Great Powers instructed that Indo-China be divided into the independent states of Cambodia, Laos and Vietnam. Vietnam was to be divided in two at the seventeenth parallel, and all foreign troops were to leave the country. Free elections were to be held in 1956 and a multi-party system of government created, then Vietnam would be reunited. The Americans were critical of the French, calling the French Premier a 'peace-at-any-price man,' and refused either to play a principal role in the negotiations or to sign the Geneva Agreement. However, a spokesman for the US government did say it would take a dim view of any 'violation of the armistice', although it also promised to refrain from threatening or using force.

In the North of Vietnam, Ho Chi Minh created a communist government, while in the South, Ngo Dinh Diem created the Republic of Vietnam which was supported by the USA. Yet this was not a satisfactory state of affairs as Dien's government was nationalist, Catholic, anti-communist and nepotistic, ruled by and for himself, his family and friends. The elections referred to in the Geneva Agreement were never held because Diem feared that elections in the North would be rigged by the communists. The USA ignored this violation of the Geneva Agreement, possibly because of the domestic situation at the time where anti-communism had become something of an obsession. In 1954, the South East Asia Treaty Organization (SEATO) was formed whose members – Australia, France, New Zealand, Pakistan, the Philippines, Thailand, the UK and the USA – all pledged to protect the countries of South-East Asia from the spread of communism.

The domino theory

The Secretary of State under President Eisenhower was John Foster Dulles, a vehement anti-communist who adhered to the 'domino theory' – if one pro-Western government in Asia fell to communism it could, in turn, 'push over' its neighbours into the arms of the communists one by one like a line of dominoes.

In Washington, Eisenhower warned the incoming President Kennedy of the dangers of South-East Asia becoming a communist area; Vietnam could turn out to be another 'domino' which could lead to the fall of all the other countries in the area, and even India, which could then threaten Europe. Kennedy was well aware of the area's importance and as early as 1956 he had stated in a speech: 'Vietnam represents the cornerstone of the Free World in Southeast Asia...We cannot ignore its needs' (*The Cold War*, C. B. Jones, Hodder and Stoughton, 2004) (see also page 186).

13 The guerrillas return

Ho Chi Minh's government in the North was so authoritarian that millions of refugees fled to the South, but along with these refugees came a more dangerous group of migrants. From 1960 onwards, guerrilla troops (the National Front for the Liberation of South Vietnam) were being trained in the North. These guerrillas were known as the Vietcong (Vietnamese Communists) and terrorized villages in the South in order to obtain food, shelter, information and recruits to the communist cause. The Vietcong received supplies from the North along a series of routes known as the 'Ho Chi Minh Trail' which passed through the jungle and highlands of neighbouring Laos. Kennedy warned that the communist threat was growing: 'Our problems are critical...The news will be worse before it gets better.'

Neither the Vietnamese police force nor the Army of the Republic of Vietnam (ARVN) had the necessary training to deal with the Vietcong and the situation seemed to be lapsing into chaos. Although the USA viewed the activities of North Vietnam as threatening the free world, Washington was uncertain how best to react to the rise of communism in the area. It should be remembered that Kennedy was preoccupied with problems in Cuba and Berlin at the time, consequently the President refused to send US combat forces to South-East Asia but was happy to send military advisers to train South Vietnam in how to deal with domestic insurgents. There were 3,000 US military personnel in Vietnam by the end of 1961, but during 1962 the situation worsened, and the numbers increased to over 11,500 after Kennedy created the American Military Assistance Command.

The idea behind the advice from the US advisers was that the South Vietnamese government would take the initiative, forcing the Vietcong out into the open to fight the ARVN. They even went so far as to devise a plan to place Vietnamese peasants into 'villages' surrounded by stockades, known as 'strategic hamlets', which would then deprive the Vietcong of the villagers' support on which they depended for food, shelter and recruits. This plan was unpopular with the South Vietnamese peasants, and may well have contributed more recruits to the Vietcong cause. It is estimated that of the 8,000 strategic hamlets, only 1,000 were judged to be secure. The Vietcong were dangerous as the clash at Ap Bac in January 1963 proved; at a price of only three Vietcong lives, 61 South Vietnamese were killed, 100 wounded and five helicopters destroyed.

Opposition to Diem's regime

Diem's government become increasingly unpopular in the South: government officials from the cities were placed in charge of the countryside even though their knowledge and understanding of farming was minimal; Diem had become more and more intolerant of other religions and the Buddhists were singled out for particular attention – their pagodas raided, shrines destroyed and monks arrested. This persecution became so bad that several Buddhist monks doused themselves in petrol and set themselves alight – their self-immolation a public protest about Diem's policies. The prize-winning photograph of the Buddhist monk Father 'Spreading Virtue' overwhelmed by flames deeply affected president Kennedy, and he became increasingly opposed to Diem's regime.

An assistant Secretary of State for the Far East drafted a telegram to the US Ambassador in Saigon suggesting that the search begin for a successor to Diem. This was hastily approved by the President and his advisers but was interpreted by Ambassador Lodge as orders to organize a coup against Diem; orders were issued accordingly to the CIA station in Saigon. The following week saw heated disagreements in Washington about the wisdom of this course of action and Kennedy cabled the Ambassador warning him that he should be prepared to call a halt at the very last minute should Kennedy decide to reverse his previous decision.

Diem was unaware of this plotting and refused to accept that his regime was repressing the Vietnamese people. Washington announced its intention to withdraw 1,000 military personnel from the country by the end of 1963, but on 1 November 1963 a coup led by South Vietnamese rebel generals seized the presidential palace and key services in Saigon. Diem, faced with this fait accompli, agreed to stand down, left the palace and sought refuge in a church. From here, Diem and his brother were persuaded to go to the rebel headquarters in an armoured personnel carrier. When the doors of the vehicle were opened, the bodies of Diem and his brother with their hands tied behind their backs were found – they had been shot. On being told of the murders, President Kennedy was visibly shaken – within three weeks he too had been assassinated.

President Lyndon B. Johnson 1963–9

When Lyndon B. Johnson became President in November 1963, he was faced with several options on Vietnam: he could negotiate an agreement with the North about the future of Vietnam; send in the Marines; pull out of the area and watch the 'dominoes fall'; or continue with the same policy as his predecessor. Johnson decided on the latter course of action. Privately, he admitted that he felt Vietnam was not worth fighting for, yet he acknowledged that there seemed to be no way out of the quagmire. Historians have gone so far as to devise a theory known as the 'quagmire' theory to explain why the USA became increasingly involved in Vietnam. At each step taken by the USA there was the hope that by escalating involvement the conflict could be brought to an end; in reality, instead of bringing the conflict to a conclusion, the USA became more and more bogged down. Rather than leading to victory, each step led to a greater investment of money, troops, and prestige which continued and escalated the struggle.

Other historians have devised the 'stalemate' theory which argues that the USA had invested such a lot in Vietnam that each regime escalated the conflict in an attempt to avoid defeat, willing to accept stalemate rather than risk a humiliating defeat. Certainly it was almost impossible, given the anti-communist atmosphere in the USA during the 1950s and 1960s, for any President to withdraw from Vietnam and risk loss of face. In addition, any President brave enough to have withdrawn from Vietnam would have to have explained why so many human, military and financial resources had been wasted – what President would have wanted to explain that to the electorate?

It was President Johnson who finally decided that the only way the USA could win was by sending in tens of thousands of troops, and so he that took the USA in a different, dangerous direction.

The Gulf of Tonkin

In August 1964, North Vietnamese patrol boats fired upon US naval vessels that were conducting surveillance in international waters in the Gulf of Tonkin. The USA had been spying on Soviet-built anti-aircraft missile bases and radar stations along the Gulf of Tonkin. South Vietnamese patrol boats had attacked these stations while the USS *Maddox* had monitored events in order to assess the effect that this type of attack would have on these bases. On 2 August, there had been a skirmish when the *Maddox* had been fired on by a North Vietnamese torpedo vessel during which one of the torpedo boats was sunk and the other two were damaged. Two days later, reports came through of further attacks and the US government reacted with outrage at this unprovoked aggression.

It is unlikely that the second encounter ever took place; the *Maddox* had been pounded by a tropical storm and had intercepted messages which implied that they were about to be attacked by North Vietnamese torpedo boats. The destroyers' equipment had been affected by the storm, leading the crews to believe that torpedoes had been fired at them. Air support from a nearby carrier could find no evidence of a North Vietnamese naval attack on one of the destroyers in the area – the *Turner Joy* – which claimed to have been attacked, but Johnson, anxious to reinvigorate the presidential election campaign, immediately ordered the first bombing of North Vietnamese bases in retaliation. He also went before Congress to seek a resolution which would give him the power to take necessary measures to defend US forces and to prevent further aggression. The proposed resolution went further and gave the President the sole responsibility for determining when peace and security had been established in the area. On 7 August, after a superficial debate, Congress passed the Gulf of Tonkin resolution which gave Johnson the authority to conduct the conflict in any way he saw fit. When Johnson won the presidential election, he gained a public mandate for his plan to take a firm stand against communism in South-East Asia.

In December 1964, Johnson gave orders to bomb the Ho Chi Minh Trail, but not North Vietnam. On 6 February 1965, the Vietcong attacked the US base at Pleiku causing much damage to aircraft and personnel. This attack outraged public opinion in the USA and gave Johnson the excuse he needed to bomb the North.

Operation Rolling Thunder

On 11 February 1965, a joint air attack was launched by the USA and ARVN on key military and industrial targets in North Vietnam. This attack was of such intensity that it was called 'Operation Rolling Thunder'. The aim of the bombing was, as Johnson himself said: 'To increase the confidence of the brave people of South Vietnam, to convince the leaders of North Vietnam that we will not be defeated, and to reduce the flow of men and supplies from the North.'

It was hoped that this campaign would eliminate the need to commit US troops to the war on the ground, and became Johnson's main weapon in trying to force the North Vietnamese government into peace talks. There was no declaration of war on North Vietnam for fear that the US might get involved in a war with China, but even so the bombing campaign was a serious escalation of the war. In fact, according to Charles Kamps in his book *The History of the Vietnam War*, (1968), because Operation Rolling Thunder did not bomb North Vietnam's biggest cities, Hanoi and Haiphong, for fear the USSR be drawn into the conflict, it created large safe areas: '...which protected 80% of North Vietnam's industry and 75% of its population'.

The first six months of air raids on restricted targets had little effect, and the flow of men and resources from North to South continued. In 1966, saturation bombing replaced selective bombing using B-52 bombers which flew at an altitude of more than 15,000 m (49,215 ft) high and carried 28 two-tonne bombs. These planes flew so high that they could neither be seen nor heard from the ground, which gave the people on the ground little chance to shelter. The bombs left gigantic craters and destroyed anything within 0.5 km (0.8 miles) of the impact. It is estimated that by 1970 the Americans had dropped more bombs on Vietnam than they had on any other previous target; more explosives even than were dropped by all nations during the Second World War. Yet the morale of the North Vietnamese remained high, strengthening the areas around Hanoi and Haiphong with anti-aircraft guns, surface to air missiles (SAM) supplied by the USSR, and Soviet Mig-17 and Mig-21PF fighters with air to air missiles. On a huge billboard in the centre of Hanoi, the number of US planes shot down was revised almost daily.

Increasing ground troops

In the spring of 1965, 3,500 US marines were sent to protect the US bomber base in Danang following a request by General William Westmoreland. These marines were not advisers but fully-equipped soldiers ready for war. This negated Johnson's promise to the American people: 'We are not about to send American boys nine or ten thousand miles away from home to do what Asian boys ought to be doing for themselves'.

In 1964, there were 16,000 US troops in South Vietnam; by 1966 there were 268,000; by January 1968 the number had reached over 500,000. The War had become 'Americanized'.

General Westmoreland, the commanding General in Vietnam, had three main objectives: to defend American bases and installations; to initiate search and destroy missions on the Vietcong; and to conduct 'mopping up' operations against the remaining communists. He pursued these objectives against a background of continued bombing, but there was also some attempt made to 'win the hearts and minds' of the Vietnamese population. The Americans supplied aid in an attempt to stabilize the countryside by making the peasants prosperous and loyal to the non-communist regime. They built schools, dug wells and provided tools, seed, cattle, chickens and pigs to enable farmers to re-establish themselves. The pacification programme was partially successful, but because it was devised in haste and was not given enough time to develop, often the 'pacification' was little more than bullying of village communities. Furthermore, the Vietcong's influence could return at any time, especially if US actions were extreme and alienated the people.

In reality, the overall aim of the US forces in Vietnam was simple, almost arithmetical: to kill as many communists as possible. Yet even though the body count was high, the Vietcong continued to attract willing recruits. As Ho Chi Minh said: 'You may kill ten of my men for every one I kill of yours. But even at those odds, you will lose and I will win' (*The Cold War*, C. B. Jones, Hodder and Stoughton, 2004). It was clear the Vietcong and North Vietnamese were prepared to accept huge losses rather than accept defeat, unlike the US. While the huge financial and human cost of the war put pressure on the US to bring the war to a speedy conclusion, the Vietcong, fighting a low-tech war on home ground, could afford to continue their guerrilla attacks for years.

As there was no discernable front line in the war, General Westmoreland established a series of supply bases along the coast. These were as large as some towns, were heavily fortified and had their own airport and harbour, which allowed them to be supplied from the sea if necessary. These huge bases supplied smaller 'firebases' – local strongholds from which units went out on 'search and destroy' missions.

Much use was made of helicopters to overcome the problems of transporting troops through Vietnam's swamps, paddy fields and hilly jungles. In addition, the helicopters were used as gunships armed with rocket launchers and machine guns and as transport for heavy goods such as vehicles, ammunition, boats and supplies. They were an integral part of the search and destroy missions, moving troops into position while saturating the ground with machine-gun fire and rockets.

Search and destroy

In spite of the increase in the number of US troops, the Vietcong continued to extend its hold on the countryside. The guerrillas were joined by regular soldiers from the North Vietnamese Army (NVA) who gradually moved into the South in 1965. The Vietcong tended to be recruited from the people who had lived in or escaped from South Vietnam while the North Vietnamese Army (NVA) was recruited from among the North Vietnamese people. The Vietcong and NVA would first infiltrate the country and mix with the people, gaining their support by threats or by persuasion; once established, small units would commence a series of guerrilla attacks against the US and ARVN forces. Because the Vietcong and NVA were heavily outnumbered, direct confrontation was avoided and tactics such as ambushes, traps, camouflage and attacks on isolated units were used instead. Conventional fighting using tanks and artillery was only used in certain circumstances such as the Tet Offensive of 1968 (see p. 207).

In 1966, the Americans began a series of missions designed to hunt down NVA units and members of the Vietcong; these were the search and destroy missions. Army units were sent into the villages and countryside to seek out and destroy any Vietcong they could find, frequently using helicopters which could land the troops close to the villages and areas they were going to search, thus giving the Vietcong little warning of an attack. These missions would go through a village with a fine-tooth comb, often burning down the whole village if suspicious equipment or food supplies were found. As it was so difficult to distinguish between the VC and ordinary villagers it became all too easy for US GIs to shoot first and ask questions later. With the average age of GIs being 19, inexperience and nervousness led to mistakes on these search and destroy missions. The use of drugs by US troops as an escape from the horrors of war was routine; heroin from Laos was easily available and smoking marijuana or dope was commonplace. Atrocities took place which turned the Vietnamese people against the Americans and the American public against the war. The Vietcong followed a similar policy to the US search and destroy, but named rather more obviously 'Search and Kill' missions. As one soldier noted, 'It was us looking for him, looking for us, looking for him.'

Vietcong tactics

In order to protect themselves from air attack, the Vietcong began to dig tunnels. At first these were simple dug-outs, but these became increasingly sophisticated – some even having hospitals, kitchens, storerooms and sleeping accommodation. The US claimed that these tunnels were evidence that the Vietcong were so demoralized by the US bombing raids that they were being forced to live underground; in fact the sophisticated nature of the tunnel complexes and the skilful way in which they were used by the Vietcong was evidence that, far from being demoralized, the Vietcong had adapted to the circumstances in which they found themselves and continued to fight undeterred.

Vietcong booby-traps were feared by the US GIs. Some were simply holes dug in paths, which were hidden and could break a leg or ankle – not fatal but enough to disable US soldiers and put them out of action. More deadly was the use of the punji trap – a hole with bamboo or metal spikes at the bottom, frequently covered with poison designed to injure and cause blood poisoning this could prove fatal if not treated quickly. A Bouncing Betty was a concealed mine which exploded up into the air and in all directions, taking with it the hapless GIs who were in its vicinity. One GI recalled hearing a Bouncing Betty going off, rushing to help the party who had been attacked, to find out of the eight men in that unit only two had survived; the rest were a 'mixture of skin, red meat and white bones'. The Vietcong often used grenades with the pins removed, but with the firing mechanism secured temporarily with a rubber band; these could be placed in tin cans and attached to a trip wire, or placed inside a fuel tank until the rubber band perished in the petrol and caused an unexpected explosion.

The Vietcong were supplied via the Ho Chi Minh Trail, a 1,000-km (1609-mile) route from North to South through the forested highland region on the borders of Vietnam, Laos and Cambodia. The trail was a complex series of paths with a workforce of 40,000 people which kept the traffic flowing along it. US planes found it difficult to spot the trail as it was protected by canopies of trees with dense tropical foliage. Most supplies were transported by bicycle or carried on the backs of porters, therefore bombing of roads and means of communication had little effect on the supply chain. Nevertheless, Washington was reluctant to cease bombing for fear that the USA would look weak. In the South, in an attempt to deprive the Vietcong of their forest cover, the Americans employed chemical herbicides to defoliate the trees and destroy the rice crops on which the Vietcong depended for food. The most notorious of these defoliants was 'Agent Orange' – a defoliant which contained dioxin, a carcinogenic substance which poisoned not only the rivers and streams and the Vietnamese people, but also the US personnel who loaded the chemical barrels onto the planes. The long-term effect of Agent Orange was to pollute the rivers and streams and the fragile eco-system, and also the Vietnamese people. By the end of the war, over 25,000 sq km (9,622 sq miles) of rainforest and crop land and the mangrove swamps of the Mekong Delta had been devastated by defoliants administered by the special air force crews that flew the defoliation missions. These crews were known as the 'Ranch Hands' and their motto was, 'Only we can prevent forests'.

The My Lai massacre 1968

On 16 March 1968, nine black helicopter gunships landed near to a small Vietnamese costal village, My Lai. Three platoons of US soldiers left the helicopters to conduct a search and destroy mission, and for the next two hours one of the platoons, led by Lieutenant William Calley, killed a large number of the village's 700 inhabitants in cold blood – the exact number is unknown; official figures put it at 175, but it could have been as high as 500. The villagers were all assumed to be Vietcong sympathizers, and the soldiers were given the order to kill and destroy everything that was in the village – there were to be no prisoners. Although the massacre took place in March 1968, the facts did not come to light until November 1969 when one of the participants in the massacre was interviewed on US television. Public opinion demanded an official enquiry, and the evidence from the men who had taken part together with photographs taken by an official US army photographer confirmed that the massacre had indeed taken place. The soldiers reacted to the public outcry in a variety of ways; some expressed remorse, others admitted their guilt, some put the blame on others, most claimed they were only obeying orders. Lieutenant Calley stated that it was, 'No big deal, Sir'. He was sentenced to life imprisonment with hard labour, but was released having served only three years. To some, Calley was a hero, and a song called 'The Battle Hymn of Lt. Calley,' sold 200,000 copies, but to the majority of the American people, news of the massacre was so horrific that they began to question the wisdom of continuing the war.

The Tet offensive 1968

In January every year the Vietnamese celebrate the Tet festival, which marks the lunar New Year, and January 1968 was no exception. The 500,000 US soldiers stationed in Vietnam had become complacent, and were convinced they were winning the war, having won every set piece battle up until then. North and South Vietnam both celebrated the Tet festival, and a ceasefire was observed by both sides for one week. However, on the 31 January the communists launched a co-ordinated rocket and mortar attack on over 100 cities (including the capital Saigon), towns and military bases all over South Vietnam. The noise of these attacks was disguised by the sounds of fireworks and merry-making, and as a result troops found it difficult to distinguish between the two and difficult to retaliate. The fighting had spilled over from the countryside into the towns and spread across the whole of South Vietnam. Vietcong guerrillas fought pitched battles with US and ARVN forces in the Saigon streets and even launched a massive suicide attack on the US Embassy. One US military base in Khesanh was surrounded and vastly outnumbered, and there were fears that it would suffer the same fate as Dien Bien Phu. That it did not was more to do with luck than anything else.

The Tet offensive had been a new departure for the communists and had exposed their soldiers to direct action against the enemy. They had expected to gain the support of the people of South Vietnam; this did not happen. Over 100,000 people were killed during the offensive. It was a serious setback for the Vietcong, killing at least 30,000 of them and dealing a blow from which it never recovered. Therafter, the major role was taken by the NVA.

In the USA, the public was horrified. As Walter Cronkite, a leading US newscaster observed: 'What the hell is going on? I thought we were winning the war?'

The US army was convinced they were winning the war and that the Tet offensive had been a victory for the US troops; the US media did not agree and decided that the war could not be won – the politicians agreed with them. In fact, the Tet offensive was not the success for the communists that it appeared to be because it did not ignite a popular rising throughout South Vietnam and huge numbers of the Vietcong's best troops had been lost. The communist's resources had been severely weakened and their ability to strike in future reduced; but in propaganda terms, the Tet offensive had been a resounding success.

Protest and the media

In the USA public opposition to the war in Vietnam first became vocal when the government was forced to draft more than 11 times as many young men into the army as they had done previously; in October 1968, 33,000 were drafted. The number of draft-dodgers increased, with many burning their draft cards, escaping to Europe or Canada, obtaining medical certificates or getting married. As one newspaper correspondent put it, 'Everybody's got an angle.' Muhammad Ali, the world heavyweight boxing champion, had his boxing title taken away from him because he resisted the draft. Many white, educated and well-off middle-class Americans were able to avoid the draft while the poorer Americans, many of them black, were unable to escape. Over 25 per cent of the foot soldiers, or 'grunts' as they were known, came from families with incomes below the poverty line, and a disproportionate number of these, 10.6 per cent, were black.

As the fighting grew more intense, the numbers of 'body bags' returning from Vietnam grew, reaching a peak in May 1968 when 562 US soldiers were killed in a single week. Increasingly, the public became convinced that the sacrifice made by these soldiers was pointless, and riots and demonstrations against the war were seen across the USA and in front of US Embassies worldwide. Public opinion in the USA turned decisively against the war as the chant, 'Hey, hey LBJ; how many kids did you kill today?' indicated. Johnson was said to be heart-broken when he heard this chant and, on 31 March 1968, he made a television broadcast announcing that the USA would stop all bombing above the twentieth parallel, in the hope that peace talks might be encouraged to take place. Johnson also announced his decision not to run in the forthcoming presidential elections in November; Hubert Humphrey was the Democrat's choice as presidential candidate while Richard Nixon was nominated as the Republican candidate.

It should be remembered that the 1960s was generally a time of protest for the young, who questioned everything the older generation held to be sacred, but when Vietnam veterans also began to protest against the war, older people began to take notice – after all these were no draft-dodgers. On 25 April 1971, a huge crowd of some 300,000 took part in the Veterans' march in Washington DC and many threw the medals they had won in Vietnam onto the steps of the Capitol, a gesture which deeply shocked many Americans.

Peace talks

Preliminary peace talks had begun in Paris in May 1968, following the Tet offensive in January of that year, but soon ran aground on the issue of who was to sit at the negotiating table. President Thieu of South Vietnam refused to negotiate if the Vietcong were present, and was encouraged by Nixon who promised him a better deal under the Republicans. On 5 November, Nixon was narrowly elected President, but his 'new team' with 'fresh ideas' did not end the fighting in Vietnam for another five years.

Vietnamization

In June 1969, the new US President decided on a process of Vietnamization – the South Vietnamese were to take over their own defence and the responsibility for conducting the war. The first US troops were withdrawn and, in 1970, the US pulled out a further 150,000 ground fighting troops while continuing its air support to the South. This move was not greeted with approval by the US commanders in the field as they still believed they could win the war. Nixon was in a difficult situation as public opinion grew more and more vocal and anti-war, especially after the Kent State University massacre in May 1970 where four students were killed by the National Guard (see Chapter 14).

By the end of 1971, only 140,000 US soldiers remained in Vietnam, and Nixon had promised that they too would be withdrawn by 1972. This had a disastrous effect on the morale of the troops: many tried to avoid taking part in search and destroy missions; some attacked or even murdered overenthusiastic officers; many deserted; some wore peace symbols on their helmets; and drugs such as alcohol, heroin and marijuana continued to be a refuge for many, a way of coping with the horror of it all.

In March 1972, the NVA invaded the South in a massive campaign led by 100 Soviet tanks expecting an easy victory as so many US troops had been withdrawn. Nixon retaliated by ordering a massive bombing campaign, code name Linebacker, which devastated the North Vietnamese infrastructure using B-52 bombers and 'smart bombs' guided by lasers. In spite of worldwide protests, Nixon knew that it was unlikely that either the USSR or China would come to Hanoi's aid as he had arranged summit meetings with both countries earlier in the year. In August 1972, the Politburo in Hanoi voted to authorize a negotiated settlement and proposed a ceasefire, well aware that they could extract better terms by casting Nixon in the role of peacemaker, thus boosting his image in the eyes of the US public in time for the presidential election in November; Nixon won the election with a landslide result. A month later peace negotiations broke down. Nixon attempted to force Hanoi into an agreement with a B-52 bombing campaign for 12 days over Christmas; it was described as, 'the most murderous aerial bombardment in the history of the world' according to one US Senator, and over 36,000 tonnes of bombs were dropped in a matter of days. Hanoi returned to the negotiating table.

Within a month, a ceasefire agreement was signed in Paris. These Paris Accords led to the withdrawal of US troops and the return of prisoners; Vietcong troops were allowed to remain in the South against Thieu's wishes; the South was to continue to receive US economic aid and military assistance should Hanoi resume military action; the most important issue of who would govern South Vietnam was left unresolved, and the agreement was unsupervised which meant that there was little that could be done should either side break the terms of the agreement. On March 29 1973 the last group of US soldiers left Vietnam, and to many Americans that was the end of the war. Aid to South Vietnam was reduced as many believed it was no longer necessary because a ceasefire had been signed. The US navy mine sweepers cleared mines in North Vietnamese waters and 600 US Prisoners of War were returned by the North. Later that year Dr Henry Kissinger (Nixon's chief foreign policy adviser and negotiator) and Le Duc Tho (North Vietnam's chief negotiator at the Paris peace talks) were jointly awarded the Nobel Peace Prize for their work in negotiating the ceasefire.

Renewal of war

The Vietnamese people still had to endure fighting for another two years. The aid promised to the South began to falter as Nixon and his regime became entangled in the Watergate affair. South Vietnam suffered massive inflation, huge unemployment and terrible corruption, which led to the growth of internal unrest and dissatisfaction with the government. In 1975, the North launched yet another attack, capturing the Central Highlands and advancing inexorably towards Saigon. The same year also saw the triumph of communist armies in Laos and Cambodia. The domino effect so feared by Eisenhower had indeed come to pass.

In Saigon there were scenes of chaos as Americans and Vietnamese tried to flee the city as the communists advanced. The last helicopters containing Americans and some Vietnamese took off from the rooftop of the US Embassy in Saigon on 29 April 1975.

The terrible sight of South Vietnamese refugees trying to cling on to the overloaded helicopters, some falling to their deaths, was watched on television around the world. People held up their children over the barbed wire fence encircling the US Embassy, asking Americans to take them. On 30 April, a North Vietnamese tank crashed through the gates of South Vietnam's presidential palace and Vietnam was reunited under communist rule: a humiliating end to the USA's longest war.

Why did the US fail in Vietnam?

The tactics used by the US military in Vietnam were, by and large, inappropriate, and many of the US commanders, trained in conventional warfare, could find no answer to the problem posed by the Vietcong's guerrilla tactics. Modern technology such as helicopters, laser-guided missiles, radar, napalm and other chemical weapons were unable to protect foot soldiers from the low-tech weapons such as the Bouncing Betty, the punji trap or the ambushes. The US military had failed to learn the lessons of the Blitz during the Second World War; neither Londoners nor the South Vietnamese were cowed by the air bombardments but instead became more determined to defeat the enemy. The US soldiers, average age 19, were unwilling conscripts, inexperienced and unused to the type of climate and conditions in the Vietnamese countryside. They were fighting in a land which was different in every way to their own, unable to distinguish between friend or foe, unable to speak the language and lacking in the same incentive to fight for their homeland as the Vietcong and the NVA. The efforts made by the US to win the hearts and minds of the Vietnamese people were minimal, and the brutal tactics of the ARVN and US troops searching for the Vietcong contrasted with the tactics employed by the guerrillas.

Following events such as the Tet offensive, the massacre at My Lai and the shooting of students at the Kent State University, the US media turned against the war. Their hard-hitting photographs, newsreels, reportage and comment turned more and more Americans against continued US involvement in the conflict. The use of the body count as a measure of US success sickened ordinary Americans and, as the US body bag count rose, so too did opposition to the war.

Effects of the war

In Vietnam there had been huge casualties, with approximately 2–3 million Vietnamese, Cambodians and Laotians losing their lives. The USA's chemical weapons, Agent Orange and napalm, had poisoned the area; drugs and prostitution, developed to cater for the GIs' rest and recreation, polluted the major cities; refugees fled from the country in their hundreds of thousands, many fleeing by sea as 'boat people'.

By joining Comecon in 1978, Vietnam received aid from the Soviet Union, but this also led to opposition from both China and the USA. When Cambodia (Kampuchea) was invaded by Vietnam in 1978, China retaliated by declaring war on Vietnam in 1979. By 1983 the Soviets were spending the equivalent of $3 million a day to support Vietnam, and further support was provided to Laos.

In the USA, the reverberations of the Vietnam War manifested themselves, until recently, in the public reluctance of the USA to intervene in the internal affairs of other countries; the war in Iraq has caused many Americans to question the wisdom of remaining in the country for fear continued US presence develops into another Vietnam.

The huge cost of the Vietnam War caused taxes and inflation to rise, and this meant cutbacks in spending on social reforms; Johnson's plans for a 'Great Society' based on welfare reform had to be put on hold. The war had devastating social effects on US society: the sale of drugs in Vietnam fed back into the USA and exacerbated an existing problem; marriages fell apart because of post-traumatic stress disorder – nearly 500,000 ex-servicemen suffered serious psychological problems. The medical effects of chemicals such as Agent Orange were profound; soldiers who had handled the chemical were more likely to develop cancer and have children born with deformities. Instead of being greeted as returning heroes, veterans were shunned by society – rejected as a reminder of a war that failed to win. Some companies discriminated against them, refusing to employ veterans as they might have taken part in some of the atrocities shown on the television. As Gloria Emerson observed, 'Vietnam is now our word, meaning an American failure, a short-hand for disaster…a loathsome jungle where our army of children fought an army of fanatics' *Winners and Losers: Battles retreats, Gains, Losses and Ruins from the Vietnam War*, Norton, 1985.

An anti-war movement developed in the USA amongst the young, and critics blamed the war for the disrespect for authority which developed amongst the young in the 1970s. During the war, thousands of young men burned their 'draft' cards and refused to fight, and sit-ins and demonstrations in universities caught the attention of students all over the world who followed suit. The peaceful student demonstration at Kent State University, Ohio in 1970 saw the National Guard opening fire and killing four students who had not even been part of the anti-war demonstration. It seemed that the government was ignoring the very American Constitution which they claimed was the blueprint for democracy. When this is taken in conjunction with the Watergate scandal, small wonder the American people began to distrust their own politicians.

Vietnam was blamed for the increase in tensions between blacks and whites since many African Americans believed that their young men had done a disproportionate amount of the fighting in Vietnam; African-American soldiers in Vietnam had often written on their helmets slogans such as, 'No Gook [Vietnamese] ever called me nigger'.

The televising of the war and its atrocities led to the American people questioning their whole ethos; how could a GI set fire to the homes of helpless peasants with such a cavalier attitude as seen in a CBS news report televised on 5 August 1965? The nightly reports of the carnage and destruction may have desensitized the American people, but it also led them to question the rightness of their cause, especially as US forces in Vietnam were accused of committing war crimes by using tactics such as dropping 4 million tonnes of bombs, killing and disfiguring people with napalm, and using Agent Orange and other poisons against non-combatants.

Vietnam had a great effect on US culture. Pop songs emphasizing the need for peace and protesting against war were inspired by the conflict, and songs by Bob Dylan and Country Joe MacDonald and the Fish expressed youth's resentment of the war in Vietnam. In the cinema only one major film about Vietnam was made during the war – *The Green Berets* (1968) starring John Wayne – but from the late 1970s there followed a stream of films based on the conflict. *Coming Home* (1978), *The Deer Hunter* (1978) and *Apocalypse Now* (1979) all underlined the futility of war and the damage it inflicted on US society.

Perhaps one of the most enduring images of the Vietnam War is a photograph taken by Nick Ut. In it a young girl is running down a road; she is naked and her clothes have been burned off in an American napalm attack. Behind her one can see the village of Trang Bang, now a mass of grey smoke. Today, the young girl in the photograph, Kim Phuc Phan Thi, has forgiven and publicly pardoned the person who launched the napalm bombing of her village, and she has dedicated her life to promoting peace. Her foundation helps children who are victims of war, providing medical and psychological counselling to help them overcome their traumatic experiences.

In the USA most people knew someone or had a member of their family who had taken part in the war. Many found it difficult to rekindle their relationships with these veterans at the end of the war, perhaps unconsciously blaming the soldiers for the US defeat and viewing them as 'losers,' no matter how bravely they fought. It was only with the dedication in 1982 of the Vietnam Veterans' Memorial in Washington that old wounds began to heal.

Nixon and Watergate

This chapter will cover:
- Nixon – domestic policy in an age of 'stagflation'
- foreign policy – détente and Vietnamization
- the Watergate affair – discovery and impeachment.

The scene of Richard Nixon being ushered into the presidential helicopter, *Marine One*, waiting for him on the lawn of the White House, pausing only to shake hands with his staff before getting into the helicopter and leaving office, inspired James Taylor to write the song 'Line 'em all up':

> I remember Richard Nixon back in '74
> And the final scene at the white house door
> And the staff lined up to say good-bye
> Tiny tear in his shifty little eye
> He said nobody knows me
> Nobody understands
> These little people were good to me
> Oh I'm gonna shake some hands

(James Taylor, 'Line 'em all up' on the album
Hourglass, 1997)

What had brought about this hurried, premature departure of Richard Milhous Nixon from his presidential post?

Richard Milhous Nixon began his long political career in 1947 when he was elected to the House of Representatives. By 1952, Nixon had been chosen as Dwight Eisenhower's vice-presidential running mate, but not before he was involved in a scandal that led to the infamous Checkers Speech. In this speech, Nixon denied that he had been guilty of financial irregularities and brought a tear to the nation's eye when he spoke of one well-wisher's gift to his children, a cocker spaniel: 'Black and white and spotted, and our little girl Tricia, the six year old named it Checkers. And you know, the kids like all kids love the dog and I just want to say this right now that regardless of what they say about it, we're gonna keep him.' As a piece of propaganda, the speech was priceless and ensured that Nixon was retained on the Republican ticket. Eisenhower went on to victory and an overwhelming defeat of opposing candidate Adlai Stevenson.

Nixon served as Vice-President for eight years, but lost the 1960 election to John F. Kennedy following an election debate in which Nixon was judged by radio listeners to have won, but which television viewers believed he had lost because of his appearance on the television. The handsome, debonair Kennedy seemed completely at home in the debate while Nixon's five o'clock shadow and profuse sweating under the studio lights gave him an untrustworthy appearance. Nixon recovered from political defeat to be chosen again as the Republican Party's candidate at the 1968 election. Nixon was inaugurated as the nation's thirth-seventh President on January 20 1969 having narrowly defeated the Democrat Hubert Humphrey. Nixon claimed toas having represent middle America which he called 'the silent majority', but his attempts to follow a conservative domestic policy were foiled by the Democrat dominated Congress. He set out to change the voting behaviour of the Congress by adopting policies designed to appeal to the white middle-class voters in the South, such as attempting to limit desegregation in schools. The Supreme Court ruled against this in the *Swann v. Charlotte Mecklenburg Board of Education* (1971) ruling.

A decade of protest

The issues of civil rights, Black Power and the Vietnam War had led to an increase in radical groups throughout the country, and the early 1970s saw the rise of the feminist and gay movements, each demanding equality.

Groups protesting against the Vietnam War became more vocal and more violent following the invasion of Cambodia in 1970. Increasing numbers of student groups became involved in protest marches and demonstrations at colleges and universities across the nation, and, as previously mentioned in Chapter 13, in some states the National Guard was called out to deal with these protests. As the National Guard was staffed with part-time soldiers, inexperienced in crowd control, it was inevitable that clashes would result in fatalities. The worst of these was at Kent State University, Ohio where protesting students set fire to one of the university buildings on 2 May 1970. Although the situation had calmed down, on Monday 4 May 1970, guardsmen carrying loaded rifles with fixed bayonets lined up to face the protesting students. Using loud hailers the guardsmen urged students to evacuate the area; the students refused. Guardsmen then began firing tear-gas at the crowd, but quickly ran out of supplies and began to retreat up the hill on the campus as students hurled stones at them. At the top some knelt, took aim, and fired at the students. At first the demonstrators believed they were firing blanks but a sudden realization that the bullets were live caused students to run for cover or dive flat on the floor. The silence which followed the volley of shots was broken by screams as the students realized that four of their number were dead and ten others wounded. The massacre sparked off hundreds of other protests as college students showed their anger. As one of them asked, 'Have we come to such a state in this country that a young girl has to be shot because she disagrees deeply with the actions of her government?' It was not only the disregard for life shown by the guardsmen that angered the nation, but also Nixon's reference to the dead students as 'college bums'.

The anti-war protesters were not the only student opposition Nixon faced. Many young people began to feel alienated from the values of their parents' generation and the consumerism of mainstream society, and embraced a new sub-culture described by Professor Timothy Leary as 'Tune in, turn on, drop out'. Long hair, eclectic dress, rock music, drugs, communes, flower power and wishes for love and peace became distinctive features of the hippy movement which came together en masse at a festival in Woodstock in August 1969. To the older generation, this younger generation was a threat to the American Way and led to a conservative backlash in politics.

The 'new left' was considered by Nixon to be a major threat to US society, and he exploited the apparent danger for his own ends using the CIA and FBI against left-wing groups. These government agencies launched 'Operation Chaos' and 'Cointelpro' against these groups and in particular against the Black Panthers. In truth, the groups were so divided amongst themselves that they were more of a hindrance than a revolutionary menace. Some small groups did advocate revolution and were responsible for a series of bombings; groups such as the Motherfuckers and Crazies urged anarchy; the Weathermen threatened violence to all and sundry but were most successful at destroying themselves as when three of them miscalculated and blew themselves up.

The rise of the feminist movement was to have more far-reaching effects than any of the above groups. In 1963, Betty Friedan wrote *The Feminine Mystique*, which claimed women had been brainwashed into believing that their place lay at home and that motherhood and housekeeping was the best thing they could aim for. This had certainly been the argument in Farnham and Lundgren's book *Modern Women: The Lost Sex* (1957), which blamed the problems of modern society on 'neurotic' career women. Friedan herself had given up her career as a psychologist to marry and raise a family and spoke with some authority of what she called, 'the silent question:' 'Is this all?'"

She advocated women who felt trapped within their traditional role to reject this conditioning and develop themselves through education and work outside the home. In 1966, Friedan founded the National Organization of Women (NOW) to support the campaign for the same civil, political and social rights for both men and women. This campaign for sexual equality was aided by Congress and the Supreme Court: the passing of the Educational Amendments Act (1972) initiated affirmative action programmes to ensure educational opportunities for women; the Equal Rights Amendment Act (1972) would have ensured equal rights in the Constitution had the states ratified it; the *Roe v. Wade* judgement (1973) legalized abortion in spite of violent protests by Catholics and fundamentalist Protestants.

Economic policies

Because of the cost of the Vietnam War and the rise in the cost of oil, the US economy was experiencing a period of inflation and unemployment. Inflation rose from 3 per cent in 1967, to 9 per cent in 1973; unemployment stood at 3.3 per cent in 1969 and rose to 5.6 per cent in 1972. The result was a period of recession from 1971–4. Nixon began his 'New Economic Policy' in 1971 in an attempt to deal with inflation. All wage and price increases were frozen for three months, the fixed exchange rate system was abandoned (which devalued the dollar, making US exports cheaper and imports dearer), import duties were placed on certain commodities such as Japanese cars, and taxes were reduced. These measures improved the economy sufficiently for Nixon to be re-elected in 1972.

Nixon and foreign policy

The ten years from 1969 to 1979 became the decade of détente, or a relaxation of tension between the Great Powers. Détente was a popular policy in the USA because it had the potential to drive a wedge between the USSR and China, draw attention away from Vietnam and develop better relations with China. Such a policy could also be to the USA's advantage in the fight against communism in Vietnam as both the Soviets and the Chinese were supplying arms to North Vietnam.

During the 1960s, it seemed unlikely that relations between the USA and the People's Republic of China would improve, especially since China was opposed to US involvement in Vietnam. The split between China and the USSR, however, led the US to change its policy, believing that by cultivating China's friendship, the USSR and China might be driven still further apart. President Nixon began by hinting publicly to *Time* magazine in October 1970, 'If there is anything I want to do before I die, it is go to China' and, in April 1971, the USA lifted its trade embargo with China and the US table-tennis team used 'ping-pong' to further US diplomacy. On 25 October 1971, China was admitted to the UN and Taiwan was expelled, a move which the US had blocked for years. Henry Kissinger (Nixon's National Security Adviser and later Secretary of State) had visited China secretly to prepare the way for an official visit to China by Nixon in February 1972. Amid huge media coverage, Nixon and Mao shook hands and toasted each other, taking plenty of time for photo opportunities in the Great Hall of the People in Beijing's Tiananmen Square and on the Great Wall of China. Trade and travel agreements followed, Chinese leaders visited the USA in 1979, and US firms were set up in China. In the same year, the USA recognized Communist China as the legal government of China.

The USA's new policy towards China was part of a wider picture, the artist of which was Henry Kissinger. Kissinger appreciated that the USA could no longer contain communism by force alone; the arms race was producing increasing numbers of nuclear weapons which were not only dangerous but expensive.

Immediately following Nixon's inauguration in January 1969, the Soviets expressed a willingness to begin discussions on arms limitations and, in November the same year, the USA and the USSR began talks for the Strategic Arms Limitation Treaty (SALT) which aimed to slow down the arms race by limiting the stock of long-range nuclear weapons held by each side. These talks took place in Helsinki and Vienna from 1969 until 1972. The two powers eventually signed SALT I in 1972. They agreed to reduce their anti-ballistic missile (ABM) systems and to limit the number of their offensive missiles and bombers. Each side was allowed to have 100 ABMs on each of two sites and, in order to ensure that these conditions were being maintained, both countries were permitted to use spy satellites.

In March 1972, President Nixon became the first US President to visit Moscow. In the same year, the USSR purchased 400 million bushels of US wheat worth $700 million – nearly the entire US surplus grain reserve. European firms helped to build the natural gas pipeline from Siberia to the West and, on 17 July 1975, three American Apollo astronauts met two Soviet Soyuz cosmonauts in space. Not everyone agreed with Nixon's policy of détente. To many, it came perilously close to being soft on communism.

The Middle East

In the Middle East, the USA and the USSR had backed opposing sides – the USA had backed Israel while the USSR backed the Arab nations and Egypt. When Egypt launched an attack on Israel in 1973 during the Yom Kippur war, there was a danger that both super powers might be drawn into the struggle.

Although Nixon sent arms to Israel, he also sent Kissinger to Moscow to work on a truce and thus save détente. A truce was agreed, but the Israelis refused to abide by it and the USSR made it clear that they were willing to enforce the truce militarily. This would not only have upset the Jewish vote in the USA, but would have given the Soviets a foothold in the Middle East. In order to make his opposition clear, Nixon placed all US bases on Defcon 3 military alert – it seemed the Middle East had the potential to draw the super powers into a direct conflict. Moscow did not overreact to the US action, and within two days the alert had been lifted. A few days later the USA compelled Israel to accept the ceasefire and President Sadat of Egypt agreed to accept a UN multi-national force to monitor the ceasefire.

The USA had achieved a resounding diplomatic victory – both sides in the Middle East looked to the USA to mediate and the USSR seemed to have lost influence in the area. Other Arab countries were not so easily cowed; the USA's offer of a $2.2 billion arms deal with Israel was unacceptable to the Arab world and this, together with the outcome of the Yom Kippur war and resentment of the low prices paid to them by the West for their oil led to the eight Arab members of the Organization of Petroleum Exporting Countries (OPEC) imposing cutbacks in oil supplies to the USA. From 1971 to 1981 the price of oil rose almost 20-fold leading to economic chaos in countries heavily dependent on oil. These countries experienced a strange combination of inflation and recession as production costs and unemployment rose. In the peace talks following the Yom Kippur war, the USA's need for oil outweighed her support for Israel, and the result was a more favourable settlement for Egypt.

Vietnam

In Vietnam, Nixon devised the 'Nixon Doctrine' whereby the USA would give aid to countries which faced internal communist revolt but would not commit troops to the task. Yet to pull out of Vietnam would smack of defeat, hence Nixon's decision to pursue a course of Vietnamization – the ARVN would take increasing responsibility for the fighting. This had a devastating effect on the morale of the US and ARVN troops. Nixon's 'madman strategy' involved dropping hundreds of thousands of tonnes of explosives on North Vietnam in an attempt to make the North Vietnamese think that the US President was mad enough to drop a nuclear bomb on them should they not come to the negotiating table. In 1970, US troops also invaded neutral Cambodia in order to wipe out bases and supply routes which the North Vietnamese army had established in the country. This led to a huge increase in the numbers of anti-war protests throughout the USA. Nixon did have some success eventually persuading the Vietnamese to the negotiating table although negotiations dragged on until the Paris Accords on 27 January 1973. The US withdrew its troops from Vietnam, Laos and Cambodia; there was a full exchange of prisoners; an international commission was established to oversee the ceasefire; and an attempt was made to organize free elections. By 1975, North Vietnam had taken over the South and Vietnam was united under communist rule.

Nixon and the presidency

Nixon had come to the post of President in 1968 at a time of increasing chaos and disorder, with race riots, anti-war demonstrations and the political assassinations of Martin Luther King and Robert Kennedy. He had promised to listen to, 'the voice of the great majority of Americans, the forgotten Americans, the non-shouters, the non-demonstrators,' the Americans he called the 'silent majority'.

Nixon's period in the White House marked the zenith of a phenomenon that US author and historian, Arthur Schlesinger, called 'the imperial presidency'. This meant that over a long period of time, dating back to the time of Franklin D. Roosevelt, the post of President had been steadily amassing more and more power. In international terms, the US President could in theory launch a nuclear war which could end the world by pressing one button. In national terms, the power of the President was limited by the Constitution but there were ways and means to circumvent the Constitution as Roosevelt had demonstrated with his New Deal, and as the Gulf of Tonkin incident (see Chapter 13) had shown. After the Second World War, several agencies had been created which enabled the President to extend his power: the CIA, originally a counter-intelligence agency for use outside the USA; the National Security Agency (NSA) created by presidential decree in 1952 to gather intelligence; and the Defense Intelligence Agency (DIA) created in 1961 which co-ordinated the intelligence-gathering of the armed forces and which had collected millions of dossiers on US radicals, students and politicians by the 1970s. The FBI had been established in 1908 to deal with federal crime, but under its director J. Edgar Hoover (1924–72), it was used for surveillance of those US citizens suspected of being communists, radicals or civil rights supporters. The President had these agencies at his disposal and had the power, therefore, to spy on others. This was not a new phenomenon: Kennedy and Johnson had both bugged their opponents, and the CIA and FBI had been used for political purposes, for example, during the McCarthy witch-hunts of the 1950s. Yet under Nixon the manipulation of these agencies for political purposes reached new, unprecedented heights. In order to understand why this should be so, one need to look no further than the character and personal life of Richard Nixon.

Nixon's childhood in California had not been a privileged one; he was raised as a Quaker by a strict and sometimes brutal father and a mother whom Nixon regarded as a saint. Psychologists have claimed that this upbringing gave him a strong feeling of inferiority, resentful of those with more privileged backgrounds, particularly the West coast liberals. Nixon was suspicious of the press, whom he blamed when he lost the election for governorship of California in 1962 saying: 'Congratulations gentlemen, you won't have Richard Nixon to kick around anymore.' In addition to this, the leaking of the 'Pentagon Papers' to the *New York Times* in 1972 by Dr Daniel Ellsberg convinced him that he had enemies everywhere. The 'Pentagon Papers' were secret Defense Department documents about US involvement in the Vietnam War which showed that the government had lied to the American people about the reasons for its involvement in Vietnam and had kept certain details secret from both the public and Congress. Nixon challenged the publication of the documents in the Supreme Court but lost when the court ruled 6–3 in favour of publication.

This incident convinced Nixon of the need to ensure that leaks to the press did not happen again, and he became obsessed with secrecy.

In order to 'fix the leaks', Nixon created a secret White House unit known as the 'plumbers'. The unit's brief was to 'stop security leaks and to investigate other security matters'. A strange bunch of characters was brought together to do precisely that, including G. Gordon Liddy, counsel to the Committee to Re-elect the President (CREEP) and a former FBI agent, and E. Howard Hunt Jr., a former White House consultant, CIA employee and a writer of spy novels.

This group investigated the private lives of Nixon's critics and political enemies, and even burgled the office of Ellsberg's psychiatrist in an attempt to discover damaging information. Other opponents were kept under surveillance to collect any information which might discredit them. For example, rumours emerged about many of the leading Democrats at this time and it was believed this was part of a strategy to secure the nomination of George McGovern as the Democrat candidate against Nixon in the 1972 elections; perhaps Nixon felt he could more easily achieve a landslide victory against this liberal politician whose views on tax and welfare reform and liberal attitudes towards abortion and drugs would not appeal to the 'silent majority' of middle America.

Nixon was fixated with the idea of retaining presidential power in the 1972 election so that he might go down in history as the man who had been President during the bicentennial celebrations of the Declaration of Independence which were due in 1976. Nixon's previous experience of narrowly losing the presidential election in 1960 and narrowly winning in 1968, convinced him of the need to use any means at his disposal to ensure victory in 1972. Nixon's former Attorney General, John Mitchell, was put in charge of CREEP. Nothing was to be left to chance in the presidential election, as Nixon had said following the publication of the Pentagon Papers, 'We're up against an enemy, a conspiracy. They are using any means. We are going to use any means.'

In June 1972, five months before the presidential election, the 'plumbers' attempted to gain entry to the Democratic Party headquarters in the Watergate building. The Watergate Hotel is one of Washington's plushest hotels; it is home to former Senator Bob Dole and was once the place where Monica Lewinsky went into hiding during the scandal surrounding her relationship with President Bill Clinton. In political terms, the name 'Watergate' is synonymous with corruption and scandal. At 2.30 a.m. on 17 June 1972 at the Watergate Hotel complex, five burglars broke into the Democratic Party's National Committee offices. If it had not been for the reactions of Frank Wills, a security guard, the scandal may never have erupted. The five burglars caught at the scene were carrying cameras and electronic equipment and were intending to tap the phone of the Democratic National Committee Chairman. The five men were named as Bernard Barker (a former CIA operative), Virgilio Gonzales (a Cuban émigré and locksmith), James McCord (former FBI and CIA, and security co-ordinator for CREEP), Eugenio Martinez (Cuban émigré connected with the CIA) and Frank Sturgis (CIA connections and history of anti-Castro action).

These five men were charged with attempted burglary and attempted interception of telephone and other communications. Whether Nixon knew of the plan beforehand is not clear; he always denied any knowledge of it whatsoever. With the election getting closer, Nixon announced in August that, following an internal investigation by John Dean, 'no one in the White House staff, no one in this Administration presently employed, was involved in this bizarre incident'. He succeeded in diverting attention from the break-in during the election campaign by illegally using the CIA to prevent an investigation by the FBI. The break-in did not become a major issue in the elections held in November and Nixon was re-elected with a huge majority, 47 million to McGovern's 29 million. However, the Democrats still had majorities in both houses of Congress.

Early in 1973, the men involved in the Watergate break-in came up for trial and were found guilty of burglary and conspiracy. The trial judge, John J. Sirica, was not satisfied and believed others were also involved in the incident; sentencing was delayed to enable the defendants to co-operate in return for mitigation of their sentences. One of the burglars alleged that high-ranking White House officials were involved in the burglary, and it soon became obvious that someone on Nixon's staff had tried to silence the burglars – the media became determined to find out who.

Two reporters from the *Washington Post*, Bob Woodward and Carl Bernstein, played a major role in the initial investigations of Watergate. The two later wrote the book *All the President's Men* (1974) which was made into a Hollywood film (1976) in which Woodward and Bernstein were portrayed as the driving force behind the investigations into the Watergate break-in, uncovering links between the burglars and the White House and an illegal slush fund used by CREEP to fund illegal activities. They were aided in all this by an anonymous White House source, known as 'Deep Throat', the identity of whom they have kept secret to date.

Political investigations into the issue began in February 1973 when the Senate established a House Judiciary Committee to investigate the Watergate scandal. The public hearings of the Committee caused a sensation. The evidence of John Dean, Nixon's former White House Counsel was damning; he testified that John Mitchell had organized the break-in, with the knowledge of Bob Haldeman and John Erlichman, both White House aides. He also testified that Nixon had approved the cover-up. The Committee uncovered that during 1971, voice-activated tape recorders had been installed in the Oval office in the White House and that there existed secret White House tape recordings; this sparked a major political and legal battle between the Congress and the President as access to these tapes was demanded. Public support for the President, influenced by the extensive television coverage of the Senate investigating hearings, began to diminish, especially after Nixon dismissed Archibald Cox, the Special Prosecutor, in October 1973; Cox had attempted to subpoena the tapes but Nixon claimed that executive privilege gave him the right to retain possession of them.

Throughout 1973, the evidence against Nixon mounted and, in March 1974, Mitchell, Haldeman, Erlichman and others were sent for trial for conspiring to obstruct the Watergate investigation. In April 1974, the White House released more than 1,200 pages of edited transcripts of the Nixon tapes to the House Judiciary Committee, but the Committee insisted that the tapes themselves should be turned over. In July, the Supreme Court backed up this request and ruled that Nixon should hand over tapes of more than 54 conversations made in 1972. On 27 July 1974, the House Judiciary Committee began the process of passing the first of three articles of impeachment, charging Nixon with abuse of power, refusal to comply with the Committee's subpoenas and the obstruction of justice. The written transcripts of the conversations held on 23 June 1972 were released to the Supreme Court on 5 August 1974 and proved to be something of an eye-opener. Nixon had been in the habit of swearing profusely while plotting vengeance on his 'enemies' and he had made derogatory and racist remarks about other politicians, but more than anything the transcripts directly linked Nixon to the Watergate cover-up. As one Senator said, the tapes revealed, 'a deplorable, shabby, disgusting and immoral performance'. On 9 August 1974, Richard Nixon resigned as President of the USA and his Vice-President, Gerald Ford, was sworn in – the first person to have achieved the status of both Vice-President and President without having been elected to either of the posts by the US electorate.

figure 9 Nixon seeking cover amidst evidence of wiretapping, break-in, political sabotage, laundered FBI funds from Mexico, and other illegal activities.

(Source: National Security Blanket, *Herblock Special Report*, W. W. Norton, 1974. Image courtesy of the Prints & Photographs Division, Library of Congress.)

Nixon's departure

Nixon left Washington without apologizing or admitting his guilt. His resignation address was emotional and rambling; he shook hands with his staff and told them how proud he was of them and was ushered into the presidential helicopter, *Marine One*, which was waiting to transport him to the Andrews air force base in preparation for the journey home to California.

The effect of Watergate on US politics

The Watergate affair was the greatest scandal in US history and, coming at the same time as defeat in Vietnam, shook the confidence of the nation in the USA reputation as a free and fair democracy. Congress became determined to keep a firmer grip on the powers of the President and on the federal government and intelligence agencies, making them more accountable to the Congress and the US public. Several laws were passed which attempted to establish limits on fundraising in elections, permitted individuals to see information kept on them in federal files, required the President to tell Congress about undercover operations, and required senior government officials to disclose their finances. Congressional Committees were created to keep an eye on the intelligence agencies, making the CIA report its activities to Congress and to obtain court orders before it could implement a wiretap.

On 8 September 1974, President Gerald Ford controversially granted Richard Nixon a full pardon 'for all offences against the United States' that might have been committed while in office. The pardon brought an end to all criminal prosecutions that Nixon might have had to face concerning the Watergate scandal.

Nixon has been severely censured for bringing the office of President into disrepute and for extending the powers of the office beyond what was envisaged by the American Constitution. He was not alone; most Presidents of the USA had pushed their powers as far as possible; perhaps Nixon was just unlucky because he was caught in the act. It is difficult to feel sympathy for this dysfunctional individual who abused his power as President yet failed to see anything wrong in what he had done.

David Frost interviewed Richard Nixon in 1977 and and later said of him:

And at the end, a 'sad man who so wanted to be great' was a phrase that occurred to me as I left him the last time in San Clemente. Because, I mean, he was lonely and alone, and I mean, he was a sad man. He wasn't quite a tragic man, because there wasn't quite that nobility about it all, but you felt he was a sad man at the end. But at the same time, at that time one was particularly aware that there were people in prison because of his actions. And so that took away a little of the sympathy.'

(David Frost on *Larry King Live*, CNN, 8 January 1992)

15

Ford and Carter

This chapter will cover:
- the presidency of Gerald Ford – ending the USA's nightmare
- Jimmy Carter
- the 1970s – a forgotten decade?

On 9 August 1974, following Richard Nixon's resignation, he was escorted out of the White House by Vice-President Gerald Ford. Ford recalled the event as being a sad occasion: '...because of our long personal friendship with Dick and Pat. That's a sad situation when you see a couple that had been good friends who [were] leaving under those very tragic circumstances' (*A Time to Heal*, Harper & Row, 1979).

President Gerald Ford 1974–7

The oath of office that Ford took on 9 August 9 1974, reflected the unusual circumstances of Nixon's departure and set the tone for his presidency. Ford acknowledged, 'I assume the Presidency under extraordinary circumstances...This is an hour of history that troubles our minds and hurts our hearts,' and went on to distance himself from Nixon and the Watergate scandal by stating categorically that 'Our long national nightmare is over.'

As a congressman, Ford had enjoyed a reputation for a willingness to compromise and to make deals behind the scenes, and was generally regarded as 'a nice guy'. President Ford's priority was to regain the country's trust in the presidency and to show that there was a new, respectable regime in the White House, totally different to that of Richard Nixon's. Ford succeeded in doing precisely that – for 30 days. Unfortunately, he then made the mistake of issuing a blanket pardon for any crimes Nixon might have committed while President, before any legal proceedings had been initiated. Ford was keen to settle the whole situation quickly rather than having a long-running trial that would perpetuate all the issues raised by Watergate and possibly destabilize the country further. However, a large part of the electorate believed Ford to be part of the Nixon conspiracy and that the pardon was part of a quid pro quo deal made with Nixon before he left office. Ford never regained the national support he had enjoyed during those first 30 days. He later admitted, 'I have to say that most of my staff disagreed with me over the pardon, but I was absolutely convinced that it was the right thing to do.' In all likelihood, his decision to pardon Nixon affected his own prestige and cost him the election in 1976.

Ford was confronted with challenges of almost insurmountable proportions: mastering inflation; reviving a depressed economy; solving chronic energy shortages; and trying to ensure world peace. He viewed himself as, 'a moderate in domestic affairs, a conservative in fiscal affairs, and a dyed-in-the-wool internationalist in foreign affairs' (*A Time to Heal*, Harper & Row, 1979). These attributes can be seen in each of the pertinent aspects of Ford's policies.

Domestic policy

The US economy was hit badly when OPEC quadrupled the price of oil in December 1973. Ford's priority on the domestic front, therefore, was to find a solution to the country's economic problems. He began by attempting to curb inflation which at that time was around 7 per cent. Although this was quite low, it was sufficient to discourage investors from investing in US companies, and pushed the small investor into investing in relatively secure government bonds rather than the stock market. Ford launched a public relations exercise to draw attention to the rising inflation by appearing on television in October 1974 and asking the US public to, 'whip inflation now' (WIN). Unfortunately, Ford had few policies with which to back up this campaign. He concentrated on reducing government spending and raising taxes – the complete opposite to the type of policies many senators saw necessary, namely tax cuts and more governmental spending, if a recession were to be avoided. In his State of the Union speech in 1975, Ford had grim news for the nation: 'I must say to you that the state of the Union is not good,' and he went on to list the economic problems facing the USA. These included high unemployment, a federal deficit of $30 billion, and a national debt of over $500 billion, inflation and inefficient industry.

As the country sank into a mild recession, Ford's economic focus was forced to change and, in March 1975, Congress signed into law income tax rebates to help boost the economy, and Ford attempted to help business operate more freely by reducing business taxes and easing the controls exercised by regulatory agencies. However, because he still feared inflation, Ford vetoed a number of non-military appropriations bills that would have further increased the already heavy budgetary deficit but also might have created more jobs and stimulated the economy. In spite of these measures, the economy continued to be a problem, as Ford later remembered: 'My greatest disappointment was that I couldn't turn the switch and all of a sudden overnight go from an economic recession to an economic prosperity.'

By the time of the 1976 presidential election, unemployment had risen to 8 per cent and the jewel in the USA's crown, the car industry, was experiencing competition from Japanese cars which were more fuel efficient and therefore had become more attractive to the American consumer since the 400 per cent increase in oil prices made by OPEC in 1973.

Assassination attempts

Ford survived two attempts on his life during his term as President. On 5 September 1975, Lynette 'Squeaky' Fromme, a follower of the imprisoned cult leader Charles Manson, pointed a gun at Ford's stomach while he was in Sacramento, meeting well-wishers. Luckily, no shots were fired and nobody was injured. A mere 17 days later there was a second attempt on his life when Sara Jane Moore tried to kill Ford in San Francisco. Her attempt to shoot Ford was thwarted by a bystander, Oliver Sipple.

Foreign policy

Against the backdrop of the fall of South Vietnam in 1975, Congress and the President struggled repeatedly over presidential war powers, oversight of the CIA and covert operations, military aid appropriations, and the stationing of military personnel. In South-East Asia, Ford took steps to bolster US power and prestige after the fall of Cambodia and South Vietnam to the communists. On 14 May 1975, in a dramatic move, Ford ordered US forces to retake the *SS Mayaguez*, a US merchant ship seized by Cambodian gunboats two days earlier in international waters. The vessel was recovered and all 39 crewmen saved, but during the rescue 41 US marines lost their lives.

In the Middle East, Ford attempted to prevent war by providing aid to both Israel and Egypt, and was successful in persuading the two countries to accept an interim truce agreement.

Détente with the Soviet Union continued, particularly in the sphere of nuclear weapons when President Ford and Soviet leader Leonid Brezhnev set new limitations upon nuclear weapons. In 1975, the Helsinki Accords recognized the existing borders of Europe, and brought up the issue of human rights when the signatories agreed to respect freedom of belief and expression. The symbolic Apollo-Soyuz joint manned space flight seemed to mark a period of co-operation between the USA and the USSR.

Ford made several diplomatic trips to Japan, China and Europe and received many Heads of State during the USA's bicentennial celebrations, in 1976. During these celebrations Queen Elizabeth and Prince Philip visited the White House. Ford's son, Jack, mislaid the studs for his dress shirt while dressing for dinner and rushed to his father's room to borrow some. He stepped into the lift in some disarray – shirt all undone and hair a mess – and was surprised to be joined by the royal couple and his parents. His mother was clearly embarrassed and introduced her son to the royal guests. The Queen smiled at Jack's dishevelled appearance and commented 'I have one just like that,' referring of course to Prince Charles.

The 1976 presidential election

During the 1976 campaign, Ford gained the Republican nomination after fighting off a strong challenge by Ronald Reagan. He chose Senator Robert Dole of Kansas as his running mate, but was not seen to have much of a chance against his rival Senator Jimmy Carter, who was riding high in the opinion polls. Even Ford's campaign manager, Roger Morton, seemed to be accepting that defeat was inevitable, and when asked whether he had plans for a change of strategy he answered: 'I'm not going to rearrange the furniture on the deck of the Titanic.' However, Ford succeeded in narrowing Democrat Jimmy Carter's large lead in the polls, but finally lost one of the closest elections in history by 38,532,360 votes to 40,276,040.

Ford was seen by many as:

> ...a loser, a bumbler, a misfit President who for some reason or other...was prone to slip on airplane ramps, bump his head on helicopter entrances, entangle himself in the leashes of his family dogs, and fall from skis in front of television cameras that showed him asprawl in snow.
>
> (John Osborne in 'Ford, Gerald R.' *Encyclopaedia Britannica*, 2004)

However, Ford did succeed in demonstrating that the presidency could be run honestly, and expressed the hope that, '...historians will write that the Ford administration healed the land, that I restored public confidence in the White House and in the government'.

President James Earl Carter 1977–81

Jimmy Carter was the first President from the Deep South since the Civil War. His record of civil rights resulted in him being supported by four out of every five African Americans who voted. Carter also did well with whites in the South and Americans on low incomes. He brought a new style of leadership to the White House and broke with many of the rather stuffy traditions associated with the office. Following his inauguration, Carter walked hand in hand with his wife down Pennsylvania Avenue instead of riding in the usual motorcade. The author remembers asking an American friend what he thought of the new President, to be told that he thought it was great that the President wore blue jeans in the White House!

Domestic policy

Carter unfortunately lacked the necessary experience to deal with the Democrat dominated Congress, to such an extent that one political commentator believed that should Carter present the Pledge of Allegiance to the Congress, it would be defeated!

Carter was unsuccessful in getting the support of Congress for his national health-insurance bill or his proposals for welfare reform and controls on hospital costs. Nor were his tax-reform proposals favourably received. He failed to gain congressional approval either to merge the natural resource agencies within the Department of the Interior or to expand the economic development units in the Department of Housing and Urban Development. However, Carter did have a number of successes in domestic affairs. He reformed the Civil Service in order to improve government efficiency, and appointed record numbers of women, African Americans, and Hispanics to government jobs; he deregulated the trucking and airline industries; and he took an interest in the environment, expanding the national park system and bringing 41.5 million hectares (103 million acres) of Alaskan lands under protection.

The economy

During the presidential campaign, Carter had criticized former President Ford for his failure to control inflation and relieve unemployment, and it was these problems that Carter had pledged to address when President. He inherited an economy that was slowly emerging from a recession, and unemployment and inflation both remained high. The traditional policy of US governments was to spend their way out of recession, but this only served to increase inflation and imports. Unemployment dropped from 8 per cent to 7 per cent during Carter's first year in office and, by the end of his administration, according to the White House's official biography, Carter could claim an increase of nearly 8 million jobs and a decrease in the budget deficit, measured in percentage of the GNP. Unemployment still stood at a nationwide average of about 7.7 per cent by the time of the election campaign in 1980, but it was considerably higher in some industrial states. Unfortunately, inflation and interest rates were at near record highs; the annual inflation rate rose steadily each year from 4.8 per cent in 1976 to around 12 per cent at the time of the 1980 election campaign and interest rates were at 20 per cent. In 1978, Carter had called for voluntary limits on wage and price increases but these had little effect. Later, controls were imposed on credit by raising the interest rate to 29 per cent as the government hoped that by discouraging borrowing, it would reduce the rate of inflation.

The fuel crisis

During Carter's term, major problems emerged in the area of energy supply. The President warned that the US was wasting energy, that US resources of oil and natural gas were running out, and that supplies of petroleum from other countries were open to embargoes by the producing nations, principally by members of OPEC. Soon after taking office, Carter asked Congress to create a new Department of Energy, and proposed legislation to reduce oil consumption, increase US oil production, and encourage the use of other energy sources. Congress approved the new department and, after much debate, some of the legislation. In 1979, because of widespread shortages of gasoline, Carter proposed a long-term programme designed to solve the energy problem. He advocated a limit on imported oil, gradual removal of official restraints on the prices of domestically-produced oil, a strict programme of conservation, and development of alternative sources of energy such as solar, nuclear and geothermal power, oil and gas from shale and coal, and synthetic fuels. In what was probably his most noted domestic legislative accomplishment, Carter pushed a significant portion of his energy programme through Congress.

Foreign policy

In foreign policy, Carter took a high moral stance, proclaiming his goals to be peace, arms control, economic co-operation, and the advancement of human rights. His efforts towards bringing peace to the Middle East were widely acclaimed. In the autumn of 1978, Carter met the leaders of Egypt and Israel at Camp David, Maryland, and agreed on the basic principles for a peace treaty. On 26 March 1979, a peace treaty was signed by Israeli Premier Menachim Begin and Egyptian President Anwar el-Sadat. The Camp David Accord, as it was called, represented a high point in the Carter presidency, but 'the devil was in the detail,' and negotiations on details of the peace and its implementation progressed at a snail's pace.

In Latin America, Carter concluded new controversial treaties with Panama, which gave the country control of the Panama Canal by the year 2000. The treaties were severely criticized by conservative forces as a 'sell-out' of vital US interests, and, during the 1980 congressional and presidential campaigns this criticism had a significant impact in some areas of the South and West.

Carter's decision to establish full diplomatic relations with the People's Republic of China in 1979, and cut formal US ties with the Nationalist Chinese government of Taiwan was also an unpopular move in some quarters.

In June 1979, President Carter and the Soviet President, Leonid Brezhnev, signed the Strategic Arms Limitation Treaty (SALT II). This set limits on the numbers of Soviet and US nuclear weapons systems. This treaty met with strong opposition in Congress and was not ratified by the Senate, finally being set aside because of the Soviet invasion of Afghanistan in 1979.

Carter frequently criticized nations that violated basic human rights and announced that aid would be cut to those foreign governments guilty of human rights violations. His personal pleas on behalf of Soviet dissidents brought him into conflict with the Soviet government, who regarded his interference as unwarranted intervention in Soviet internal affairs.

Iran and Afghanistan

At the end of 1979, two issues arose that severely tested Carter's leadership. In November, 1979, student militants in Iran seized the US Embassy in Teheran and took 52 US hostages. The Iranian students demanded that the deposed Shah of Iran, who was in the

USA for medical treatment, be handed over to the government of Iran and only then would the hostages be released. To free the hostages, the USA first tried to negotiate with Iranian leaders, and then imposed economic sanctions on Iran. Seeing that these measures were not successful, Carter ordered military action – an armed rescue – but that mission also failed. Many Americans criticized Carter's handling of the hostage seizure and the lack of protection for the personnel in the US Embassy considering the anti-American attitude of the Iranian government at that time. Yet there no other reasonable alternatives available to Carter, especially in the face of Iranian threats to punish or kill the hostages. Carter's approval rating during the summer of 1980 slumped to 21 per cent, the lowest figure ever recorded by a President. In the final month of Carter's administration, negotiations with Iran, through Algerian intermediaries, finally freed the hostages on 20 January 1981, just as Ronald Reagan was inaugurated. In December 1980, the Soviets invaded Afghanistan to put down an anti-communist rebellion. In response to the Soviet action, Carter asked Congress to delay its discussion of the new SALT, limited trade with the Soviet Union, and called for a boycott of the 1980 Summer Olympic Games, held in Moscow.

The 1980 presidential election

Carter's administration was also unable to deal successfully with the country's mounting economic problems. Inflation had risen throughout Carter's presidency and, by 1980, had reached 15 per cent. The Republican nominee, Ronald Reagan, successfully built inflation and the fear of US military weakness into the major campaign issues. With the Iran hostage crisis still unresolved, Carter had little chance against Ronald Reagan and was easily defeated, receiving only 35 million votes to Reagan's 44 million. Historian Maldwyn Jones sees this as, 'the most devastating rejection of an incumbent President since Hoover's defeat in 1932...the voters...seem to have been demanding a stronger foreign policy and more decisive leadership' (*The Limits of Liberty*, OUP, 1995).

Life after the presidency

Although regarded by many as a weak and ineffective President of the USA, Carter's career on leaving office is one to be admired. He used the prestige of his former position to apply his principles of honesty to a wider stage and concentrated on one particular area in which he excelled – human rights. In 1981, Carter established the Carter Centre which sponsored programmes to promote human rights in developing countries. He also became involved in negotiating the end of human rights abuses in Nicaragua, Panama, Ethiopia and Haiti. Carter has played a leading role in keeping the Middle East peace process going and persuading North and South Korea to begin discussions; he brokered the ceasefire in Bosnia; he has fearlessly monitored elections in Panama and Nicaragua; and has even been allowed to broadcast to the citizens of Cuba criticizing Castro's civil rights record.

Both the former President and Rosalynn Carter received the Presidential Medal of Freedom in 1999 for their work in fostering peace and, in 2002, Jimmy Carter was awarded the Nobel Peace Prize for his 'untiring effort to find peaceful solutions to international conflicts, to advance democracy and human rights, and to promote economic and social development.'

The 1970s – a forgotten decade

To many, the 1970s was a decade of disillusion, cynicism and bitterness. Many Americans were disillusioned with the government and their democratic institutions because events such as the Vietnam War and Watergate had challenged their faith in the government and its leaders. Along with political disillusionment came economic stagnation, recession and poverty, which brought in its wake a declining standard of living. The 1970s became a decade of confusion and frustration, and there was a pervading feeling that the USA had lost sight of the 'American Dream'.

Many of the problems facing Americans during this period were already in existence but seemed to grow worse during the 1970s. The family appeared to be in terminal decline with one in two marriages ending in divorce, and a consequent rise in single parent households. Increasing numbers of women went out to work, both to support their families and to try to make up for their family's declining standard of living, and many social commentators blamed the increasing breakdown of the family and rise in juvenile delinquency on this.

Unemployment rose dramatically, especially in the manufacturing sector, and at the same time 70 per cent of all new jobs created were in the low-paying service sector. High inflation devalued US wages and the real income of US workers fell on average 2 per cent a year each year from 1973 to 1981. The American Dream seemed to be beyond the reach of an increasing number of Americans. It seemed that even the youth of America veered away from the hippy generation and took the safe option, or did they?

Youth in the 1970s

According to Nik Cohn in the *New York* magazine in June 1976, 'The new generation takes few risks; it graduates, looks for a job, endures. And once a week, on Saturday night, it explodes.' Cohn's article told of young people in Brooklyn's Bay Ridge district who, every weekend, escaped their humdrum existence by dancing their cares away at a local disco. Cohn's article, 'Tribal Rites of the New Saturday Night', was turned into a film in 1977 starring John Travolta and Karen Gorney. Entitled *Saturday Night Fever*, the picture was released in December 1977 and earned over $108 million by the end of 1978. Disco exploded on to the pop scene during the late 1970s in the nightclubs in Brooklyn, New York. Soon 'discotheques', as they were called, were springing up all over the country fuelled by the success of *Saturday Night Fever*. Disco was not a long lasting phenomenon and was officially declared to be 'dead' in 1979.

Cinema

In the cinema, outer space was clearly a preoccupation with the film makers as the success of Steven Spielberg's movie *Close Encounters of the Third Kind* proved in 1977. The most successful film of the 1970s was George Lucas' and Stephen Spielburg's *Star Wars* (1979) which broke all box office records for that decade with its futuristic depiction of Luke Skywalker's struggle to avenge his father's death and his fight against the Empire's Darth Vader. This film obviously caught Ronald Reagan's imagination as he named his Space Defence Initiative after it!

Television

On television, traditional shows such as *MASH*, *The Mary Tyler Moore Show*, *That Girl*, *Rhoda*, *Charlie's Angels*, *Star Trek*, *Good Times* and *Happy Days* remained popular but increasingly topics once considered taboo were aired for the first time. The comedy social satire *All in the Family* based on the British comedy *Till Death us Do Part*, covered controversial issues such as abortion, race and homosexuality. Television news broadcasts from the frontlines of the conflict in Vietnam continued to bring the horrors of war into the homes of millions of Americans and intensified anti-war sentiment in the country. The television mini-series, *Roots*, based on the book by Alex Halley about the experiences of his slave forefathers, fostered an interest in genealogy generally, a greater appreciation of the plight of African Americans, and an increased interest in African-American history.

Technology

Technology began to play an increasing role in people's lives. The video cassette recorder changed home entertainment, and the development of the floppy disc in 1970 and the microprocessor would have a profound effect on every aspect of life.

Space exploration continued: *Apollo 17*, the last manned craft to the moon, brought back 250 samples of rock and soil; and unmanned space probes explored the moon, Jupiter, Mars, Saturn, Uranus and Venus. The USSR and the USA co-operated in space when the US *Apollo 18* and the USSR's *Soyuz 19* linked up to conduct joint experiments.

Medicine made dramatic advances when the first test-tube baby was born in July 1978, ultrasound diagnostic techniques were developed, and steps were taken towards developing genetic engineering. Unfortunately this was also the decade in which the neutron bomb, which destroys living beings while leaving buildings intact, was developed.

Fads and fashion

Some of the fads to capture the imagination of Americans during this decade included the Rubik's cube, lava lamps, sea monkeys, mood rings, smiley faces, clackers, chopper bikes, romper-stompers and slime, to name but a few. The wildest fad surely was streaking nude through very public places!

In fashion, the 1960s hippy look became mainstream as men sported shoulder-length hair and non-traditional clothing became the rage, including bellbottom trousers, hipster jeans, colourful patches on clothes, hot pants, platform shoes, earth shoes, clogs, T-shirts, and gypsy dresses. Knits and denims were the most fashionable fabrics. The movie *Annie Hall* (1977) inspired a fashion trend with women for wearing men's clothing such as tweed jackets and collars and ties, but generally women wore everything from ankle-length grandmother dresses to hot pants and micro-mini skirts.

16

Ronald Reagan and the end of the Cold War

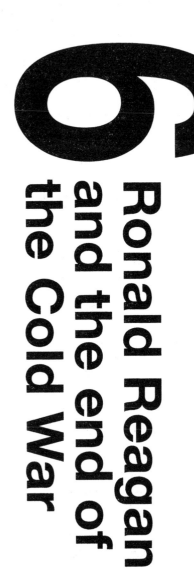

This chapter will cover:
- the Teflon President
- Irangate
- Star Wars versus the Evil Empire and the end of the Cold War.

On 6 June 2004, Ronald Reagan, President of the USA from 1980 to 1989, died at the age of 93 after a long struggle with Alzheimer's. The news of his death immediately brought statements from statesmen from all over the world paying homage to him. Among the many tributes came one from the Former British Prime Minister, Margaret Thatcher, who spoke warmly of the man many regarded as her ideological soulmate during the Cold War. She regarded President Reagan as one of her closest and dearest personal friends and believed that, 'to have achieved so much against so many odds and with such humour and humanity made Ronald Reagan a truly great American hero'. She credited him with having, 'won the Cold War for liberty…without a shot being fired'.

Former Soviet President Mikhail Gorbachev, who met Reagan on a number of occasions, called him a 'great president', thanks to whom the Soviet Union and the USA had begun a difficult but crucial dialogue which led eventually to the end of the Cold War.

The US President George W. Bush said that Reagan left behind 'a nation he restored and a world he helped save…May God bless Ronald Reagan.'

It is natural that obituaries of statesmen are generally positive and pay glowing tribute to the deceased, but those paid to Ronald Reagan were unanimous in their praise of the man known as 'the great communicator'. This unanimity was not so obvious during his lifetime. Journalistic opinions varied from the affirmative to the downright critical:

> As time goes by, it becomes clear that President Reagan was not only a great president but also one of our greatest, right up there with FDR, Lincoln and maybe George Washington.
>
> (Dana Rohrabacher, *Daily Pilot*, 7 February 2001)

> Ronald Reagan may have been a likable guy…but his administration was also flat-out the most anti-democratic, hoodwinking, lying, Constitution-flouting, despot-coddling, rich-enriching, deficit-building, environment-despoiling, health-endangering, paranoid, cynical and fundamentally corrupt one in our nation's history.
>
> (Jim Washburn, *Orange County Weekly*, Vol. 7, No. 22, February 1–7 2002)

How could this man who was President of the USA for two terms inspire such widely differing views?

Historians also tend to polarize themselves along the lines indicated above. Some regard him as a B-movie actor who stumbled by chance into politics, a profession where he could act out his cowboy fantasies in front of a nationwide audience with no real need to understand events, just the ability to learn his lines and deliver them in a convincing style at the right moment. Others believed he was one of the greatest US Presidents of the twentieth century, who single-handedly ended the Cold War which had hogged the world stage since the end of the Second World War. During his time as President, Reagan was full of contradictions. He was the USA's most ideological President in his speeches, although more pragmatic in his actions. He emphasized the need for balanced budgets, but never submitted one himself; he hated nuclear weapons, but built thousands of them and even planned the futuristic-sounding missile system 'Star Wars'; he would write cheques to some poor people who had written to him directly, but he cut the benefits of many; he successfully united the country with patriotism, but his vision of the USA alienated millions worldwide; he preached family values but was the head of a very dysfunctional family. Perhaps the best way to view these contradictions is that he was a leader with clear objectives and stubbornness when trying to achieve them, but who also had the ability to compromise when it was necessary to do so.

Ronald Reagan's style of government was laid back; according to aides, Reagan worked two to three hours per day, napped at cabinet and summit meetings, and spent more than a year of his eight years in office relaxing on his Californian ranch. *The Economist* recalled that he seemed to take his job lightly:

> He popped jelly beans in cabinet meetings, and cracked jokes, rather than getting his head into the paperwork. He liked, indeed insisted on, his afternoon nap. His favourite books were westerns, and his favourite occupation, apart from those naps, was clearing brush on his ranch on the coast of California.

(*The Economist*, June 2004)

This relaxed approach to government did not mean that Reagan was ineffective; he preferred not to get immersed in details but to concentrate on the larger picture. He was aware that some might not appreciate this and commented:

Much has been said about my management style, a style that's worked successfully for me during 8 years as Governor of California and for most of my Presidency. The way I work is to identify the problem, find the right individuals to do the job, and then let them go to it. I've found this invariably brings out the best in people. They seem to rise to their full capability, and in the long run you get more done.

(*Ronald Reagan: An American Life*, Pocket Books, 1999)

Delegation not only enabled Ronald Reagan to keep focused on the broader view but also ensured that if things went wrong he could avoid being blamed. This gave rise to the nickname the 'Teflon President' – nothing stuck to him!

Assassination attempt

President Reagan's first term did not begin well. On 30 March 1981 he made a speech to the Construction Trades Council at the Hilton Hotel in Washington DC; he recalled in his autobiography: 'My speech at the Hilton Hotel was not riotously received – I think most of the audience were Democrats – but at least they gave me polite applause. After the speech, I left the hotel through a side entrance and passed a line of press photographers and TV cameras' (*Ronald Reagan: An American Life*, Pocket Books, 1999)

It was then that Reagan was shot by John Hinckley, Jr. Hinckley was trying to attract the attention of actress Jodie Foster, having seen a scene portraying a shooting incident in the film *Taxi Driver* (1976), and had decided to shoot a public figure in order to demonstrate his love for the actress. Reagan was more seriously injured than his short hospital stay and jaunty manner indicated. The bullet missed his heart by less than 2.5 cm (1 inch); it lodged in his lung, causing it to collapse. James Baker, White House Chief of Staff from 1981–5 and Secretary of Treasury from 1985–8, recalled that even in such extreme circumstances Reagan kept his sense of humour:

> …when we arrived at the hospital and he was on a gurney there, they were wheeling him into surgery and he looked up at us and he said, 'who's minding the store?' and again when he made his famous comment about the doctors 'I hope somebody's a Republican in this crowd'. What

people I don't think appreciated at the time, was how very close he came to dying, as a consequence of that assassination attempt.

(www.ronaldreagan.com)

Reagan's wife Nancy rushed to be at her husband's side to be greeted with the immortal words: 'Honey, I forgot to duck!' It seems that prior to this incident Nancy had had a premonition that something had happened and had returned to the White House early from a luncheon engagement. She had been so rattled by the attempt on her husband's life and sought the advice of astrologer Joan Quigley who would henceforth influence the President's schedule by pointing out 'good and bad days'. Reagan's personal popularity soared following the assassination attempt and survived even the revelation that he consulted an astrologer. The courage shown by the President 'under fire' enhanced his reputation and no doubt contributed to the indulgent attitude of the Congress towards his economic policy.

Economic policy

Reagan's main objective in domestic affairs was to reduce 'big government', that is, to lessen government intervention in the affairs of US citizens, intervention which had gradually been increasing since the time of the New Deal. He believed the 'Government is not the solution to our problems, government is the problem'. In essence he attacked the ideology of the New Deal and Lyndon B. Johnson's 'Great Society' and proposed to cut federal spending, lower taxes, liberate the free market from excessive government regulation and encourage private initiative and enterprise. The priority of Reagan's first 100 days in office was to be economic recovery.

On 28 April 1981, Reagan appeared before Congress for the first time since the assassination attempt and received a hero's welcome and overwhelming support for his economic package. Inflation was in double figures and interest rates were high; the budget deficit was $79 billion or 2.7 per cent of the USA's GNP – put simply the USA was spending more than it was earning. Although there was a federal deficit of over $100 billion, Reagan managed to persuade Congress to pass a plan for a three-year reduction in income tax rates. This was followed by cuts in domestic spending. During the 1980s, Reagan's policy of reducing income taxes and federal domestic budgets became known as 'Reaganomics'.

Reaganomics

Reaganomics consisted of four key elements to reverse the high inflation, slow growth economic record of the 1970s: a restrictive monetary policy, which included a rise in interest rates, designed to stabilize the value of the dollar and end runaway inflation; a 25 per cent across-the-board tax cut (The Economic Recovery Tax Act of 1981) designed to spur savings, investment, work and economic efficiency; a promise to balance the budget through limiting domestic spending; and action to roll back government regulation.

The Omnibus Budget and Reconstruction Act (1981) reduced the level of federal spending for 1982 by $35.2 billion. In spite of the President's promise to protect entitlement programmes such as Medicare and Social Security and to make savings by targeting 'waste, fraud and abuse', most of the cuts were made in areas such as health, education and housing programmes, and therefore came in for a great deal of criticism since the cuts fell most dramatically on programmes designed to help the poor. In his diary Reagan wrote, 'I'm trying to undo LBJ's Great Society. It was his war on poverty that led us to (this) mess.'

The Economic Recovery Tax Act cut personal taxes by 25 per cent – all tax payers would benefit, but the naturally wealthy would benefit the most, indeed the speaker of the House, Tip O'Neill, vowed to fight Reagan's programme because he claimed it '(soaked) the poor to subsidize the rich'. Reagan's supporters denied that the rich benefited at the expense of the poor and noted that, 'income tax revenues *increased* during this period and the share of taxes paid by the rich *increased* also!' (www.presidentreagan.info).

Reagan hoped that tax cuts would stimulate economic growth and reduce unemployment, which would in turn reduce social security payments and create more tax payers. Yet in spite of optimism and support for Reagan's tax cuts and increased defence spending, the economy went into decline as the Federal Reserve Board raised interest rates to fight inflation. Inflation did drop from 13.5 per cent in 1980 to 5.1 per cent in 1982, but at the same time a severe recession set in, as unemployment exceeded 10 per cent for the first time in 40 years. The administration modified its economic policy after two years by proposing selected tax increases and budget cuts to control rising deficits and higher interest rates. After the economic downturn in 1982, the reduced inflation rate of less than 5 per cent sparked record economic growth, and produced one of the lowest unemployment rates in modern US history, hitting a 14-year low in June 1988. As Reagan left office, the nation was experiencing its sixth consecutive year of economic prosperity.

However, the economic gains came at a cost of a record annual deficit; by 1984 it was $203 billion. The national debt ballooned with the administration running up nearly as much debt during its first term as had been run up over the previous 200 years. The budget deficit was exacerbated by a trade deficit. Americans continued to buy more foreign-made goods than they were selling. Reagan, nevertheless, adhered to his free trade stance, and signed an agreement to that effect with Canada. He also signed, reluctantly, trade legislation designed to open foreign markets to US goods.

Social programmes

In 1981, Congress agreed to cut more than $25 billion from welfare programmes, with further cuts of $20 billion to be implemented in 1982 and 1983. These cuts reversed the traditional, liberal approach which used government expenditure to drive the economy, while at the same time safeguarding groups such as the elderly and the poor. The social programmes affected by these cuts included child nutrition, job training, Aid to Families with Dependent Children (AFDC), and food stamps.

In line with his desire to reduce the role of the federal government, Reagan attempted to shift responsibility for welfare programmes from the federal government to the state governments, and social spending decreased as a percentage of government expenditure as some programmes were transferred back to the states. For the first time since the New Deal, states began to seek their own answers to problems and power began to shift from Washington DC to the states. Table 1 shows government spending on social welfare.

table 1 federal social welfare spending

Federal			
Year	Total social welfare (billions $)	% of GNP	% of government outlays
1960	24,957	5.0	28.1
1970	77,337	8.1	40.1
1980	303,276	11.5	53.2
1981	344,066	11.6	54.0
1982	367,691	12.0	52.5
1983	398,792	12.0	51.9
1984	420,399	11.3	50.2
1985	452,860	11.5	47.8
1986	472,364	11.3	47.6
1987	499,844	11.0	50.4
1988	532,144	10.9	49.1

(Source: 'Information Please', Almanac ed., p. 64, 1991.)

The Omnibus Budget Reconciliation Act (1981) allowed states to experiment with making workfare mandatory for AFDC recipients. Workfare meant that 'employable' recipients of welfare must accept a job or participate in a work related activity in order to receive benefits. Programmes such as the Basic Skills Training programmes were aimed at providing job skills, education, and employment opportunities for welfare recipients but were criticized by many as a means of taking money from the neediest in society.

Most government agencies such as the Environmental Protection Agency, the Occupational Safety and Health Administration, the Department of Transportation, the Department of Housing and Urban Development, and the Justice Department's anti-trust division found their budgets slashed by 10 per cent in 1981. The result was that companies reduced the costs of complying with regulations designed to promote public health and safety and consumer satisfaction.

Reagan's cutbacks in welfare, real or imagined, drew many criticisms from all walks of the liberal establishment. The music artiste James Taylor was so incensed by Reagan's social security spending cuts that he released a song criticizing the administration and referring to Reagan's previous career as a film cowboy, which contained the words:

> Take all the money that we need for school
> And to keep the street people in out of the cold
> Spend it on a weapon you can never use...
> Slap leather, head for that line of trees, yeah
> Go on Ron

(James Taylor, 'Slap Leather' on *New Moon Shine*, 1991)

The AIDS epidemic

The death of the actor Rock Hudson in 1986 from HIV/AIDS was the catalyst for the Reagan administration to speak out about the epidemic which had been sweeping the USA since the first case was reported in 1981. It is believed that no public statement had been made before this because Reagan had prevented the Surgeon General from speaking out about it in deference to the religious right, who saw AIDS as a disease confined to the gay male community and who believed its 'immoral' behaviour was responsible for spreading the disease. Consequently, Reagan's administration approached the situation cautiously, viewing the epidemic as an issue for the states rather than something of concern to the federal government.

The Surgeon General's report on Acquired Immune Deficiency Syndrome emphasized the need for an AIDS education policy and the distribution of free condoms. Following the publication of the report, Reagan appointed the Watkins Commission in 1987 to look into the situation. This commission reported that there was a need for increased federal funding, which was largely ignored by Reagan's administration and by the subsequent Bush administration.

Reagan and foreign policy

Reagan firmly believed that détente had caused the USA to lose ground to the USSR, and he returned to an anti-Soviet policy which included such initiatives as expanding the USA's armed forces, developing a new type of nuclear bomb (the neutron bomb), deploying missiles including the MX, Cruise and Pershing missiles in Europe, and developing a new form of defence against nuclear attack – the Strategic Defence Initiative (SDI), or Star Wars, as it became known. He justified these initiatives by playing on the need to rid the world of communism claiming that:

> ...the march of freedom and democracy will leave Marxism-Leninism on the ash heap of history as it has left other tyrannies which stifle the freedom and muzzle the self-expression of the people. And that's why we must continue our efforts to strengthen NATO even as we move forward with our zero-option initiative in the negotiations on intermediate-range forces and our proposal for a one-third reduction in strategic ballistic missile warheads.
>
> (Announcement from the SDI from the White House, 23 March, 1983)

It was Reagan's Star Wars initiative that caused concern not only in Russia but all over the world.

Star Wars

The SDI, or Star Wars, officially announced on 23 March 1983, was an expensive programme which aimed to develop anti-missile weapons that used laser beams. It intended to make it impossible for Soviet missiles to reach US targets by creating a huge laser shield in space. This system, should it have been built, would have been in direct contravention of the Anti-Ballistic Missile treaty of 1972. This treaty had brought stability to the nuclear weapons situation by ensuring that if either side launched an attack, their own destruction would be guaranteed (mutually assured destruction or MAD). If the SDI programme succeeded in developing this shield in space it would mean that the USA could not be the victim of a 'first strike' and might feel sufficiently confident to initiate a nuclear strike. Star Wars may have been meant as a purely defensive system, but to the Soviets it was a provocative gesture, especially because so much of Reagan's rhetoric was anti-Soviet. Although it was meant as a joke during a radio microphone test, Reagan's following announcement no doubt rattled the Soviets: 'My fellow Americans, I am pleased to tell you I just signed legislation which outlaws Russia forever. The bombing will begin in five minutes.'

Grenada

Although Reagan avoided direct conflict with major communist countries such as China, he did send paratroopers into Grenada against Bernard Coard, who had overthrown the elected government of Maurice Bishop in Grenada in October 1983. However, it was not made clear at the time that Bishop was himself a Marxist. Mere days after the invasion of Grenada, NATO began its 'Able Archer' war games – games designed to test NATO's nuclear-release procedures. The Soviets believed that 'Able Archer' was a cover for a NATO attack and several nuclear-capable planes were placed on alert in East Germany. The USA failed to realize how dangerous the situation between the US and USSR had become until the Director of the CIA met the British double-agent Gordievsky who clarified the effect Reagan's public proclamations were having on the Soviet leadership. This proved to be a turning point which paved the way for talks in Reykjavik, caused the Americans to tone down their military exercises and persuaded Reagan that it was necessary to begin discussions with the USSR rather than trying to provoke them. On 10 March 1985, Mikhail Gorbachev was elected unanimously by the Politburo as the new General Secretary. He had already spoken of the need for reform within the Soviet Union, and realized that one way to fund this was by reducing spending on defence. The British Prime Minister, Margaret Thatcher, had already declared that Gorbachev was a man she could do business with, but would Reagan be able to work with him?

Reagan and Gorbachev

Arms reduction talks in Geneva between Gorbachev and Reagan in November 1985 were not a success. Each leader accused the other of dividing the world and of accelerating the arms race but, following a short walk together, the two leaders sat down beside an open fire to continue their discussions and, to the surprise of all concerned, they appeared to enjoy each other's company. A similar pattern was repeated on the second day – disagreements in the morning and personal rapport in the afternoon. A dialogue had been opened and a final joint communiqué declared that nuclear war should never be fought and that the two sides should not attempt to achieve military superiority.

In October 1986, a mini-summit was agreed between the two powers at Reykjavik, but nothing came of the meeting as Reagan refused to relinquish his dream of SDI.

In February 1987, Gorbachev and Reagan signed the INF treaty which eliminated an entire class of Soviet and US nuclear arms from Europe – the SS-20s, Cruise and Pershing missiles that had caused so much protest in Britain were to be dismantled.

Gorbachev's bombshell

On 7 December 1988, Gorbachev addressed the UN general assembly and announced unilaterally a cut of 500,000 men in the Soviet armed forces, the removal of 10,000 tanks, 8,500 artillery pieces and 800 combat aircraft from Europe, large withdrawals from Manchuria and from the border with China. The Soviets were dismantling their Cold War armoury. Reagan was convinced that US strength and determination had forced the Soviets to give in, however, Mikhail Gorbachev was of a different opinion:

> I think that Gorbachev should get credit and the changes that happened in the Soviet Union...and both in domestic and foreign policies of the Soviet Union should get credit...That was very important. But Reagan, Shultz, and George Bush, they, too, should get credit because without their work, again, we wouldn't have ended the Cold War. Also, Mitterand, Thatcher, Andriotti, Chancellor Kohl, all of them, too should get part of the credit. So I think it was an important moment when the leaders of the leading countries of the world were able to reach a mutual understanding and act responsibly. But it was all a very dramatic process.
>
> (*Mikhail Gorbachev: Memoirs*, Bantam, 1997)

Irangate

Reagan funded anti-communist groups in several countries in Latin America and in Afghanistan. In Nicaragua an anti-communist group, the Contras, was fighting the elected Marxist government of Daniel Ortega. Reagan not only funded the Contras but also undermined the democratically elected Nicaraguan government by imposing economic sanctions upon the country. It was later discovered that the USA had attempted to damage the economy by the mining of Nicaragua's harbours.

In 1986, Reagan became embroiled in mysterious deals involving the secret sale of arms to the Islamic fundamentalist government in Iran in order to gain the release of US hostages in the Lebanon. The profits made in this way were then diverted to help the Contras in Nicaragua. This plan had been concocted by Colonel Oliver North with the apparent support of senior White House aides and the tacit approval of the President. Congress had refused to vote the President the funds he wanted to give to the Contras, and when this secret dealing became known it caused public outrage because the President had seemingly circumvented Congress. Although both North and the National Security Adviser, John Poindexter, denied that the President had any direct knowledge of the deal, the affair was christened 'Irangate' by the media and damaged Reagan's reputation as he had previously told the US public he would never 'yield to terrorist blackmail'.

The Tower Commission was established to investigate Irangate, and its report published in 1987 placed much of the responsibility for the affair on Reagan's laid-back management style. As a direct result of the scandal, the White House Chief of Staff, Donald Regan together with John Poindexter, were forced to resign. Reagan survived, but the case damaged his image and gave the impression that he was not in full control of his administration. The 'Great Communicator' attempted to heal the rifts with his public in a speech on 4 March 1987 by distancing himself from the arms deal but at the same time seeming to accept responsibility:

> First, let me say I take full responsibility for my own actions and for those of my administration. As angry as I may be about activities undertaken without my knowledge, I am still accountable for those activities. As disappointed as I may be in some who served me, I'm still the one who must answer to the American people for this behaviour. And as personally distasteful as I find secret bank accounts and diverted funds – well, as the Navy would say, this happened on my watch.

In retrospect, it seems that many of Reagan's decisions in foreign affairs were flawed.

In 1981, Reagan sent Donald Rumsfeld, his Middle East envoy, to Iraq. This resulted in Reagan selling Saddam Hussein 'dual-use' items which could be used for innocent civilian purposes but which could also be put to military use, e.g., helicopters and chemicals. He also armed the Mujahideen in Afghanistan which eventually evolved into the Taliban.

The historian Robert Dallek believes that Reagan was well served by his foreign policy advisers and by circumstance:

He happened to be there at the right time, it was the right moment, the Soviet Union was going into an eclipse, it could not sustain itself with its economic and internal contradictions for all that much longer, and Reagan happened to be there and had the wisdom to take advantage of it. So, I would say he has a general design, but the fact that he appears to be so successful in foreign affairs also has to do a great deal with circumstance, with luck.

(Robert Dallek during a PBS television interview, 1991, about his book, *Ronald Reagan: The Politics of Symbolism*, 1999)

End of an era

Ronald Reagan's popularity rating at the end of his second term in office in 1989 stood at 70 per cent. He had achieved many of his objectives by the end of his tenure of the White House: the Cold War was over, and to all intents and purposes, the USA had won; the country was experiencing a period of economic prosperity; federal taxes were the lowest they had been since before the Second World War; and the role of the federal government had been curtailed. All in all, Americans had regained their self-confidence thanks to the Great Communicator who had healed the rifts between the presidency and citizens caused by the Watergate scandal and the ineffective foreign policy of Carter. His words, as he left office on 11 January 1989, sum up Reagan's achievements for the majority of the American people:

... as I walk off into the city streets, a final word to the men and women of the Reagan revolution, the men and women across America who for eight years did the work that brought America back. My friends: We did it. We weren't just marking time. We made a difference. We made the city stronger. We made the city freer, and we left her in good hands. All in all, not bad, not bad at all.

Bush and Clinton

This chapter will cover:
- Bush's U-turn on his promise of 'no new taxes'
- Desert Storm
- Clinton scandals leading to impeachment.

President George Herbert Bush 1989–93

George Herbert Bush became the forty-first President of the United States in 1989, the first Vice-President since 1837 to win a presidential election. In his inaugural speech, he spoke of a new breeze blowing through history and, as his term began, 'a chapter begins, a small and stately story of unity, diversity, and generosity – shared, and written, together.' Many wondered whether this meant he would continue his predecessor's policies.

Economic policy

Bush had campaigned on the promise that he would not be raising taxes when he became President, but his immortal words, 'Read my lips – no new taxes,' would come back to haunt him before the end of his presidential term.

Bush had inherited a large federal budget deficit from Reagan, which was compounded by an economic recession that reduced the government's income from tax revenues, and by the costly Gulf War in 1991. By 1992, the federal budget deficit had risen to $400 billion. This was to prove a major problem for Bush because of the Gramm-Rudman-Hollings Act which had been passed in December 1985. This Act had set a series of targets for eliminating the federal budget deficit by 1991. If Congress and the president failed to agree on voluntary spending reductions, the law called for automatic cuts of the necessary percentage from each item in the budget. Half of the cuts were to come from domestic spending and half from defence spending. In June 1990, Bush abandoned his campaign pledge, raised taxes and made cuts of $492 billion in domestic and military spending. Many Republican conservatives were critical of this U-turn, but a compromise deficit-reduction plan was killed by the House. As a result, the government was almost forced to shut down for lack of money, while a new budget proposal was drafted.

Unemployment figures rose in 1991 and, in an attempt to create new jobs through raising exports, Bush toured Australia and some Far East countries in January 1992 but failed to bring any significant benefits to the US. One wonders whether this had anything to do with the incident at a formal banquet in Japan when Bush became ill – and vomited on Prime Minister Kiichi Miyazawa as he cradled the President's head!

In his 1992 State of the Union address, Bush proposed ways to stimulate economic growth, including fewer government regulations on business, the cutting of certain domestic programmes that he felt should not be funded by the federal government, and a cut in capital gains tax. He also proposed tax credits for first-time house buyers and to enable poor families to acquire health insurance. In spite of Congress adopting some of his proposals, the final bill was vetoed by President Bush because the amended bill proposed to raise taxes on the wealthy.

By 1992, interest rates and inflation were at the lowest level they had been since 1982, but unemployment had risen to 7.8 per cent and 14.2 per cent of the American population was living in poverty, according to the figures issued by the Census Bureau.

In one of his first measures as President, Bush proposed legislation to bail out the nation's financially troubled savings and loan institutions which had been facing severe difficulties. Congress passed a $50 billion ten-year plan to rescue the ailing industry, but the scope and cost of the problem grew, reaching $325 billion by 1990.

Social policy

Bush's policy, America 2000, proposed the use of educational reforms to raise the numbers of pupils graduating from high school to 90 per cent, to improve basic skills such as numeracy and literacy (including adult literacy), and to raise drug-awareness by improving anti-drugs education. He also proposed a partnership between private business and schools as a means to raise academic achievement.

Under the Clean Air Act (1990) a limit was placed on the amount of a pollutant that can be in the air anywhere in the USA. The aim was to ensure that all Americans have the same basic health and environmental protections. The law allowed individual states to have stronger pollution controls, but states were not allowed to have weaker pollution controls than those set for the whole country.

Just before the election of 1992, Bush signed the Energy Policy Act which aimed to promote the development of renewable energy and the conservation of energy.

Civil rights

Rodney King, an African American, became a symbol of police brutality in March 1991 when amateur photographer George Holliday shot a video that showed several white Los Angeles police officers using their batons to beat King, who had led them on a car chase after they tried to stop him for speeding. A Los Angeles jury seemed to ignore the video evidence. When the four policemen charged with the beating were acquitted, it set off the worst riot in US history. Fifty-five people were killed in several days of rioting, looting and retaliatory attacks against whites and Asians. About 2,000 people were injured, and another 12,000 arrested. More than $1 billion worth of property was damaged and the National Guard was deployed to help police restore order. President Bush and his Vice-President, Dan Quayle, have been criticized for failing to provide decisive leadership during this time of crisis, and it was not until May that Bush implemented an emergency programme for the poor; even then the Urban Aid Supplemental Bill, which provided $1.1 billion aid for the inner cities was far lower than Congress had requested.

Bush had some success with the Americans with the Disabilities Act of 1990 which was passed on 26 July 26 1990. This was a wide-ranging civil rights law that prohibited discrimination based on disability. It affords similar protections against discrimination to the disabled as the Civil Rights Act of 1964, which made discrimination based on race, religion, sex, national origin and other characteristics illegal. Certain specific conditions are excluded, including alcoholism and trans-sexuality.

In the Supreme Court, Bush continued to follow his predecessor's tendency to appoint conservative justices. Following the resignation of US Supreme Court Justice William J. Brennan in 1990, Bush called David H. Souter of New Hampshire to the post. In 1991, he appointed Clarence Thomas, an African-American federal judge, to the court to succeed Thurgood Marshall, who was scheduled to retire. Thomas was a federal court of appeals judge with strong conservative views and his nomination was opposed by some women's and civil rights organizations. Bush continued to support his nominee, even after a former member of Thomas's staff, law professor Anita Hill, accused the judge of sexual harassment in nationally televised hearings. Thomas was eventually confirmed in his appointment with a vote of 52–48.

Foreign policy

As President, Bush had most success in foreign affairs, an area in which he had most expertise and in which Presidents have the most liberty to exercise their powers.

Yet Bush faced a dramatically changing world: the communist empire, so feared by his predecessor, broke up after the Berlin Wall fell in 1989. A series of summits with Soviet President, Mikhail Gorbachev, resulted in the signing of treaties on arms reductions and agreements on other issues, but the Soviet President was nearly ousted in an attempted coup by communist hard-liners in August 1991. Thanks to Boris Yeltsin's resistance to the coup, Gorbachev was returned to power but resigned soon after. By December 1991, the Soviet Union had ceased to exist and had become a loose confederation of independent republics. Bush recognized the new states and sought to come to terms with Yeltsin, now president of Russia.

In the spring of 1992, Bush and Yeltsin agreed to substantial cuts in nuclear weapons. Bush later admitted that the end of the Cold War had taken him by surprise: 'I hoped it would end but I wasn't sure it would end that fast...I wasn't sure the [Berlin] wall would come down. I wasn't sure Germany would be unified. I wasn't sure that the Soviet Union would have dramatically imploded as it did' (*A World Transformed: George Bush and Brent Scourcroft*, Vintage, 1999).

In Latin America, Bush raised the banner of the Monroe Doctrine. Following the killing of a US soldier in Panama in 1989, he personally ordered troops to invade the country and to capture Panama's dictator, Manuel Noriega, who was threatening the security of the Panama Canal and of Americans living there. Noriega was brought to the USA for trial as a drug trafficker.

With the collapse of communism and the end of the Cold War, the USA was deprived of a clear focus in world affairs. But in 1990 came Iraq's invasion of Kuwait and US involvement in the Persian Gulf War. Critics claimed the real motive for fighting was oil. George Bush insisted it was a matter of principle that led to his decision to send 425,000 US troops to free Kuwait: 'The evil against the good was so clear it made it very easy for me.' Bush referred to the unprovoked invasion of Kuwait, Iraq's desire to control a large portion of the world's oil reserves, and Iraq's growing nuclear-weapons potential. In January 1991,

Bush asked Congress for 'all necessary means' to expel Iraq from Kuwait. He received congressional approval to use force.

After weeks of air and missile bombardment and the 100-hour land battle dubbed 'Desert Storm', the US troops, who had been joined by 118,000 other troops from allied nations, routed Iraq's 1 million-strong army. It has been argued that President Bush made a grave mistake when he allowed Saddam Hussein to stay in power in Iraq. He followed the advice of his 'war cabinet' which included Dick Cheney as Secretary of Defence. Cheney noted that invading Iraq would get the USA 'bogged down in the quagmire' and would have led to what Bush believed would be, 'incalculable human and political costs...We would have been forced to occupy Baghdad and, in effect, rule Iraq.' Bush felt it would have been disastrous for the USA to invade and occupy the country without allies to support them.

Following the Gulf war, Saddam Hussein crushed internal revolts by Kurds and Muslims. Although Bush sent relief aid to refugees fleeing Hussein's forces, there was still a feeling that somehow the USA had been partially responsible for the situation because of their reluctance to 'finish the job'. In 1992, as Saddam Hussein's troops continued to attack Shi'ite Muslims, Bush enlisted the support of France and Britain to establish a 'no-fly zone', enforced largely by US aircraft, preventing Iraq from sending planes into the disputed territory.

The 1992 presidential election

Bush's success in the Gulf War left him with the highest approval ratings of any President in the history of the Gallup polls. By most accounts, that should have given him a second term, yet it didn't. This was because the economy had weakened, and the voters took their frustrations to the ballot box. In his 1992 campaign for re-election, Bush was cast by the Democrats as a tired relic of the Cold War who had neglected the home front and broken his pledge not to increase taxes. His opponent, Bill Clinton, presented an opportunity for change, and Bush was further hampered by the appearance of a third candidate in the presidential race, the Texan billionaire Ross Perot who proposed to bring honesty back to US politics. Bush received 37.7 of the popular vote; Clinton received 43.2 per cent and Perot, 19 per cent.

President William Jefferson Clinton 1993–2001

William Jefferson Clinton was the first 'Baby Boomer' President, that is, one that was born after the Second World War. As such, he was a complete change from the older generation of politicians. Coming after the likes of Reagan and Bush, Bill Clinton seemed a very informal character, and his frequent trips to McDonald's become almost symbolic of his ordinariness. With his sound-bite rhetoric and pioneering use of pop culture in his campaigning, Clinton was derogated as the 'MTV' President, but he was the first Democratic President since Franklin D. Roosevelt to win a second term in office, and his election brought the Democrats complete control of the political bodies of the federal government – the House of Representatives, the Senate and the presidency.

The economy

The emphasis of Clinton's presidential campaign was the economy, which was given priority over all other issues and was kept at the forefront of his aides' thoughts by a poster on the campaign office wall stating, 'It's the economy stupid!' Having campaigned on promises to improve the US economy, Clinton had to make every effort to balance the budget and keep inflation in check. To reduce the annual deficit to achieve a balanced budget, Clinton had to reduce government spending and/or raise taxes. As he was reluctant to raise the taxes of the wealthy, whose votes he had been cultivating, or to cut fund to the armed forces, Clinton had to cut other areas of federal spending. According to Howard Zinn (*The Twentieth Century: A People's History*, 1998), Clinton spent less than the previous Republican governments on health care, food stamps, education and single mothers. Alan Greenspan, who was appointed as head of the Federal Reserve System, which regulated interest rates, was anxious to avoid inflation for fear it reduced profits of holders of government bonds, and consequently attempts were made to keep wage rises in check.

On the authority of the Office of Management and Budget, in 1991 the country began to enjoy a period of continuous economic expansion which continued throughout Clinton's two terms. Unemployment fell to the lowest level in 30 years, and more than 22 million new jobs were created. Clinton succeeded in turning the largest budget deficit in US history into a surplus and in paying off $360 billion of the national debt – in 1999 the federal budget was balanced for the first time since 1969. Federal government spending did decline but so too did the federal income tax burden.

Health care

In the 1997 budget, the Clinton-Gore administration made health care one of their priorities. There were a number of innovative proposals, including extending the life of the Medicare Trust Fund and offering new opportunities for patient choice and preventive care, for example, annual mammograms, screening tests for both colorectal and cervical cancer, and a diabetes self-management programme, hailed by the American Diabetes Association as the most important advance in diabetes care since the discovery of insulin. The Health Care Plan failed to pass through Congress. It was criticized by some health care professionals because it was a piecemeal reform which even at its best would not have established a universal 'Right to Health Care' nor ever reached 100 per cent health care coverage. Others believed the Health Care Plan failed because the public didn't understand it and had not been consulted about the changes they wanted to see in this area:

> The President's reform plan was...the product of experts and experts alone. Technical experts designed it, special interests argued it, political leaders sold it, journalists more interested in its political ramifications than its contents kibitzed it, advertising attacked it. There was no way for average Americans to understand what it meant to them'.
>
> (Daniel Yankelovich, 'The Debate that wasn't: The public and the Clinton Health Care Plan', *The Brookings Review*, Summer, 1995)

Following this failure, Clinton declared the era of big government to be over and concentrated instead on legislation to improve education, to protect the jobs of parents who cared for their sick children, to restrict the sale of handguns, and to strengthen environmental laws.

Sects and terrorism

Clinton's presidency saw two tragedies unfold, which some Americans blamed on the mishandling of the Branch Davidian sect by the Clinton administration. On 28 February 1993, the Bureau of Alcohol, Tobacco and Firearms (BATF) raided the Branch Davidian sect's ranch in a rural area near Waco, Texas. The BATF conducted the raid because there had been allegations that there were illegal weapons being constructed on the property, and as the Branch Davidians were an apocalyptic sect that believed that the prophesies of the Book of Revelations were about to be enacted, the FBI was concerned particularly for the safety of the children of the sect's members. Four agents and five members of the sect were killed in the initial raid. There followed a 51-day siege which ended on 19 April when the compound was consumed by fire following the attempted use of CS gas by the FBI. The cause of the fire was disputed, but the official explanation was that Koresh, the Sect's leader, had deliberately set fire to the enclosure in an act of defiant mass suicide. Over 80 men, women and children, including Koresh, were killed. Newly appointed US Attorney General Janet Reno had approved the final assault on the recommendation of FBI officials after being told that children were being abused inside the besieged complex, and both she and Clinton came under criticism for permitting the heavy-handed approach of the BATF and for mishandling the stand-off.

On 19 April 1995, on the second anniversary of the Waco incident, just after parents had dropped off their children at day care at the Murrah Federal Building in Oklahoma City, a massive bomb inside a rental truck exploded at 9.03 a.m., blowing up half of the nine-story building. One hundred and sixty-eight people died in what was then the worst terrorist attack on US soil and a nation watched as the bodies of men, women and children were pulled from the rubble for nearly two weeks.

Just over an hour after the explosion, an Oklahoma Highway Patrol officer pulled over 27-year-old Timothy McVeigh for driving without a licence plate; McVeigh was recognized as a bombing suspect and later charged with the bombing. At his trial, the US government asserted that the motivation for the attack was to avenge the deaths of Branch Davidians at Waco, Texas, whom McVeigh believed had been murdered by agents of the federal government. McVeigh called the casualties in the bombing 'collateral damage' and compared the action to actions he had taken as a soldier during the 1991 Gulf War. McVeigh was executed on June 11 2001, by lethal injection, at the US federal prison in Terre Haute, Indiana.

Foreign policy

In January 1994, Clinton and the Russian Premier, Boris Yeltsin, signed the Kremlin Accords which stopped the use of pre-programmed aiming of nuclear missiles at targets, and also provided for the dismantling of the nuclear arsenal in the Ukraine.

Northern Ireland

The Clinton administration was not the first US administration to have involved itself in the affairs of Northern Ireland, but the USA's role in Northern Ireland changed dramatically with the election of Bill Clinton in 1992. The pull of Irish ancestry remains strong in the USA, and privately many Americans donated money to the Irish Republican cause which was spent on arms for the provisional Irish Republican Army (IRA). As part of his presidential campaign, Clinton promised Irish Americans that he would send a peace envoy to Northern Ireland, an announcement which did not please the British government. Clinton believed he could turn the IRA away from the use of terror and towards the use of the ballot box to achieve their aims. One of his most controversial decisions was to grant a US visa to Sinn Fein President, Gerry Adams, in 1994; Adams reportedly had links with the nationalist terrorist group, the IRA. Adam's visit to Washington DC strengthened Clinton's influence over the Republican leaders and reinforced the case for turning away from violence. Clinton arrived for his first official visit to Northern Ireland in November 1995, 15 months after the IRA announced its first ceasefire. After famously shaking hands with Gerry Adams on Belfast's Falls Road (the exact location now features in the official Belfast bus tour), Clinton went on to receive a rapturous reception when he turned on the Christmas tree lights in Belfast city centre. He had succeeded in capturing the imagination of the people of Northern Ireland and was able to encourage both sides of the divided community to begin talks, setting in motion the process which would lead to the Good Friday Agreement.

Senator George Mitchell, who later chaired the political talks, was not merely a token envoy but a respected and impartial figure who effectively guaranteed the White House's involvement in helping to find a political settlement in Northern Ireland, between the north and the south, and Dublin and London. As the deadline for a deal drew near, Clinton kept open a hotline to Stormont so that he could be called on to intervene in any last-minute disputes. The BBC reported that, 'Without a doubt, [Clinton] played a crucial role in the delivering of the Good Friday Agreement, and he remains recognised for this among Northern Ireland people.'

The Middle East

President Clinton, it has been argued, looked to the Middle East to make his mark as a statesman. He presided over the historic 1993 Israeli-Palestinian Declaration of Principles, the peace treaty between Jordan and Israel in 1994; the Interim Agreement on Palestinian self-rule in 1995; and the Arab-Israeli peace process which led to the Wye River Accords in 1998 – many believe it was Clinton, together with the late King Hussein of Jordan – who pulled the peace process back from the brink at the Wye River summit in 1998.

Following the Wye River agreement, the peace process fell into stalemate until President Clinton urged both parties to come together at Camp David: 'If the parties do not seize this moment there will be more hostility and more bitterness – perhaps even more violence.' At Camp David in 2000, Clinton offered a proposal for a comprehensive peace, accepted by the government of Israel but apparently rejected by Yassar Arafat.

Bosnia

The Clinton administration led diplomatic efforts to end the civil war and 'ethnic cleansing' in Bosnia, which culminated in the Dayton Peace Agreement in November 1995. This agreement brought an end to the war in the former Yugoslavia which had been in progress for the previous three years, and settled the future of Bosnia and Herzegovina. The present political structure of the two countries and their political divisions along ethnic lines were generally agreed upon as part of the Dayton Accords.

However, the Clinton administration was criticized because its intervention in the Balkans was hesitant and belated. It came in 1995, only when the UN's peacekeeping operation was in trouble.

In other trouble spots, Clinton was less enthusiastic, perhaps because of the memory of the Battle of Mogadishu where, in October 1993, 18 US soldiers were killed on a mission intended to capture a local warlord. This incident had a negative effect on US foreign policy and on Clinton's willingness to commit troops abroad.

During the Rwandan genocide, the USA along with many other countries, refused to intervene militarily. In Sierra Leone and

East Timor, the Clinton administration encouraged countries like Nigeria and Australia to lead the peacekeeping effort, rather than commit troops of its own.

President Clinton launched the process of expanding NATO from a Cold War alliance to a haven for the new post-communist democracies, with new partners and members being admitted, including Hungary, Poland and the Czech Republic.

Iraq

The Clinton administration attempted to contain Iraq's power by supporting an effective inspection regime, which succeeded in destroying more chemical and biological weapons stock, missiles, warheads and laboratory facilities than had been destroyed in the 1991 Gulf War. Iraq was bombed for the failed attack on former President Bush and for hampering weapons inspection programmes. Clinton also supported the Oil for Food programme, which provided funding to Iraq to address the humanitarian needs of the Iraqi people.

Although Clinton visited more foreign countries than any other President and displayed a more sophisticated understanding of international affairs than most of his predecessors, his interventionist instincts were limited by political considerations at home in the USA. The US public would not consider the introduction of US troops abroad because of the Vietnam legacy of a fear of foreign entanglements.

Impeachment

As early as the 1992 presidential election campaign, rumours abounded about Clinton's adulterous relationships. These surfaced and increased with Paula Jones' accusations of sexual harassment in 1998. Mrs Jones was a former Arkansas state clerk who alleged that when Clinton was Governor of Arkansas in 1991, she was summoned to his room at the Excelsior Hotel in Little Rock by a state trooper. She was then propositioned by Senator Clinton but claims that she refused his offer, was told to keep quiet about the whole incident, and that she was later demoted at work as a result of her refusal. Mrs Jones filed a formal complaint against President Clinton in May 1994 alleging sexual harassment and defamation of character but, in April 1998, the case was thrown out by Federal Judge Susan Webber Wright saying that Jones' lawyers had failed to provide enough evidence to prove it could win at trial.

Gennifer Flowers, a former nightclub singer, became the focus of attention during Clinton's 1992 election campaign. She alleged at the time that she had an affair with Bill Clinton for 12 years while he was Governor of Arkansas. She sold tapes of their telephone conversations and said that he offered her a job in local government in exchange for sexual favours.

Former White House volunteer, Kathleen Willey, also complained of sexual harassment by Clinton when she went to ask advice about her financial difficulties, but Clinton denied the accusations in spite of Willey's deposition in 1993.

Monica Lewinsky was an unpaid intern when it was alleged that President Clinton first took an interest in her. It is claimed the two had an affair which lasted a year. Following recorded conversations between Linda Tripp and Monica Lewinsky in January 1998, Clinton's sex life became the focus of his public image.

These sexual liaisons became entangled with the Kenneth Starr investigation into the Whitewater affair.

The Whitewater scandal

It was learned that after the death of White House Counsel Vincent Foster, certain documents concerning the Whitewater Development Corporation of Arkansas had been removed from his office by White House Chief Counsel Bernard Nussbaum. President Clinton and his wife, Hillary, had invested in this corporation and were subsequently accused of fraud in connection with this investment.

At Clinton's request, an independent counsel was appointed in 1994 by the Department of Justice to investigate the legality of the Whitewater transactions, whereupon further accusations surfaced. However, the Clintons were cleared of any wrongdoing.

In 1998, the new independent counsel, Kenneth Starr, began investigating the Paula Jones accusations of sexual harassment and sent a report to Congress in which he charged Clinton with perjury, obstruction of justice, witness tampering, and abuse of authority in the Paula Jones lawsuit. The report also contained details of Clinton's liaisons with Monica Lewinsky. Starr was criticized for expanding the investigation beyond its initial scope and for the graphic nature of the report.

Clinton was impeached by the House of Representatives on 19 December 1998, on charges of perjury to a grand jury and

figure 10 Bill Clinton and Monica Lewinsky

(Source: Balance, *Herblock: A Cartoonist Life*, Times Books, 1998. Image courtesy of the Prints & Photographs Division, Library of Congress.)

obstruction of justice, and tried by the Senate in January 1999. He was only the second US President to be impeached, the other being Andrew Johnson in 1868.

Clinton's supporters claimed that the charges made against Clinton had nothing to do with his official duties and therefore did not amount to the severity of wrongdoing required for the impeachment and removal of a sitting President. In their opinion, the wide-ranging investigation was a witch-hunt of the President's personal life by the right wing. On the other hand, Clinton's opponents argued that as the President was effectively the chief law enforcement officer, his repeated lies and false testimony in a court of law were grounds for removal.

Impeachment proceedings began on 7 January 1999, and Clinton was finally acquitted by the Senate on both counts on 12 February 1999. It is interesting to note that the votes for and against impeachment fell along party lines with only Republicans voting for impeachment.

Political scandals

There were a number of other political scandals associated with Clinton's administration including Travelgate, the improper firing of staff in the White House travel office; Filegate, the failure of the White House to ask permission before handling personnel files; Pardongate, the US Attorney's office investigation into Bill Clinton's decision to commute the sentences of four men convicted of stealing millions in government funds; Chinagate, involving the Democrats accepting money which actually came not from an individual but from the Chinese government; and Troopergate, where state troopers procured women for the President.

Achievements

Bill Clinton had the potential to be one of the greatest and most successful Presidents that the US had ever seen. He was a working-class boy who succeeded in going to Georgetown University to study international affairs, attaining a BS degree in 1968, winning a Rhodes scholarship to Oxford University, and graduating from Yale Law School in 1973. Clinton's achievements in office were many and varied; he ushered in a period of prosperity which the USA had not seen for many years – he could point to the lowest unemployment rate in modern times, the lowest inflation and a budget in surplus.

Clinton appealed to a wide sector of American people: Toni Morrison called Clinton, 'the first Black president,' as he 'displays every trope of blackness: single-parent household, born poor, working-class, saxophone-playing, McDonald's-and-junk-food-loving boy from Arkansas'; he appealed particularly to 'Generation X' voters, the children of Baby-Boomers, young voters, many voting for the first time; he even appealed to the 'soccer mom' vote. Yet he also failed to live up to his potential, preferring to squander his reputation on cheap thrills. *The Economist*, January 2001, summed up Clinton's presidency thus: 'In these past weeks, as the focus has shifted to another inexperienced but less clever southern governor, there is a huge sense of talent wasted. With more discipline and less self-indulgence, how good eight years of Bill Clinton could have been.'

18

the end of the millennium

This chapter will cover:
- events at the end of the
  twentieth century
- dramatic events in 2001.

As the millennium approached, pundits took stock of the century which was reaching its conclusion and looked forward to the twenty-first century. Others predicted the end of the world, and considerable effort was taken by business and government to prepare for the effects of a supposed inherent fault in microprocessor chips whose internal clocks would be unable to function when the year changed from 1999 to 2000. For most people, however, the end of the year was a time of excitement – a once in a lifetime event to be enjoyed. The huge crowd that packed Times Square in New York included people from around the world, and as they counted down the seconds until midnight, they all became part of the nation's biggest celebration. The drop of the huge crystal ball in Times Square set off an explosion of fireworks, cheering and kisses as the millennium came to the US mainland, and with it new challenges.

On New Year's Eve, people gathered in many public spaces in cities across the world and Washington DC was no exception; President Clinton was due to speak from the steps of the Lincoln Memorial. He spoke just moments before midnight but the crowd in Washington, anxious for the New Year and the start of the new millennium, barely paid attention as the President who led the USA from the twentieth century into the twenty-first century asked the American nation: 'If the story of the 20th century is the triumph of freedom, what will the story of the 21st century be? Let it be the triumph of freedom, wisely used, to bring peace to a world in which we honor our differences and even more, our common humanity'.

Instead, children blew bubbles, were hoisted onto shoulders for a better view, shook cans of 'silly string', and prepared paper streamers for the moment when the countdown ended.

Fortunately, the dire warnings of the FBI's project Megiddo, which had advised police chiefs across the country that the Bureau had discovered evidence of religious extremists, racists, cults and other groups preparing for violence as New Year's Eve approached and had urged law enforcement agencies to view the dawn of the next millennium as a catalyst for criminal activities, had not been fulfilled. The predicted catastrophe caused by the so-called 'millennium bug' failed to appear – aircraft did not fall out of the sky, electrical equipment continued to operate, no people were trapped in lifts and the planet did not grind to a halt.

A little over one year later, in 2001, a new President was inaugurated. George W. Bush, son of former President George

Herbert Bush, became the forty-third President of the USA. Bush had won the presidential election against his Democrat rival, Al Gore, by only five electoral votes (Bush 271, Gore 266), and it was the first election contest since 1888 in which the successful candidate lost the popular vote but won the electoral college vote and, with it the presidency. Bush's inaugural speech, made on 20 January 2001, in hindsight seems prophetic:

> The enemies of liberty and our country should make no mistake. America remains engaged in the world, by history and by choice, shaping a balance of power that favors freedom. We will defend our allies and our interests. We will show purpose without arrogance. We will meet aggression and bad faith with resolve and strength. And to all nations, we will speak for the values that gave our nation birth.

The difference in tone and emphasis between the two speeches is prophetic of the change that was to be wrought, so forcefully, on the culture and attitude of the United States later in 2001.

Bush in office

President George Bush began his term in office by implementing a tax cut, the Economic Growth and Tax Relief Reconciliation Act of 2001, claiming that it would increase the pace of economic recovery and job creation although his opponents alleged these cuts actually favoured the wealthy and certain special interest groups.

In June 2001, while on his first visit to Europe in his role as President, Bush came under attack for his rejection of the Kyoto Protocol. This Protocol, aimed at reducing global warming by reducing the emission of carbon dioxide into the atmosphere, was rejected by the Senate as it would exempt certain nations such as China even though these nations were themselves polluters on a large scale, since they were classified as developing nations.

In foreign affairs Bush had spoken of closer links between the USA and Latin American countries such as Mexico, and of a wish not to become involved in 'nation building ' nor in petty military engagements. However, administration was to focus intently on Middle Eastern policy following the events of September 2001.

11 September 2001

It was a beautiful morning with a clear blue sky, which gave no clue to the events about to unfold. All over New York, everyday rituals were being conducted: parents waved off their children on the yellow school buses; families bade their goodbyes as they went their separate ways to work, shop, meet friends or simply to enjoy the day as the season slowly turned from summer to autumn. All were oblivious to the fact that US history was about to be changed forever.

This peaceful scene was shattered at 8.45 a.m. when American Airlines Flight 11 out of Boston, Massachusetts, crashed into the north tower of the World Trade Center, tore a gaping hole in the building and set it on fire. At 9.03 a.m. United Airlines Flight 175 from Boston crashed into the south tower of the World Trade Center and exploded. At 9.43 a.m., American Airlines Flight 77 crashed into the Pentagon. At 10.05 a.m., the south tower of the World Trade Center collapsed, hurtling into the streets below. A massive cloud of dust and debris formed and slowly drifted away from the building into the surrounding area. At 10.10 a.m., United Airlines Flight 93 crashed in Somerset County, Pennsylvania, south-east of Pittsburgh. The fourth airplane failed to reach its target, believed to be the White House or Capitol Hill in Washington DC thanks to the bravery of the passengers on board who attempted to overpower the hijackers. At 10.28 a.m., the World Trade Center's north tower collapsed from the top down. There were no survivors from the hijacked planes, and the death toll in the World Trade Center and the Pentagon came to nearly 3,000.

These terrorist attacks which took place on 11 September 2001 (9/11), were the first time that mainland USA had been attacked by a foreign foe. The attacks involved the hijacking of four commercial airlines by members of al-Qaeda, a militant Islamist terrorist group. These four, fully fuelled airplanes became, in effect, flying bombs which were deliberately flown and crashed into pre-chosen targets.

Rescue and recovery

Within minutes of the first plane striking the World Trade Center north tower, New York City firefighters rushed to the scene. Because of problems with radio communication, many firefighters lost touch with the command centres and failed to hear the orders to evacuate the building. When the towers

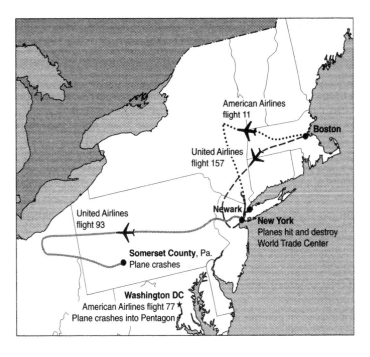

figure 11 11 September 2001 attacks

collapsed, hundreds were killed or trapped beneath the debris. Local media reported that about 350 firefighters were missing – more than the total number lost to the service in the whole of the USA since 1977.

The experiences of the firefighters were captured on film by Jules and Gedeon Naudet who were, at the time of the attacks, filming the experiences of a new recruit in the New York Fire Department and, by chance, captured the only known film footage of the first plane hitting the towers.

Volunteers began to stream into the area, known as 'Ground Zero', soon after the towers collapsed, determined to help in any way they could. During the first few days, people with skills as diverse as demolition, engineering, medicine and counselling worked alongside the American Red Cross and disaster relief specialists during the rescue and recovery effort.

The rescue operation also received help from foreign governments, some eager to repay the USA for the help it had sent them in time of crisis: Belgium sent a medical team specializing in the treatment of burns; Turkey, which received millions of dollars of US aid after it was struck by earthquakes in 1999, sent a specialist search-and-rescue team; Japan, also hit by devastating earthquakes, offered expert assistance; and the Dalai Lama donated $30,000 to the US relief effort as thanks for the US support of Tibet.

Responsibility

The responsibility for the terrorist attacks of 9/11 has been shown to lie with the militant Islamic group, al-Qaeda, but immediately after the tragedy no one was completely certain which terrorist group was responsible. It was claimed initially that the Democratic Front for the Liberation of Palestine was responsible, but this was denied by a senior leader of the group, and the attacks were denounced by Yasser Arafat, the Palestinian leader.

Claims were made that the Taliban, the Islamic government of Afghanistan, was responsible, but this group also publicly denounced the attacks. In fact, all world leaders whether allies, rivals or enemies of the USA denounced the attacks of 9/11. The only exception being Saddam Hussein, the leader of Iraq at that time; he claimed that the attacks were the harvest reaped by the USA for its crimes against humanity.

Al-Qaeda, although not explicitly claiming responsibility for the attacks, did hint at their involvement and praised those who had carried out the attacks. The US government declared the group and its leader, Osama bin Laden, as the prime suspects. This declaration seems to have been upheld following the arrest of two of the group's members, Khalid Mohammed and Ramzi Binalshibh, and an interview with a leading journalist on the Arabic television station al Jazeera. In 2004, the US government commission investigating the attacks concluded that they had been planned and executed by al-Qaeda operatives.

On 29 October 2004, in a videotape aired on al Jazeera, Osama bin Laden claimed responsibility for the attacks stating:

> We decided to destroy towers in America…God knows that it had not occurred to our mind to attack the towers, but after our patience ran out and we saw the injustice

and inflexibility of the American-Israeli alliance toward our people in Palestine and Lebanon, this came to my mind.

The war on terrorism

The 9/11 attacks led to what President George W. Bush called the 'war on terror'. Not only did the US government increase measures against terrorist groups but also against the governments and countries accused of harbouring them. As a direct consequence of this 'war on terror', the US government targeted the Taliban government of Afghanistan who refused to give up the chief suspect Osama bin Laden to the US authorities. On 7 October 2001, the USA and its ally Britain began the invasion of Afghanistan by launching bombs and cruise missiles against Taliban military and communications facilities, and suspected terrorist training camps in Afghanistan. By 5 December, the Taliban government had been replaced by a 30-member power sharing interim government, and the country occupied by a contingent of international peacekeepers.

Iraq

In 2002, President Bush pressed the UN to send weapons inspectors to Iraq in order to inspect the progress being made in disarming and disposing of the country's so-called Weapons of Mass Destruction (WMDs). The UN Security Council Resolution 1441 allowed inspectors, led by Hans Blix, to investigate allegations that Saddam Hussein was in fact developing WMDs rather than dismantling them. These inspectors were forced to leave the country in 2003 without being able to verify or rule out the existence of WMDs. It became clear that Bush would not be able to persuade the UN Security Council to vote for a further resolution and, instead, he gathered together a group of approximately 40 countries who would support a war against Iraq.

In March 2003, the USA invaded Iraq because of its unwillingness to implement the UN Resolution and because of the country's refusal to co-operate with the weapons inspectors. The immediate goal of the invasion was to ensure that Iraq could not develop or deploy WMDs and, to this end, it was also necessary to topple the country's ruler, the dictator Saddam

Hussein. The war has come under much criticism from many quarters, including the Secretary General of the UN, Kofi Annan, who called the conflict an illegal act. The Iraqi armed forces collapsed in the face of the superior fire power of the USA and its allies, but the problems in Iraq continue to mount. To date, no WMDs have been found, and it has been claimed that these were in fact figments of the imagination created as a pretext for war. To some extent these claims have been supported by investigations by the Senate Select Committee on Intelligence.

On 12 January 2005 a White House spokesman admitted that the search for weapons of mass destruction in Iraq had concluded without any evidence of the banned weapons.

conclusion

> We will stand mighty for peace and freedom, and
> maintain a strong defence against terror and
> destruction. Our children will sleep free from the threat
> of nuclear, chemical or biological weapons...And the
> world's greatest democracy will lead a whole world of
> democracies.

In 2004, Bill Clinton's words at the close of the twentieth
century seem to have a hollow ring to them.

The 'American Century' closed in the way that it had begun –
with the flight of an airplane. The flight of the Wright
brothers at Kittyhawk in 1905 promised so much. The three
flights on 9/11 destroyed so much.

glossary

American constitution A legal document stating the rights and freedoms of the people of America and the limitations on the power of the government.

Apollo Project Manned lunar landing programme.

baby boom Period of population growth following the Second World War.

CIA Central Intelligence Agency – a counter-intelligence agency for use originally outside the USA.

Cold War Conflict between Democratic West and Communist East which attempted to avoid an actual 'hot' war for fear of the use of nuclear weapons.

congress Group of politicians elected by the people which is responsible for making laws.

D-Day Allied landings in occupied France in order to liberate Europe from Nazi rule.

Defcon 3 Highest state of nuclear alert for American forces.

democrats Members or supporters of the Democratic party, one of the two major political parties in the USA.

dust bowl Area of flat grasslands where a prolonged drought and strong winds blew away the topsoil making the area unfertile.

Enola Gay The plane which carried the atomic bomb dropped on Hiroshima.

FBI Federal Bureau of Intelligence – main role is to deal with federal crimes.

federal government The central government which is responsible for matters concerning the country as a whole.

fundamentalists Religious groups who take the events described in the Bible or other sacred texts literally.

ghetto Areas in a city where groups of people of a particular race, nationality or religion live almost isolated from the rest of the city.

homesteaders People who claimed free land in the West following the 1862 Homestead Act.

Jim Crow laws A music-hall character dressed in rags with a blacked up face who came to symbolise a white view of black people. Name later applied to the segregation laws in the South.

Ku Klux Klan A terrorist group which believed in White supremacy and was anti-African American, anti-Semitic and anti-Catholic.

League of Nations Association of states which aimed to cooperate with each to ensure peace and security and avoid world war.

little boy An atomic bomb.

Monroe Doctrine A statement made in 1923 that any attack on the continent of America would be viewed as an attack on the USA.

progressivism A political movement which was anxious to improve American politics and society at the beginning of the twentieth century.

prohibition A law which forbade the sale and consumption of alcohol.

Red Scare Fear that anarchists and communists were plotting revolution in the USA.

Republicans Members or supporters of the Republican party, one of the two major political parties in the USA.

rugged individualism People succeeded by their own hard work and not relying on the government for help.

socialists People who believe in a more equal society and in extending the role of the state in the economy.

Star Wars Strategic Defense Initiative – a proposed defence against nuclear attack.

state government Each state within the USA has its own local government with particular powers and laws.

Stormont Since 1974 the administrative headquarters for Secretaries of State of Northern Ireland. Now the home of the Northern Ireland Assembly.

Supreme Court Judicial branch of the federal government which ensures all legislation passed by Congress is constitutional.

tariffs Taxes placed on imported goods to protect home industries.

The Depression A period of economic hardship.

the New Deal Policies intended to provide relief from the effects of the Depression, rebuild the US economy and reform the economic system.

Treaty of Versailles Peace Treaty forced upon Germany by the victorious Allies following the First World War.

Vietnamization Getting the Army of the Republic of Vietnam to take responsibility for the fighting in Vietnam.

WASPs White Anglo-Saxon Protestants.

Western Front Main area of fighting in Western Europe during the First World War.

abbreviations

AAA Agricultural Adjustment Administration
ABM anti-ballistic missile
AEF American Expeditionary Force
AFDC Aid to Families with Dependent Children
ARVN Army of the Republican of Vietnam
BATF Bureau of Alcohol, Tobacco and Firearms
BEF Bonus Expeditionary Force
CCC Civilian Conservation Corps
CPI Committee on Public Information
CIA Central Intelligence Agency
CIO Congress of Industrial Organizations
CORE Congress for Racial Equality
CREEP Committee to Re-elect the President
CWA Civil Works Administration
DIA Defense Intelligence Agency
ExComm Executive Committee of the National Security Council
FERA Federal Emergency Relief Administration
FBI Federal Bureau of Investigation
FDR Franklin Delano Roosevelt
FCA Farm Credit Administration
FEPC Fair Employment Practice Committee
FSA Farm Security Administration
GIs abbreviation of government or general issue
GNP Gross National Product
HOLC Home Owners Loan Corporation
ICC Interstate Commerce Commission
HUAC The House Un-American Activities Committee

INF Intermediate Range Nuclear Force Treaty
IRA Irish Republican Army
IRS Internal Revenue Service
NAACP National Association for the Advancement of Colored People
NATO North Atlantic Treaty Organization
NIRA National Industry Recovery Act
NLRB National Labor Relations Board
NOW National Organization of Women
NRA National Recovery Administration
NSA National Security Agency
NVA North Vietnamese Army
NWLB National War Labor Board
NYA National Youth Administration
OEEC Organization of European Economic Co-operation
OPA Office of Price Administration
OPEC Organization of Petroleum Exporting Countries
PWA Public Works Administration
RA Resettlement Administration
RFC Reconstruction Finance Corporation
SALT Strategic Arms Limitation Treaty
SCLC Southern Christian Leadership Conference
SDI Strategic Defense Initiative
SEATO South East Asia Treaty Organization
SEC Securities and Exchange Commission
SNCC Student Non-Violence Coordinating Committee
TVA Tennessee Valley Authority
UN United Nations
UNIA Universal Negro Improvement Association
Vietcong Vietnamese Communists
WAC Women's Army Corps
WAFS Women's Auxiliary Ferrying Squadron
WASPs White Anglo-Saxon Protestants
WIN 'whip inflation now'
WMDs Weapons of Mass Destruction
WPA Works Progress Administration

taking it further

Books

Ambrose, Stephen. *Nixon Volumes 1 and 2*, Simon and Schuster, 1989.

Branch, Taylor. *Parting the Waters: Martin Luther King and the Civil Rights Movement 1954-1963*, Macmillan, 1991.

Brogan, Hugh. *The Longman History of The United States*, Longman, 1999.

Bryson, Bill. *Made in America*, Black Swan, 1998.

Carter, Paul. *The Twenties in America*, Harlan Davidson, 1975.

Clinton, Bill. *My Life*, Knopf, 2004.

Cooke, Alistair. *Alistair Cooke's America*, BBC, 1973.

Ford, Gerald. *A Time to Heal*, Harper and Row, 1979.

Galbraith, J.K. *The Great Crash*, Hamish Hamilton, 1955.

Giglio, J.N. *The Presidency of John F. Kennedy*, Kansas University Press, 1991,

Gorbachev, Mikhail. *Memoirs*, Bantam, 1997.

Hamilton, Nigel. *Bill Clinton and American Journey*, Random House, 2003.

Hersh, Seymour. *The Dark Side of Camelot*, Back Bay books, 1998.

Jones, Maldwyn. *American Immigration*, University of Chicago Press, 1960.

Jones, Maldwyn. *The Limits of Liberty*, OUP, 1995.

Lacey, Robert. *Ford: The Men and the Machines*, Little, Brown and Co., 1986.

Leuchtenburg, William. *Franklin D. Roosevelt and the New Deal, 1932–1940,* Harper Collins, 1963.

Lightbody, Bradley. *The Cold War,* Routledge, 1999.

Lowe, Peter. *The Korean War,* Longman, 1997.

Manchester, William. *Death of a President,* Galahad, 1988.

Reagan, Ronald. *An American Life,* Pocket books, 1999.

Reichard, Gary. *Politics as Usual: the age of Truman and Eisenhower,* Harlan Davidson, 1988.

Sanders, Vivienne. *The USA and Vietnam, 1945–1975,* Hodder and Stoughton 1999.

Smith Matthew. *The Second Plot,* Main Stream Publishing, 2003.

Terkel, S. *Hard Times: An Oral History of the Great Depression,* 1970.

Traynor, John. *Mastering Modern United States History,* Palgrave, 2001.

Walker, Martin. *Makers of the American Century,* Vintage, 2001.

Zinn, Howard. *A People's History of the United States,* HarperPerennial, 1990.

Websites

www.americanpresident,org
www.cnn.com/SPECIALS/cold.war/
www.eisenhower.utexas.edu
www.fdrlibrary.marist.edu/index.html
www.jfklibrary.org
www.koreanwar.org/
www.lbjlib.utexas.edu
www.ronaldreagan.info
www.spartacus.schoolnet.co.uk/USAcivilrights.htm
www.spartacus.schoolnet.co.uk/USAmccarthyism.htm
www.theodoreroosevelt.org
www.trumanlibrary.org
www.vietnamwar.net/
www.yale.edu/lawweb/avalon/avalon.htm

index

the cold war
0340 884940 £8.99

nazi germany
0340 884908 £8.99

the middle east
0340 884916 £8.99

the second world war
0340 884932 £8.99

special forces
0340 884924 £8.99

the first world war
0340 884894 £8.99

the british monarchy
0340 889276 £8.99

twentieth century usa
0340 900938 £8.99

the history of ireland
0340 890010 £8.99

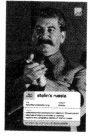

stalin's russia
0340 889314 £8.99

Why not try another book from
the **teach yourself** series?
Read on to sample a
chapter from **The Second World War**.

teach yourself ®

teach yourself

the second world war

goal
sample another book

category
history

content
- understand the development of the war
- explore this important period in world history
- discover the details of this astounding story

be where you want to be with **teach yourself**

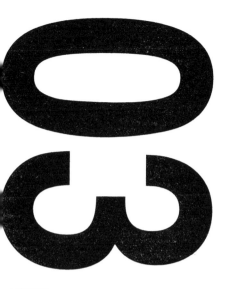

03

Britain alone

This chapter will cover:
- the Battle of Britain and the Blitz
- the search for allies.

Soon after 5.00 p.m. on 7 September 1940, over 300 German bombers, escorted by twice that number of fighters, attacked the East End of London. They bombed Woolwich Arsenal, a power station, a gas works, the docks and the City. Two hours later, another 200 bombers appeared. The bombing continued throughout the night, the last attack taking place soon after 4.00 a.m. German pilots, returning to their bases in France, spoke of London being an 'ocean of flames'. 'This is the historic hour when our air force for the first time delivers its blows right into the enemy's heart,' declared Herman Göring. More than 400 people were killed and 1,600 badly injured. The attack, the first mass bombing raid on Britain, marked a change of tactics. Rather than focusing their attack on the destruction of the RAF, the Germans had gone for a softer target. In so doing they were committing a major blunder that may have cost them victory in the Second World War.

'The Battle of France is over,' Winston Churchill declared on 18 June 1940, 'I expect that the Battle of Britain is about to begin.' Britain seemed to stand very little chance of winning this battle. If it was not quite alone – there was the support of the Dominions (Australia, Canada, South Africa, New Zealand, but not Eire) and other parts of the Empire – Britain's position seemed hopeless. By the summer of 1940, Nazi Germany dominated western and central Europe. Some states not taken over by Hitler were effectively German satellites (like Slovakia) or allies (like Hungary). Although Sweden and Switzerland remained democratic and neutral, they were tied to the German economic system. German military success during 1939–40 had been achieved at a trifling cost in men and materials. Most Germans assumed the war was effectively over. Final victory over Britain seemed just a matter of time. Yet Britain managed to survive. Why? What hope did it have during 1940–1?

The Battle of Britain

If the speed and scale of German victory left Britain stunned, it also left Hitler undecided as to how to use his triumph. He had never desired war with Britain. In early July, without much enthusiasm, he ordered plans to be made for an invasion of Britain. He hoped that the invasion – code named Operation Sealion – would not be necessary. In a speech on 19 July, Hitler offered peace terms to Britain. In return for recognition of Germany's hegemony in Europe, Britain would be allowed to maintain her empire and navy. He believed he had little to gain from Britain's defeat. In August he told his chief generals, 'Germany is not striving to smash Britain because the beneficiaries will not be Germany but Japan in the East, Russia in India, Italy in the Mediterranean and America in world trade'. Hitler's thoughts were already focused more on Russia than on Britain. Even while Sealion was being planned, German troops began to move eastwards.

Churchill's cabinet did not totally brush aside the possibility of peace. Churchill, himself, however, had no intention of 'parleying' with Hitler. Instead, he exhorted the British people to fight on. Many have stressed the importance of Churchill's oratory in strengthening British resolve. He was more modest, 'It was the nation and the race dwelling all round the globe that had the lion's heart. I had the luck to be called on to give the roar'. The 'Dunkirk spirit' was certainly not something that was conjured up by Churchill. Most Britons were determined to continue the war. Nevertheless, Churchill's 'roar' was important. Confidently citing history, he convinced his fellow countrymen that the war could be won.

Churchill was determined to preserve Britain's position as a great power. Yet he never really faced up to the mismatch between British resources and British commitments. Nor did he look far into the future. He seemed to think, like Hitler, that most problems could be overcome by will power. It is possible to question his judgement to fight on. If he had made peace in 1940, British power might have been left intact while Stalin and Hitler slugged it out in the East – to Britain's benefit. In many respects, Churchill's decision to continue the war was irrational. Britain by itself could not defeat Germany. Churchill's only hope was that Germany and Russia would fall out or that the USA would enter the war on Britain's side. Alliance with Russia would link Britain with a regime which was just as evil as that of Hitler's. Alliance with the USA was unlikely to benefit Britain's long-term interests. By continuing the war, it may be that Churchill bankrupted Britain and mortgaged her future to the USA. It should be said that this was probably a better fate than putting trust in Hitler and becoming a client state of Nazi Germany.

In July, Churchill signalled his determination to fight on. He regarded the French fleet, anchored at Mers-el-Kebir, as a potential menace. Although the Franco–German armistice terms agreed that the fleet should remain in French hands, there was a real danger that Hitler might seize it. On 3 July, Churchill ordered its destruction. The British attack on July 5 resulted in three capital ships being put out of action. One thousand two hundred and fifty French sailors were killed. The US President, Franklin D. Roosevelt (FDR), approved Britain's action. It did much to convince him of Churchill's resolve to continue the war. Thus, Britain was worth supporting. The attack, nevertheless, soured Britain's relations with Vichy France. Petain's government broke off diplomatic relations with Britain.

Given that Churchill would not make peace, Hitler had little alternative but to make war. Still, he remained half-hearted about Sealion, so much so that he did not direct the campaign personally. Instead, after a whistle-stop tour of France, he returned to Germany to ponder the future. The German high command structure was such that when Hitler's attention wandered, there was no one with the drive or vision to pick up the reins. In historian A. J. P. Taylor's view, Sealion was a mixture of 'improvisation and bluff'. In Britain, however, the German threat was taken seriously. Home Guard units, armed with a variety of makeshift weapons, prepared for invasion. Army chiefs doubted whether they could hold up German forces once they had landed. Navy chiefs doubted whether they could prevent a landing if the *Luftwaffe* controlled the air. Thus, as the Chiefs of Staff reported, 'all depends on the air force'.

German thinking was much the same. The *Wehrmacht* was confident of conquering Britain if it could get its forces ashore. The German navy, decimated in the Norwegian campaign, was in no position to protect an invasion force. Only the *Luftwaffe* could prevent the Royal Navy destroying German landing forces. In late July, Hitler gave orders for a massed air offensive against Britain, to be followed by a cross-Channel assault in September, 'if we have the impression that the English are smashed'. Barges and coastal steamers were assembled in Belgium and northern France. The Germans were working to a tight schedule. British aerial resistance would have to be broken quickly, allowing time for the *Luftwaffe* to bomb the Royal Navy out of the Channel. By October bad weather would make an invasion impossible. Thus, everything depended on the conflict between the *Luftwaffe* and the RAF. This conflict, fought over the skies of southern England in the late summer and early autumn of 1940, is known as the Battle of Britain.

Göring was confident of success – with good reason. In July, the *Luftwaffe* had some 2,600 planes and 10,000 trained pilots, compared to the RAF's 1,000 planes and 1,500 trained pilots. Nonetheless, the *Luftwaffe* also faced serious problems. Given that it was making use of captured enemy airfields in Belgium and northern France, every local facility – of supply, repair, signals – had to be adjusted to German needs. Nor were *Luftwaffe* leaders clear on strategy. Was the aim to bomb British industry, population centres, radar stations, airfields or the Royal Navy, or was it essentially to destroy British fighters? German planes had to fly scores of kilometres before coming to grips with the RAF. German Messerschmitt fighters (Me109s and Me110s) lacked the range to operate over more than a corner of southern England. RAF Fighter Command, by contrast, was operating from home bases and over home territory. This meant its planes could stay aloft longer. Moreover, RAF pilots who had to bail out often lived to fight another day. German aircrews died or became prisoners.

Perhaps the main problem was that Göring and other German leaders underestimated the RAF's strength. They assumed that Britain could only produce 200 fighters per month. In fact, British factories turned out over 400 Spitfires and Hurricanes a month between July and November. (The Germans only built an average of 200 fighters a month in the same period.) Fighter Command thus fought the Battle of Britain on something like equal terms. It managed throughout to keep 600 fighters serviceable daily. The *Luftwaffe* was never able to concentrate more than 800 fighters against them. The RAF's main problem was lack of experienced pilots, not lack of aircraft. *Luftwaffe* leaders believed that their fighters were superior to both the Spitfire and the Hurricane. The reality was that the Hurricane was almost as good as, and the Spitfire technically superior to, the Me109 and the Me110 in speed and firepower. German leaders also underestimated the RAF's integrated warning system, not least the 50 radar stations which lined the British coast from the Orkneys to Land's End. These stations picked up incoming planes from a distance of about 120 kilometres (75 miles) and could make accurate estimates of their numbers and altitude. (Radar was a British invention, credit for which belonged to Robert Watson-Watt.) Once the planes reached the coast, they were followed by the Royal Observer Corps. Information was relayed to RAF Fighter Command Headquarters at Bentley Priory near London and then sent to the four Fighter Command Groups. Swift analysis of information enabled RAF fighters to be airborne by the time German planes were over their airfields.

Fighter Command was directed by Air Chief Marshal Sir Hugh Dowding. During the Battle of France, he had done everything possible to preserve Fighter Command for what he believed to be its essential role – the defence of Britain. Dowding's aim now was to stop the *Luftwaffe* winning air superiority. To this end, he deployed less than half of his fighters in southern England. His northern squadrons, out of range of German bombers, represented a reserve that he could feed into the battle. He believed that his prime task was to protect his airfields and his communications system. It was therefore essential to shoot down bombers before they released their bombs, rather than concentrating on their fighter escorts. There was opposition to Dowding's strategy from men like Air Marshal Leigh-Mallory and swashbuckling Squadron-Leader Douglas Bader. They believed Dowding should throw all his planes at the *Luftwaffe*'s fighters.

The Battle of Britain had no formal beginning or end, but most historians agree that it lasted from mid-July to mid-September. The opening round of the battle occurred over the Channel with attacks on British merchant shipping and western coastal towns. The Royal Navy, which had to be beaten if the *Wehrmacht* was to invade, remained untouched. Fighter Command, however, suffered heavy losses. The air war over the Channel showed that German tactics were superior and German pilots were better trained. Nevertheless, the RAF was quick to learn.

On 1 August, Hitler ordered the *Luftwaffe* to, 'overpower the English air force with all the forces at its command in the shortest possible time'. The objectives were planes, airbases, and aircraft factories. Göring fixed 'Eagle Day' for 7 August. Beset by bad weather, it stuttered into life on 8 August. Throughout the week, the Germans claimed that the 'exchange ratio' was in its favour. However, German losses were running so high that Göring now ordered the *Luftwaffe* to concentrate its efforts on airfields. He also increased the proportion of fighters to bombers. Bad weather delayed the start of this effort. Not until 24 August did the RAF feel its effect. In the following fortnight, airfields in the south of England suffered extensive damage. By early September, the RAF was perilously close to defeat. Between 24 August and 6 September, Fighter Command lost 290 aircraft. The *Luftwaffe* lost 380 aircraft, only half of which were fighters. For two weeks the RAF was losing more planes than it could replace. A serious pilot shortage was also developing: 231 pilots were killed or wounded with only half that number coming from training units.

At this critical moment, the *Luftwaffe* switched tactics and changed its target to airfields further inland and to bombing London. This was a major blunder. It was partly a retaliation for a British bombing raid on Berlin. The raid was ineffective but it enraged Göring (he had announced that he would eat his hat if a single bomb fell on the German capital). The change of strategy was also the result of poor intelligence. German leaders were convinced that the RAF was down to its last reserves. They hoped that an attack on London would force British fighters north of the capital to give battle. Consequently, dense formations of German bombers, protected by phalanxes of fighters, attacked London from 7 September. The diversion of the attacks gave the RAF a welcome respite. Moreover, London was a more distant target for the *Luftwaffe* than south-eastern airfields. This gave Fighter Command more time to marshal its fighters to intercept. It also reduced the flying time of the Messerschmitts. For ten days in mid-September, the skies of southern England were filled by German planes heading towards London to be intercepted by RAF fighters. On 15 September, the *Luftwaffe* sent the largest force yet – 200 bombers with a heavy fighter escort. Dowding threw all his planes into a counter-attack. The RAF destroyed nearly 60 German planes (not the 183 claimed at the time). The RAF lost 26 planes; it was clearly not beaten. German air supremacy had not been achieved. On 17 September, Hitler announced the postponement of Sealion. Nazi Germany had suffered its first defeat. The legacy of that defeat would be long delayed. However, the survival of Britain which it assured helped to determine the downfall of Hitler's Germany.

By simply remaining a viable force, the RAF won the Battle of Britain. The victory was largely due to 3,000 RAF pilots. The majority were British, but Canadians, Australians, New Zealanders, South Africans, Americans, Czechs and Poles also flew British fighters. 'Never,' said Churchill, 'had so much been owed by so many to so few.' The 'few' shot down 1,300 German planes between July and September. The RAF lost 800 planes (and 500 pilots). Moreover, the RAF lost more fighters than the *Luftwaffe*. It was the loss of 600 German bombers which made the balance sheet read so favourably for the RAF. While the Battle of Britain was won in the air, it was also won on the ground in the aircraft factories. Britain had more fighters ready for action in October than in July, despite the losses over the summer. Dowding, the main architect of British success, was shabbily treated. Churchill, convinced he lacked flair, replaced him in November. He was given 24 hours to clear his desk.

The *Luftwaffe* assault continued through September but instead of airfields, its main targets were now British cities. The aim was to break British morale. Between September 1940 and May 1941, the Germans dropped 35,000 tons of bombs, over half of them on London. After November, all the bombing was done at night. (Daylight raids resulted in heavy losses of planes.) The RAF had no effective defence against night bombers. Even with pilots stuffed full of carrots that were supposed to improve night vision, British fighters stood little chance of intercepting the bombers. Some 45,000 people died in the 'Blitz'- far less than had been feared. British propaganda depicted cheery and defiant citizens clearing up the debris after nights of heavy bombing. This image was part myth. The bombing often caused panic and confusion. Yet the 'spirit of the Blitz' was not all propaganda. German bombing did not shatter civilian morale. Indeed, arguably the British people became more united in the face of the shared peril. Nor did the Blitz cause major economic damage. Even in Coventry, which suffered one of the heaviest raids, most of the factories were in full production within a few days. All the Blitz succeeded in doing was generating a long-lasting anger among most Britons and a determination to seek revenge.

Bombing was not the only, nor perhaps even the most serious, threat that Britain faced. Its ability to continue to feed the population, arm the troops and supply its ships, aircraft and tanks with fuel depended upon being able to keep its shipping lanes open. There were various ways in which the Germans could threaten British shipping. German bombers, based in France and Norway, were soon taking a heavy toll. Mines, whether laid by aircraft, surface ship or submarine, were a constant menace. German battleships and cruisers provided the most spectacular but, given the Royal Navy's strength, least effective threat. The greatest threat came from submarines. In April 1941, nearly 700,000 tons of shipping was lost – far more than British shipyards could replace. So severe was the crisis in Britain, the scale of rations had to be cut. By mid-1941 Britain was near to losing what Churchill called the 'Battle of the Atlantic' and, thus, close to losing the war. (Chapter 10 deals with the U-boat threat in more detail.)

The search for allies

Churchill was sustained by a supreme confidence that the USA would come into the war. This confidence was not particularly well founded. Certainly, FDR sympathized with the British cause. In late 1939, he persuaded Congress to allow the Allies to purchase arms on a 'cash and carry' basis. He knew, however, that most Americans had no wish to get involved in war with Germany. Given the strong isolationist lobby in Congress, he had to proceed cautiously. For a few weeks after the fall of France, US military leaders were reluctant to send arms to Britain: if Britain surrendered, US supplies would fall into German hands and might eventually be used against the USA. Once it was clear that Britain intended to fight on, FDR determined to do everything possible to help. Most Americans agreed with him. They saw Hitler's success as a looming threat to the USA, and judged that Britain's survival was essential to the US's own security. In August 1940, America provided Britain with 50 destroyers in return for the right to establish bases in British possessions in the Caribbean. Although most of the US ships needed considerable repair, the destroyer deal was an important gesture and an indication of FDR's intent. That intent was kept under wraps in the autumn of 1940 in the run-up to the presidential election. His opponent Wendell Willkie played on the fear that FDR was leading the USA into war. FDR declared his determination to preserve peace, 'Your boys are not going to be sent into any foreign wars,' he said in the campaign. After his re-election success, FDR's support for Britain became more overt.

Churchill clamoured for war material. 'Give us the tools,' he declared, 'and we will finish the job'. Unfortunately Britain was not in a position to pay for the tools. By late 1940, she was out of dollars and yet dependent on US imports. In March 1941, Congress was persuaded to pass the Lend-Lease Act which gave FDR the power to make huge quantities of US resources available to Britain. Arrangements for repayment were to be made later. This, FDR explained, was like a man who lends his neighbour a garden hose to put out a fire. The USA, he announced, would become 'the great arsenal of democracy'. By mid-1941, the USA was hardly neutral. US troops had taken over from a British garrison in Iceland, and US warships were escorting convoys bound for Britain halfway across the Atlantic. However, most Americans still had no wish to get involved in the war. Hitler, having no wish to fight the USA, ignored US breaches of neutrality. Thus, there was no certainty when – or even if – the USA would join the war on Britain's side.

Churchill's other great hope was Russia. Despite his anti-Bolshevik record, the idea of an alliance with Russia appealed to his sense of history. Yet Stafford Cripps, sent to Moscow to try to improve Anglo-Russian relations, was kept at arms length by Stalin. Britain had nothing to offer Russia as adequate compensation for a break with Germany. Cripps wrote gloomily in August 1940 that if the Russians had to choose between the two sides, 'there is no doubt whatever they would choose Germany'. Nonetheless, German-Soviet relations did give Britain some hope. Stalin, who had hoped for a long war of attrition, was concerned by the quick fall of France. Determined to gain some advantage from the situation, he annexed the Baltic States and parts of Romania in June 1940. These acquisitions angered Hitler. He loathed communism and dreamed of winning *lebensraum* in the East. By September, his high command was considering an attack on Russia. Large numbers of troops were heading eastwards. Nevertheless, Hitler kept his options open. In November, he met Russian Foreign Minister Molotov in Berlin and proposed that Russia should join with Germany, Italy and Japan in dividing the world. Germany would take most of Europe, Italy the Mediterranean, Japan the Far East, and the USSR Persia and India. Molotov showed no interest. He was more concerned about the situation in Finland, Bulgaria and Romania, and determined to hold Germany strictly to the terms of the Nazi–Soviet Pact, which defined their respective spheres of influence in eastern and southern Europe. This was enough to convince Hitler that 'the final struggle with Bolshevism' was inevitable. The decision to attack Russia was fixed in December 1940. Six months were to elapse before the forces necessary to implement it were set in motion.

Meanwhile, Hitler had tried to find other allies against Britain. In October 1940, he met Spanish dictator Franco, hoping to persuade him to join the Axis and attack Gibraltar. The loss of Gibraltar would have seriously weakened Britain in the Mediterranean. Franco, not trusting Hitler, and under considerable economic pressure from the USA not to get any closer to the Axis powers, failed to be won over. Petain, whom Hitler met the following day, proved equally unresponsive. Nor did Japan join the war against Britain. However, the Japanese government did sign the Tripartite Pact with Germany and Italy in September 1940. This bound the signatories to come to each other's assistance if any of them were attacked.